Digital Scenography

Performance + Design is a series of monographs and essay collections that explore understandings of performance design and scenography, examining the potential of the visual, spatial, material and environmental to shape performative encounters and to offer sites for imaginative exchange. This series focuses on design both for and as performance in a variety of contexts including theatre, art installations, museum displays, mega-events, site-specific and community-based performance, street theatre, design of public space, festivals, protests and state-sanctioned spectacle.

Performance + Design takes as its starting point the growth of scenography and the expansion from theatre or stage design to a wider notion of scenography as a spatial practice. As such, it recognizes the recent accompanying interest from a number of converging scholarly disciplines (theatre, performance, art, architecture, design) and examines twenty-first-century practices of performance design in the context of debates about post-dramatic theatre, aesthetic representation, visual and material culture, spectatorship, participation and co-authorship.

Series Editors
Stephen Di Benedetto, Joslin McKinney and Scott Palmer

Contemporary Scenography: Practices and Aesthetics in German Theatre, Arts and Design
Birgit Wiens 978-1-3500-6447-8

Consuming Scenography: The Theatricality of the Shopping Mall
Nebojša Tabački 978-1-3501-1089-2

The History and Theory of Environmental Scenography: Second Edition
Arnold Aronson 978-1-4742-8396-0

Immersion and Participation in Punchdrunk's Theatrical Worlds
Carina E. I. Westling 978-1-3501-0194-4

Sounds Effects: Theatre, Drama and Hearing in the Modern World
Ross Brown 978-1-3500-4590-3

Scenography Expanded: An Introduction to Contemporary Performance Design
Edited by Joslin McKinney and Scott Palmer 978-1-4742-4439-8

The Model as Performance: Staging Space in Theatre and Architecture
Thea Brejzek and Lawrence Wallen 978-1-4742-7138-7

Sites of Transformation: Applied and Socially Engaged Scenography in Rural Landscapes
Louise Ann Wilson 978-1-3501-0444-0

Digital Scenography

30 Years of Experimentation and Innovation in Performance and Interactive Media

NÉILL O'DWYER

methuen | drama
LONDON • NEW YORK • OXFORD • NEW DELHI • SYDNEY

METHUEN DRAMA
Bloomsbury Publishing Plc
50 Bedford Square, London, WC1B 3DP, UK
1385 Broadway, New York, NY 10018, USA
29 Earlsfort Terrace, Dublin 2, Ireland

BLOOMSBURY, METHUEN DRAMA and the Methuen Drama logo
are trademarks of Bloomsbury Publishing Plc

First published in hardback in Great Britain 2021
This paperback edition published 2023

Copyright © Néill O'Dwyer, 2021, 2023

Néill O'Dwyer has asserted his right under the Copyright, Designs
and Patents Act, 1988, to be identified as the author of this work.

For legal purposes the Acknowledgements on pp. xii–xiii constitute
an extension of this copyright page.

Cover design by Burge Agency
Photograph: *D.A.V.E.*, by Klaus Obermaier (© Marianne Weiss)

All rights reserved. No part of this publication may be reproduced or
transmitted in any form or by any means, electronic or mechanical,
including photocopying, recording, or any information storage or retrieval
system, without prior permission in writing from the publishers.

Bloomsbury Publishing Plc does not have any control over, or responsibility for,
any third-party websites referred to or in this book. All internet addresses given in this
book were correct at the time of going to press. The author and publisher regret any
inconvenience caused if addresses have changed or sites have ceased to exist,
but can accept no responsibility for any such changes.

A catalogue record for this book is available from the British Library.

A catalog record for this book is available from the Library of Congress.

ISBN: HB: 978-1-3501-0731-1
       PB: 978-1-3502-3275-4
       ePDF: 978-1-3501-0733-5
       eBook: 978-1-3501-0732-8

Series: Performance and Design

Typeset by Integra Software Services Pvt. Ltd.

To find out more about our authors and books visit www.bloomsbury.com
and sign up for our newsletters.

*This book is dedicated to the memory of my father, Paul O'Dwyer,
my architect.*

Contents

List of Illustrations x
Acknowledgements xii

   Introduction 1
   Historical Background 2
   Yet Another Recuperation of the Theory of the Avant-Garde 4
   Contextualization of Digital Scenography 9
   Epochal Rupture of Digital Technology and Global Interconnectivity 17
   Methodology 18
   Through-Lines 20

1 Avant-Garde and Invention in Early Digital Scenography: Troika Ranch 25

   Introduction 25
   Background 26
   The Need (1989) 27
   Tactile Diaries (1990) 29
   Mise-en-scène 31
   Technical Description 33
   Project Background and Avant-Garde Tendencies 35
   Teleacting and Democratization of Video Broadcasting 36
   Rupture and the Pharmacology of Digital Telecommunications 39
   Experimentalism, Invention and Procedure 41
   Systems Art 43
   Technological Transformations of Methods 44
   Towards *In Plane* 45
   Individuation and Influences on Troika Ranch 47
   In Plane 49
   A Final Thought on Troika Ranch 51

2 Scenography of the Cyborg: Stelarc's *Extra Ear* 53

   Introduction 53
   Themes and Concepts 54

Extra Ear: Description 57
Leroi-Gourhan, Evolution and the Technical Tendency 61
Technicity 63
Towards Technical Individuation 64
A General Organology 66
Technical Evolution 68
Preindividual Milieu and Epiphylogenesis 69
Stelarc's *Extra Ear*, Post-evolution and Organ Functions 70
Subversion and Rupture 71
Sociocultural Impact 72

3 Innovations in Motion-Tracking and Projection-Mapping: Klaus Obermaier 79

D.A.V.E. 80
Technical Determinacy in *D.A.V.E.* 84
Vivisector 86
Description 87
The Ambivalences of Digital Scenography 91
Apparition 93
Responsive Scenography 94
Projection-Mapping 97
Socio-political Metaphors of *Apparition* 99
Symbiosis or Organology? 101

4 Responsive Environments and Choreographing Indeterminacy: Chunky Move 105

Introduction 105
Description 106
Grammatization 108
Specificities of Digital Scenography 111
Sublime Aesthetics of *Mortal Engine* 116
Performing Digital Individuations: Organology 119
Delegation of Responsibilities: Towards AI 122
The Pharmacology of the Second 'Scenographic Turn' 122
Expanding the Theoretical Lens 125

5 Architectural Projection-Mapping: OnionLab Beaming on a Grand Scale 127

Introduction 127
A-Cero 15th Anniversary: Description 127

Theodor Adorno: Aesthetic Theory and the Culture Industry 130
From the Culture Industry to the Programme Industry 132
Symbolic Misery 134
Desire 136
Desire and the Programme Industry 138
Blade Runner 2049: 'Everything You Want to Hear/See' and the Horror of Joi 139
The Pharmacology of Software as Art Material 141
Computer Vision: A Digital Resource 143
The Pharmacology of Software as an Art Material 145
Summing Up Projection-Mapping and the Programming Industries 146

6 Ubiquitous Computing, Behavioural Profiling, Big Data and Machine Learning: Blast Theory 149

Introduction 149
Karen 152
Description 152
Mise-en-scène 153
Dramaturgy 155
Durational Time, Intermittence and Subversion of the Author–Audience Relation 156
Algorithmic Governmentality and 24/7 Capitalism 159
A New Critical Vocabulary for the New Economy 163
The Goal of Art in the Hyperindustrial Economy 163
Bifurcation Points in the Hyperindustrial Economy 165
Eliciting the New Specificities 166

Conclusion: Towards a Nascent Grammar of Digital Scenography 169

Political Agency 170
Singularity 172
(In)determinism 173
Innovative Repurposing 174
Digital Specificity 175
Noetic Reactivation 176
Increasing Technological Performativity 177
A Final Word 179

Notes 180
Bibliography 191
Index 203

List of Illustrations

1.1 Photo: Steve Gunther. *Tactile Diaries*, Dawn Stoppiello donning the MidiDancer (courtesy of Troika Ranch) 28

1.2 Photo: Steve Gunther. *Tactile Diaries*, Scene 1, Writing. Performers: Dawn Stoppiello and Ilaan Egeland (courtesy of Troika Ranch) 31

1.3 Photo: Mark Coniglio. *In Plane*. Performer: Dawn Stoppiello (courtesy of Troika Ranch) 50

2.1 Photo: Nina Sellars. Stelarc – Ear on Arm, 2006 (courtesy of Nina Sellars and Stelarc) 58

2.2 a) Photo (left): Nina Sellars. Stelarc Extra Ear Surgery – surgical implantation procedure, 2006 (courtesy of Nina Sellars and Stelarc). b) Photo (right): Nina Sellars. Medpor scaffold, just prior to its insertion, 2006 (courtesy of Nina Sellars and Stelarc) 60

3.1 Photo: Felix Noebauer. *D.A.V.E., Deformation* (courtesy of Felix Noebauer and Klaus Obermaier) 82

3.2 Photo: Marianne Weiss. *D.A.V.E., Red Orb* (courtesy of Klaus Obermaier) 83

3.3 Photo: Klaus Obermaier. *Vivisector*, pixelated bodies (courtesy of Klaus Obermaier) 87

LIST OF ILLUSTRATIONS

3.4 Photo: Klaus Obermaier. *Vivisector*, disembodied limbs (courtesy of Klaus Obermaier) 90

3.5 Photo: Klaus Obermaier. *Apparition, Particles* (courtesy of Klaus Obermaier) 96

3.6 Photo: Klaus Obermaier. *Apparition, Lines* (courtesy of Klaus Obermaier) 97

3.7 Photo: Klaus Obermaier. *Apparition, Text* (courtesy of Klaus Obermaier) 100

4.1 Screenshot: *Kalypso* software (courtesy of Frieder Weiss) 107

4.2 Photo: Andrew Curtis. Performer: Harriet Ritchie (courtesy of Chunky Move) 117

4.3 Photo: Andrew Curtis. Performer: Antony Hamilton (courtesy of Chunky Move) 121

5.1 Photo: *A-Cero 15th Anniversary* (courtesy of OnionLab) 129

5.2 Photo: *A-Cero 15th Anniversary* (courtesy of OnionLab) 130

6.1 Photo: Multiple-choice interface for *Karen* (courtesy of Blast Theory) 153

6.2 Screenshot: *Karen*. Performer: Claire Cage (courtesy of Blast Theory) 155

Acknowledgements

The book emerged from my ongoing relations with the Scenography Working Groups at the International Federation of Theatre Research (IFTR) and to a lesser extent Theatre and Performance Research Association (TaPRA). I would like to extend my thanks to all my colleagues in the working groups, especially to Scott Palmer, for identifying the significance, originality and topical nature of my research. I would also like to thank the series editors, Scott Palmer, Joselyn McKinney and Stephen di Bennedetto, for their guidance and support in developing the book and reviewing the content. I would also like to thank the anonymous peer reviewers, whoever you are.

In no particular order, I would particularly like to acknowledge the support of the following people who were, and still are, central to my research and writing processes: Nicholas Johnson in the Department of Drama at Trinity College Dublin (TCD), for his supervision of the project; Aljosa Smolic of V-SENSE (supported by Science Foundation Ireland [grant number 15/RP/2776]) in the School of Computer Science and Statistics (TCD), for ongoing mentoring, the provision of research time dedicated to the completion of the book and encouraging the expansion of my research under the rubric of his computer vision focused research; Noel Fitzpatrick and all my friends and colleagues in the Digital Studies Seminar in the Graduate School of Creative Arts and Media (GradCAM) at the Technological University of Dublin (TUDublin); Bernard Stiegler (who sadly passed away during the closing stages of this book project, but whose thought extends towards infinity), Vincent Puig and all the great people at l'Institut de Recherche et d'Innovation (l'IRI) at the Pompidou Centre in Paris; and all the staff at the Irish Research Council (IRC) for providing me with the competitive postdoctoral research fellowship award (grant number GOIPD/2017/902), which afforded me the luxury of immersing myself full-time in this book project and without which its completion would have been nigh impossible. I also want to sincerely thank Matthew Causey Professor Emeritus of the School of Creative Arts at TCD, whose seminars and supervision of my dissertation (completed in 2016) still stand as invaluable pieces of academic direction. I want to thank Olga Clancy for proof-reading the completed manuscript. Finally, I want to thank Mark Dudgeon and Lara Bateman for their help and support in developing and producing this book and for always being available to respond to my many questions.

ACKNOWLEDGEMENTS

I would like to extend my deep gratitude to all the artists and photographers who participated in the interviews, offered feedback on my writing and provided images, all of which comprise a crucial foundation of the research and content of the book. In order of appearance these wonderful people are: Dawn Stoppiello and Mark Coniglio (Troika Ranch); Stelarc and Nina Sellars; Klaus Obermaier, Marianne Weiss and Felix Noebauer; Frieder Weiss, Gideon Obarzanek and Chunky Move; Aleix Fernandez and Tamara Sefcovicova of OnionLab; and Matt Adams and his colleagues at Blast Theory. Some of the interview content and research from Chapters 3 and 4 date back to conversations with three of the artists (Klaus Obermaier, Gideon Obarzanek and Frieder Weiss) that began in 2012. Some of the ideas in Chapter 3 were first published in a book section entitled 'The Cultural Critique of Bernard Stiegler: Reflecting on the Computational Performance of Klaus Obermaier' in *The Performing Subject in the Space of Technology* (2015) as part of Palgrave McMillan's Series in Performance and Technology. I would like to thank the series editors Susan Broadhurst and Josephine Machon and Palgrave's editorial assistant for Literature and Theatre & Performance, Jack Heeney, for allowing me to develop and extend these ideas. Some of the reworked material from Chapter 4 first appeared in 'The Scenographic Turn: The Pharmacology of the Digitisation of Scenography', *Theatre and Performance Design* 1, no. 1–2 (2015): 48–63. https://doi.org/10.1080/23322551.2015.1023667. This content and research are developed and extended with the kind permission of the Editors-in-Chief Jane Collins and Arnold Aronson, to whom I am deeply grateful.

Finally, I would like to thank my beautiful, patient wife and children who have suffered me during this intensive period of writing and to whom I am ever indebted for their love and emotional and moral support. And I would like to thank my mother, my siblings and my much adored father who passed away during the writing process and to whom this book is dedicated.

Introduction

This book charts a genealogy of scenographic innovations, afforded by the invention of the microchip and the new capacity for light-speed calculation. It focuses on the shift that has taken place in performance practice and process through the introduction of digital technologies – a shift analogous in magnitude to that imposed by mechanical technologies. To consider these developments the book uses a two-pronged theoretical strategy consisting of digital media theory and scenographic scholarship, the goal of which is to produce a nascent vocabulary, or grammar, of digital scenography that is epistemologically and pedagogically useful for scholars and practitioners in defining their work and engaging in the discursive economy of the field.

The book makes much use of technological theories from the Continental philosophical canon, especially those of Bernard Stiegler, because he draws such a hard line between the analogue and the digital. Stiegler asserts that society is experiencing the 'second mechanical turn of sensibility' (Stiegler 2011b: 4), which describes a shift in the way individuals and collectives think, operate, interact and self-organize under the profound influence of digital technology. Based on the thesis that the 'first scenographic turn' occurred under the auspices of electrical lighting and the ingenuities of Adolphe Appia (Palmer 2015), Stiegler's thesis can be extended to assert that *the second scenographic turn* has happened under digital technologies and is validated by the genealogy charted in this book. Techno-evolution – constituted by specialist subject areas like bandwidth, nanotechnologies, processing power, artificial intelligence and biomechanical engineering – continues to accelerate, creating ever more opportunities for techno-cultural innovation. But the acceleration of cyclical automata to astounding speeds, millions of times faster than that of mechanical technology, is a techno-evolutionary 'phenomenon that artists and the art-going public have never had the time or space to digest and reconcile' (O'Dwyer 2015b: 49).

This book also harnesses the 'expanded' understanding of scenography as an interdisciplinary field that champions audio-visual, participatory, immersive, site-specific and design-led approaches to performance practice (McKinney and Palmer 2017). The goal is to celebrate performances that are conceived and devised through design processes, where the dramaturgical vision is guided by the mise-en-scène, the availability of certain materials and environmental conditions, all of which are pivotally influential on the experience (Brejzek 2011; Lotker and Gough 2013). This expanded conceptualization of scenography therefore resonates with aspects of Hans-Thies Lehmann's thesis on 'postdramatic theatre', for example, by advocating polysemic, open-ended performance systems and opposing traditional values that reinforce the hierarchy of the text (Lehmann 2006). During the last fifteen years, scenography and performance design have experienced a rich burgeoning in their practical and theoretical avenues of exploration, evinced by a strong representation in peer-reviewed journals (Lotker and Gough 2013; Collins and Aronson 2015) and the publication of numerous scholarly books (Aronson 2005; Mckinney 2009; Collins and Nisbet 2010; Oudsten 2012; Baugh 2014). This upsurge in scholarship is composed of, on one hand, critical readings of performance design that use a scenographic lens for decoding performances, and on the other hand, a design-led approach to practice-as-research (PaR) in performance (Piccini and Kershaw 2004; Allegue et al. 2009). Both approaches testify to an enthusiastic engagement with scenography as a fertile epistemic territory in which art-making and appreciation synergistically enliven each other, providing rich, varied, engaging and contemporary aesthetic experiences.

On the spectator side, there is an increasing public interest in performances that seek to enhance audience engagement through immersive, tactile, experiential, exploratory and location-based theatre, all of which heavily depend on an innovative approach to mise-en-scène using new materials, technologies and techniques. This book responds to these new conditions of the performing arts, by providing a bracketed genealogical study composed of both historical material facts and cutting-edge theoretical analyses. In this regard, the goal is to produce a nascent grammar of specifically digital scenography that will arm practitioners and scholars with a suitable vocabulary for articulating and reading design-led performance work and will, therefore, help open new 'lines of flight' (Deleuze and Guattari 2004: 226) for a new genre of performance practice burgeoning in the digital era.

Historical Background

The theoretical axis and historical bracketing of this book are organized around the occurrence of two major historical-material *Events*,[1] the invention of the electronic microchip and the intervention of the internet. This book draws a line between the invention of digital (cybernetic[2]) technology, which dates back to the post-Second World War period of the late 1940s, and the intervention of the World Wide Web, which was rolled out publicly in the early 1990s. The former represents a material, physical invention and the latter represents a sort of evolutionary leap in means of mass intersubjectivity. It is not arbitrary that the watershed in the mass-production of computational hardware (c. 1990) should broadly coincide with the launch of the internet. The overarching narrative of this book focuses on the idea that contemporary socio-economics, politics and culture have been fundamentally altered and reconditioned by these two historically profound technological innovations.

Following the mass availability of digital hardware and software, every epistemic field has experienced a reorganizational shift in how it operates. The broad flexibility and applicability of digital technologies to every knowledge area have created new opportunities, as well as closures – excitement and worry. This is especially true of the performing arts. While there are new opportunities for interdisciplinary collaboration – particularly between the arts and sciences – there are also expressions of doubt by professionals who feel occupationally destabilized by the tectonic shifts. Theatre is inclusive and collaborative by its nature and has always encompassed various sectors of art, design and technology. Now, by embracing digital technologies, it continues to assert its ability to span traditional doctrinal divides by including subjects from science, technology and engineering. Scenography is the domain that nurtures this epistemic symbiosis. Through its dialogical functioning, the digital fundamentally differs from analogue technology, thereby occasioning new ways of telling stories and engaging audiences. Digital technologies are constantly evolving, increasing in power, efficiency and the capacity for processing huge amounts of data in real time. This affords representational techniques in live theatre that were previously only available to the film and gaming sectors following laborious post-production processes. As the practice of organizing space, scenography has been the leading subsector of performance to include techno-scientific knowledge areas, embrace the new specificities of digital technologies and rethink performance and storytelling in the digital age.

The repercussions of the digital technological revolution are profound and ongoing. Like all areas of contemporary culture, performance has been vastly transformed in terms of the type of work being made, new working processes and the topical new themes afforded by a digitally buttressed society. During the early- to mid-1990s 'a disparate group of artists emerging from the worlds of electronic music, video art, performance art, and theatre ... began to integrate new digital technologies into live performance' (Saltz 2013: 421). It was a period of cybercultural burgeoning, which occasioned a utopian enthusiasm advocated by its theoretical and practical proponents.

For example, theorists like Donna Haraway and N. Katherine Hayles saw cyberspace as a new subjective space, a blank canvas bereft of ideological preconceptions and prejudices, where rules could be rewritten and old, traditional, patriarchal and misogynistic ideologies could be eroded, perhaps even erased. However, a series of economic collapses, namely the dot-com bust in 1999 and the global economic collapse of 2008, have provided a clarity that only the crystal-clear lenses of historical hindsight can provide. We must not place all our faith in technology. We cannot be 'watched over by machines of loving grace' (Brautigan 1967: 1). The future of humanity cannot be set to autopilot. And transhumanism is not cool anymore. Nevertheless, integrated circuit technology now forms the basis of daily existence for most citizens in industrialized economies.

Following on from the excellent humanities-based groundwork that has charted the canon of technologically engaged performance at the turn of the twenty-first century (Birringer 1998; Giannachi 2004; Causey 2006; Dixon and Smith 2007) and the aforementioned work on the expanded conceptualization of scenography, this book seeks to highlight, examine and chart ground-breaking digital scenographic work created during the last thirty years (c. 1990–present) – since Tim Berners Lee invented the global cultural phenomenon of the internet. It focuses on a selection of pioneering performance makers that seek to break new ground and open up new dialogues by employing the latest innovations in digital technology. Given the internet's new facilitation for global networking and dissemination, it is no surprise that a spate of innovative creative activities, investigating the potential of digital technologies in the performing arts, should coincide with Berners Lee's invention. In addition, the drop in prices of (previously inaccessible) broadcast-quality audio-visual technologies – normally only within the reach of wealthy government institutions and media corporations – meant that independent artists and amateurs could widely practise new media and develop expressive techniques from the grassroots. This accessibility to new tools and techniques facilitated a new epoch of unbridled experimentalism that is unavoidably described as avant-garde.

Yet Another Recuperation of the Theory of the Avant-Garde

The historical avant-garde is often the go-to theoretical discourse for analyses of technological art; this genealogy is no exception. The discourse is inescapable when discussing the reorganization of creative practice in the aftermath of a technological revolution. Each of the artists examined in this book – Troika Ranch, Stelarc, Klaus Obermaier, Chunky Move, OnionLab and Blast Theory – merits a commendation for their pioneering scenographic innovations and brave explorations of an unknown field. While this book does not attempt to labour the point by tracing the history of the avant-garde through the twentieth century, it does draw on some of its key theoretical characteristics: experimentalism, activism, antagonism and its inherent link to technology.

The theory of the avant-garde enjoys a rich and, at times, polemical discourse that can be traced through an important, influential discursive economy (Poggioli 1968; Adorno 1970; Russell 1981; Bürger 1984; Mann 1991; Lyotard 1992). Any invocation of the term demands that it be clearly defined and its usage contextualized because for practising artists, every bit as much as historians and critics, definition is a process of positioning work. For Poggioli, who posits that the avant-garde can be largely categorized as activistic and antagonistic art movements that challenge normative sociocultural conditions, definition is its most important facet. Whereas Russell contends that Poggioli's categories should be gathered under the single category of 'aesthetic activism', which always produces an 'activist art' that is 'inherently political' (Russell 1981: 13). Bürger only validates one type of activism: that which is directed against the institution of art, 'and denies authentic avant-garde status to any movement that does not demonstrate such opposition' (Mann 1991: 8). Bürger's thesis builds on the aesthetic theory of Adorno, who interprets the avant-garde as an aesthetic pursuit of innovative, inventive subject-object relations that challenge the status quo, thereby furnishing the work with an immanent socio-political subjectivity. The nexus of Bürger's argument includes a delineation of the failure of the activism at the heart of avant-garde praxis, its assimilation to the institution and the recursion of self-reflexive theorizing. And this theme is taken up again by Mann who maintains that the avant-garde is ambiguously bound to the notion of recuperation. For Bürger, and Mann thereafter, socio-political concerns are a constant constituent of the avant-garde, and they are recuperated periodically throughout the history of modern art. It is the strategies for engaging them that continually evolve, and this mutability is reflexively determined by the inherent and inseparable embeddedness of economic and technological subjectivities at the heart of avant-garde praxis. In this regard, this book follows the transhistorical and recursive nature of the avant-garde, by employing the term as a means for understanding what the state of the art is in the durations that constitute the said period of this genealogy (1990–2020).

Adopting an avant-garde methodology is not without criticism. In reviewing scholarship from the field of technology and performance, David Saltz offers an important criticism: almost all digital media theorists 'bind digital performance to the historical avant-garde and, more recently, post-dramatic theatre, excluding popular and literary theatre from their purview' (Saltz 2013: 431). Many scholars historicize as far back as Richard Wagner, yet they fail to acknowledge the important role that popular cultural practitioners, like Lincoln J. Carter, Windsor McKay or William Dudley, play in advancing the field. Saltz continues:

> This anti-populist bias impoverishes the breadth of examples, conflating technological innovation with a particular tradition of aesthetic innovation, and limits and distorts our understanding of the artistic, political, and philosophical implications of new technologies.
>
> (Saltz 2013: 431–2)

The problem of repetition is implicit in Saltz's criticism. His fear is linked to the possible homogenization of critical discourse occasioned by a diminishing pool of literature that could result in the stupefaction of scholarship itself. This book on digital scenography attempts to address Saltz's concerns by synthesizing the separate but overlapping discourses of avant-garde theory, technological philosophy and scenographic analyses. In reflecting upon Mann's book, Philip Auslander cogitates seriously on the idea of abandoning avant-garde theory on the basis that it is overused:

> The real problem is that if we (i.e., critics, theorists) were to relinquish the vocabulary of critical discourse on the avantgarde, the discourse of oppositional art, or critical art, on the grounds that postmodern culture has rendered such terms impossible or irrelevant, *what would be left to say about the art we want most to address?*
>
> (Auslander 1993: 197)

For Auslander, the issue most at stake for the discursive economy is not homogenization through repetition, but the worrying eventuality of a complete abandonment of the pragmatics of critical discourse – the cessation of recuperation. This would paradoxically cast avant-garde critical theorists into the nihilistic domain of total silence. Every occurrence of an avant-garde movement is fundamentally underpinned by a conflict between provocation and compliance. The avant-garde is not straightforwardly the resistant or cooperative aspect of a movement; rather, it is the conceptual vehicle through which the binarism is articulated. What is most crucial is that questions continue to be asked, that dominant socio-political and power structures continue to be challenged. It is this logic that allows Mann to make the assertion that the avant-garde is always already dead and recuperated. That which commands the death of the avant-garde is the very thing that sustains and prolongs its life cycle: 'The discourse of the avant-garde is its death and in death it continues to reproduce itself as a death-discourse' (Mann 1991: 40). This is what he means by theory-death. Arguing for the recuperation of critical theory and praxis is the key concept in Mann's meta-critical analysis. He wrote the book precisely so that we could get past the urge to endorse or disparage another tirade of utopian, revolutionary rhetoric, and to debunk the accusation that it is outmoded to invoke the term 'avant-garde' and its legacy of discursive encumbrances.

This book also aims to respond to David Saltz's criticism concerning the overuse of an avant-garde theoretical framework to the neglect of populism, which may impoverish the breadth of discourse, ultimately distorting 'our understanding of the artistic, political, and philosophical implications of new technologies' (Saltz 2013: 432). While the relations between technological innovation and the avant-garde aesthetic tradition are certainly valid and strong, 'it should not be the only genre studied within the purview of media and performance scholarship, to the exclusion of others' (Rouse 2018: 374). Although this book maintains an avant-gardist aesthetics of technical innovation at its core, it also attempts to respond to the concerns regarding the oversight of populist innovations. Chapters 5 and 6 discuss aspects of technical innovation in the popular culture industries and the extraordinary level of spectacular sophistication that they have contributed to the field, through big budgets. This discussion considers the ambivalent internal tensions between the avant-garde and the culture industry, and the influential role that technology plays in mass mobilization, distraction and political persuasion. Philosophical, (bio)political and critical theory writings facilitate this discourse, which is generally salient throughout the book.

The aporia of invoking an avant-garde framework constitutes the basis and justification for yet another engagement with the aesthetic theory and ideological critique in this book. The genealogical approach demonstrates how the circular metanarrative of critical discourse fits to the digital era, which moves from activist praxis, through assimilation to the institution, to self-reflexive theorizing, and, finally, to the repetition of the cycle at a higher level. Mann's appeal for a reactivation of avant-garde discourse at a new level is paralleled in Bernard Stiegler's recuperation of the concept in his aesthetic programme. He is analogously more concerned with the issue that *critical questions continue to be asked*, than whether an attributive noun, a strategy, a theory or a methodology is outmoded. In his attempt to rejuvenate the avant-garde, Stiegler rethinks the concept in terms of a quasi-scientific grammar.

Stiegler maintains that the overarching trajectory of contemporary art is dependent on 'new articulations of the avant-garde' (Desmond et al. 2015: 73) and the need for 'a new concept of critique' (Desmond et al. 2015: 74). He calls for a recuperation of oppositional criticism in the domain of practice, and an engagement with new paradigms of critical discourse. Stiegler's two-pronged strategy, and his willingness to invoke the concept of the avant-garde, strengthens the decision to analyse digital scenography through an avant-garde lens, and it invalidates convictions that avant-garde discourse is exhausted. He writes: 'I understand the potential of creative territories: as the possibility of an *avant-garde* territory, that is, an area capable of inventing a new cultural, social, economic and political model' (Stiegler 2010b: 13–14). Stiegler identifies the potential of artistic praxis to facilitate a more wholesome intersubjective milieu with reinvigorated dialogue between social, cultural, political and economic actors, thus positioning himself as a proponent of keeping avant-garde discourse alive. Stiegler's aesthetics sides with Deleuze by encouraging a reactivation of the political aspect of creative practice with a view to invigorating a rejuvenated conception of socio-economics and politics, thereby 'contributing to the invention of a people' (Deleuze 2005: 209). This is nothing new; indeed, the entire discourse of Continental aesthetics, since Hegel, has been focused on its relationship to politics. The fact that they are inextricably linked is unchanging; the thing that is variable is *how* they are linked, *how* they interoperate and cross-pollinate. This is precisely what this genealogy of digital scenography hopes to elucidate. This historical mapping of the digital scenographic microsphere aims to open a better understanding of developments in the sociocultural and political macrosphere – how they are mutable, fluid and contingent on one another. Examined through an avant-garde lens, their relationship reveals the emergence of the deeper problem of increasing efficacy in the material domain that has profound socio-political and aesthetic repercussions. Finally, despite Stiegler's analysis of the new, sophisticated relations between digital technology and culture, he weighs in heavily on the side of philosophical theorizing and fails to supply either a cohesive 'genealogy of the sensible' (Stiegler 2011b: 139) or a substantial aesthetic analysis of avant-gardist work. As such, there are still incommensurable gaps between his pure technological philosophy and the historicist lens deployed by art critics, which this book intends to fill.

The issue that most avant-garde theorists fail to analyse, in great depth, is the colossal impact that the modern technologies of automatic reproducibility have had on the Western sociocultural landscape, where such an aesthetics could be conceived and flourish. Each theorist *does* acknowledge Marx's theory of dialectical materialism, the proletarianization of the worker under the aegis of new technologies and the role this socio-technological development plays in the formation of an artistic-political activism. However, they simultaneously skirt around a deep discussion of technical epistemology and avoid becoming embroiled in discourse that could tease out the influence of technology on psychosocial ontology. These incommensurable gaps can be addressed by synthesizing avant-garde theory, scenographic methodologies and technological philosophy, thereby offering an original aesthetic reflection on contemporary performance. This book presents the story of performative artistic activism, assimilation and recursion through the tripartite lens of avant-garde theory, technological philosophy and scenography. By charting the development of digital scenography over the last thirty years, this book offers a historicist narrative that evaluates how periodic evolutionary leaps in the technical domain initiate transformations in psychosocial awareness that are revealed by art, showing the fundamental, original and inescapable bind between art and politics. The power of theatre is that it has always 'been virtual, a space of illusory immediacy' (Causey 2006: 15), a mirror of material culture. This book shows the pivotal role of scenography in the contemporary digital-cultural iteration of representing reality.

Contextualization of Digital Scenography

The widely supported theory that mass accessibility to digital technologies affords a reversal of the mode of knowledge creation and transmission from top–down to bottom–up (Haraway 1991b; Landow 1992; Hayles 1999; Ascott 2003; Stiegler 2010b) is evinced by the breadth of digital art created by a tech-savvy cohort of creative practitioners. The transmission of ideas over electronic networks means that they spread quicker and in a (non-linear) way that is fundamentally different from previous epochs. Traditionally, modes of dissemination followed a radial pattern of transmission, emanating from an epicentre; in global electronic networks they spread in a way that is more akin to a virus – a metastasis. This is evinced by the concurrent emergence of disparate grassroots digital avant-garde activities in North America, the UK, Europe and Australia, which indicate an overtaking of media enterprises by independent practitioners, in terms of technical and cultural innovation. Because of the socio-economic conditions arising from geospatial proximity to commercial technological innovators, artists in North America were notably on the cusp of the digital revolution. Troika Ranch (CalArts) and Georges Coates Performance Works (San Francisco) are two notable examples of early pioneers that benefited from operating within the Californian catchment. However, other North American practitioners like Laurie Anderson (New York), Robert Lepage's Ex Machina (Québec) and the Wooster Group (New York) were quick to adopt and integrate new digital technologies into the fabric of their repertoire. The logic of digital network metastases determined that there was a co-emergence of similar investigations in the UK, Europe and Australia. Artists of note are: Stelarc (Australia), Orlan (France), Jeffrey Shaw (Germany), Miller Puckette (France), Klaus Obermaier (Austria), Chunky Move (Australia), Blast Theory (UK), Symbiotica (Australia), to mention a few. Crucially, many of these important practitioners were supported by a network of media art research centres – e.g. ZKM (Germany) and IRCAM (France) – established to support investigations into the potential for digital technologies in creative expression. Given that the temporal scope of this genealogy encompasses a plethora of rich, varied digital performances, it would be ideal to examine the work of all these artists. However, this book does not aim to be an encyclopaedia; on the contrary, several works are examined in detail to cogitate on working processes, methodologies and practices in digital performance and scenography. In anticipation of the inevitable criticism of works included in, and omitted from, this volume, it is important to define the selection criteria. The artists/works selected are chosen on the basis that they satisfy *all* the following criteria:

1. They are clearly identifiable as scenographic, spatial practice or design-led performances that challenge traditional performance formats; that is, spatial concepts are integral to the performance and it only makes sense through their consideration.
2. They are exploratory and pursue practice-as-research methodologies that demonstrate experimentalism and are a pioneering contribution to the field of digital scenography.
3. They represent a scientific–artistic (technological–epistemological) hybrid invention by re-harnessing, reconfiguring and re-purposing technologies, techniques and working processes towards unforeseen cultural applications; that is, they rewire circuits of knowledge by redefining rules of engagement and representation.
4. They elicit the specificities of digital technology[3] to interrogate new possibilities for performance design and storytelling, thereby opening an aesthetic questioning concerning subject–object dialogue that constitutes the fabric of contemporary identity and ideology.

By these criteria, the cross-section of objects that qualify for discussion is significantly narrowed. For example, the first criterion serves to ensure that the works selected are apt to scholarly definitions of scenography's moderation of the relationship between stage technologies, the mise-en-scène and the performance. Christopher Baugh posits that the technologies employed are not simply a means to an end; they are frequently 'used as ends in themselves, where the gasp of awe and amazement at their operation has been a significant aspect of the experience of performance' (Baugh 2014: 1). Lotker and Gough buttress this thought by asserting that 'scenographies are environments that not only determine the context of performative actions, but [... also] inspire us to act and ... directly form our actions' (Lotker and Gough 2013: 3). Scenography should not be conceived as designing a setting that simply contextualizes themes and illustrates actions; it is 'a body (a discipline, a method, a foundation) in its own right. It is a discipline that has its own logic, its own distinctive rules' (Lotker and Gough 2013). This position is supported by Palmer and McKinney, who advocate 'scenography not simply as a by-product of theatre but as a mode of encounter and exchange founded on spatial and material relations between bodies, objects and environments' (McKinney and Palmer 2017: 2). Scenography is not something simply observed by audiences; it is an environment, a world to be experienced, engaged and encountered kinaesthetically, physically and viscerally. It is inherent to and inseparable from the performance. This book mobilizes these definitions of scenographic practice and focuses on performances that employ digital technologies, not only for the mise-en-scène, but also as a key component of the art idea.

The said definitions of scenography resonate with the contemporary discourse on technologically engaged performance, which, depending on nomenclatorial preferences, can be classified using various terms: *multimedia*, *intermedial*, *cyborg/cybernetic*, *new/digital media*, *virtual* etc. These inconsistencies in phrasal formulations reflect contentions around what are understood as the field's defining parameters, and they highlight its infancy, breadth, richness, plurivocality and diversity. Rosemary Klich and Edward Scheer prefer the adjective *multimedia* and populate their taxonomy with performances 'that creatively utilise [...] media technologies as an integral component of the overall work' (Scheer and Klich 2011: 17). Chris Salter presents a broad survey of 'experimental artistic practices of performance' that consciously and intentionally engage technology generally, 'so that they are inseparable from the form and operation of the work' (Salter 2010: xxxvi). Both definitions announce a position that resonates with the aforementioned views that scenography is integral and causal to the conceptual development of performance work. This book aims to debunk preconceptions that technologies are tools that serve scenographic ends by drawing on the notion that digital materials inspire new actions, influence new conceptualizations of work, and afford new rules, methodologies and working processes that constitute original mise-en-scène in contemporary performance.

The first criterion also ensures that this book focuses on performances and that the subject matter does not meander into other creative areas, like the visual and plastic arts. However, some further clarification is required because many artistic niches are constituted by digital technologies, for means of both fabrication and idea communication. At the level of communication, it is pertinent to ask: at what point does the human recede into the background, so that the technology itself emerges as the thing in question, and the audience's experience of it is performative, as opposed to ancillary? To address this question, it is useful to consider Salter's precondition for 'situated action' (Salter 2010: xxxiv), which he uses for setting-out the scope of performances that qualify for his study. He specifies that his objects of discussion must demonstrate 'physical, real-time situatedness involving collective, co-present spectating, witnessing and/or participation within the framework of a spatiotemporal event' (Salter 2010). It is a notion which he derives from Lucy Suchman's anthropological analysis of human–machine interaction and it considerably tightens the scope of his book because he uses it as a pretext for eliminating purely internet-based, networked or telepresent performance, which he dismisses as 'anytime, anyplace simulation' (Salter 2010). However, this position is arguably contradictory because the framework of an internet-based performance encompasses co-presence on a planetary scale, and wherever there is a cognitive spectator paying attention there is a physical body behind it, regardless of distances. It also contradicts definitions of performance held by many other digital performance practitioners and scholars, who validate and endorse non-present performances. Furthermore, it forecloses an important discussion relating to the centrality of online performance in critiquing networked, reticular culture and its ability to subvert and explore dominant and emerging cultural conceptions of identity and subjectivity. Global connectivity is *the* quintessential characteristic of digital culture. Networked performances are some of the best examples of how performance practice can elicit the *specificities* of digital culture, and they are crucial to the rapidly expanding phenomenon of engaging content through mobile devices. The theme of global connectivity bookends this volume. The first chapter examines a networked performance by Troika Ranch, and the last chapter discusses a mobile app-drama by Blast Theory. It is demonstrated that reticulated society is a rich and rewarding domain for contemporary performances. Far from dismissing performances on the basis of mediated presence and latency, a more valuable approach is to cogitate the subversion they channel by giving precedence to the *what* over the *who*.

Scheer and Klich's and Salter's books offer valuable contributions to scholarship. They examine cross-sections of work that reach back to the early/mid-twentieth century, which is important for historiography and contextualization within the larger frame of performance studies. Their emphasis on avant-gardist experimentalism resonates with my second criterion for qualification, which requires *practice-as-research, experimentalism* and that the works are a *pioneering contribution to the field*. Both books trace narratives through historic figures/movements like Richard Wagner, Étienne-Jules Marey and Eadweard Muybridge, Marcel Duchamp, Dada, Futurism, Constructivism, Bauhaus, John Cage, Happenings, Fluxus, Nam June Paik, Robert Wilson, Richard Foreman, Laurie Anderson, the Wooster Group, Lightwork, the Builders Association, Rockeby, Robert Lepage and George Coates, among others. The ingenuity and influence of these practitioners are undeniable, and many of them find their way into Steve Dixon and Barry

Smith's compendious volume, *Digital Performance: A History of New Media in Theater, Dance, Performance Art, and Installation* (2007). This is probably the most exhaustive study of the field so far and undoubtedly influenced the aforementioned authors. The overarching argument of their book is that digital performances essentially emerged from the legacy of the avant-garde, and the experimentalism demonstrated by those practitioners continues to occupy a pivotal role in influencing content, themes, techniques and methods in the digital age. Katheryn Farley notes that the abrupt and slightly pessimistic ending to the book belies the authors' 'Herculean undertaking' and the hopes they have for the continuation of a rich and productive niche of performance practice (Farley 2007: 691). The expansive purview of all three books compels methodologies that cover much ground but become consumed with general descriptions and listings of facts, thereby curtailing deep analyses of the works' internal tensions.[4] However, the expansive genealogy is important for emphasizing the value of historical avant-garde practices. In the context of these books, the worth of producing yet another historiographical study that spans the breath of twentieth-century performance is questionable. In an attempt to focus the discourse, this book keeps the scope of research within the digital realm, thereby delineating a digital avant-garde.

The third criterion is a corollary to the second, in that it asks for plurivocal, hybrid performances that integrate the sciences and demonstrate inventiveness. While it is one thing to produce a performance work that is avant-gardist in nature, this does not necessarily mean that the work demonstrates these qualities; indeed, there are definitions of the avant-garde that do not consider technology. Looking at the aforementioned list of avant-garde artists/movements, how many of those that continue to practise in the digital age have actually developed ground-breaking technologies, with a view to fundamentally challenging not just the performance–spectator paradigm, but also the techno-scientific landscape generally? Each of the artists discussed in this book has developed bespoke hard/software, thereby augmenting the performance spectacle, expanding the field and establishing themselves as inventors.

The goal of adding the fourth criterion is to absolutely refine the selection of objects to a handful of quintessentially digital works. This final criterion, demanding works that *elicit the specificities of digital technology*, focuses the scope to a subset of performances that are only possible in the digital age, thereby distinguishing this book from much of the competing scholarship in the field. The way the digital materials are employed should interrogate the essence of the medium, bringing fundamentally new subjectivities to the forum. This perspective displays affinities with *Mapping Intermediality in Performance* (2011),[5] which focuses acutely on the effect of digital media on performance and theatre. In the introduction, Robin Nelson importantly asserts that by numerically encoding and binarizing all types of data (be they textual, visual, oral, sonic or gestural), digital media furnish convergence between various artforms and afford 'the capacity to manipulate data in real time in a way which was not possible with earlier analogue technologies such as film' (Bay-Cheng et al. 2011: 16). This statement identifies the essence of digital material and summarizes the type of performances examined in this book. The emphasis on the discontinuities between analogue and digital technologies is expounded in their thinking of the development as an 'intermedial turn' (Bay-Cheng et al. 2011: 11). The discrete nature of digital media opens new practical and thematic opportunities on the stage that have potentialities analogous to Appia's anarchic innovations under the aegis of electrical lighting which profoundly transformed the 'very concept of theatre' (Appia and Beacham 1993: 264).

To satisfy the fourth criterion, a computer is required for processing data and performing operations, so that the performance is driven in a way that analogue audio-visual technologies could not achieve. Although illustrious in terms of stage-craft, influence and rich content, we can, with a certain regret, exclude the work of some of the aforementioned avant-garde practitioners, whose oeuvres span the *intermedial turn*. Although many of them champion the integration of audio-visual technologies in theatre and performance, that does not necessarily mean they *elicit the specificities of digital technology*; many employments of digital technology do not significantly differ from what was already possible with analogue techniques. For example, locating multiple screens/projections in performances is seen in the digital experiments of Richard Foreman, the Wooster Group, Robert Wilson and so on. But this was already achievable using analogue recording and visualization technologies. And while many recent works *do* elicit digital specificities, respond to digital culture and evoke digital subjectivities, many practitioners still fall foul of criterion number two: they should *pioneer experimentation with digital technologies*. The forging of new ground in theatre, scenography and storytelling in the mid- to late twentieth century is profound, but for qualification in this volume the centrality of *inventing* specifically digital techniques is paramount. Anyway, much of the really interesting experimental productions in this period fall outside of the temporal scope of this volume, and there is already significant scholarship on them, so there is no need to continue resurrecting existing comprehensive analysis.[6]

Although some analogue works are referenced in this book for historicizing purposes, the discussion primarily focuses on contemporary digital, or so-called postdigital (Berry and Dieter 2015; Causey 2016) culture. It is preferable to classify the earlier works as postmodern performances, understood for example in terms of Johannes Bringer's 'architecture of perception', where 'postmodern experimental performance generally presupposes our conflicted sensory experiences ... of the technological scene and mobilizes audio-visual techniques of abstraction against the no longer clearly defined/confined phenomenological reality of the stage' (Birringer 1985: 227), or Matthew Causey's 'New Media performance', which he describes as 'the inclusion of the televisual screen in performance, and the practice of performance' (Causey 1999: 385). There is a marked differentiation between postmodern performance and digital media performance, which establishes a central tenet of this book: *simply displaying videos or imagery using a digital projector, or screen, does not straightforwardly qualify a performance, set design, prop or costume as digital scenography.* By 1987, Josette Feral was already declaring that the incorporation of media devices into contemporary performance had become both commonplace and widespread, establishing a new normative 'aesthetic form which today signals the contemporaneity of the performance' (Feral and Bermingham 1987: 469). The dominant representational regime culminated in a postmodern assault on the senses that gave way to a new digitally afforded aesthetic that prioritizes 'the capacity to control [... over] a fascination with a fetishised object of desire' (Nichols 1988: 33). This shift parallels the altered conditions of perception in digital culture, in which control enters into a dialectical relationship with collectivity (Nichols 1988: 22) that gives rise to another uniquely digital specificity: the networked spectator. The increasing predominance of reticulation in contemporary spectating is the main reason for extending the definition of digital performance beyond Salter's criterion of *situated action*, and it moots the cyber/cybernetic/cyborg nomenclature of technological performance.

Internet-based performances are symptomatic of networked society's shift towards cyberspace and reticulated virtual reality, envisioned in the mid- to late 1990s by utopian theorizing towards equality and democracy. The writings of Hayles (1999) and Haraway (1991b) were profoundly influential in opening new discourses that reconsider the relationship between bodies and technologies. They challenge outdated notions of the fixed subject and expound the potential for disembodied intersubjectivity to erode traditionalist patriarchal ideological structures and democratize society. Discussing performances based on their ability to subvert and critique dominant notions of subjectivity and identity is precisely the ambit of the philosophical *Cyborg Theatre: Corporeal/Technological Intersections in Multimedia Performance* (Parker-Starbuck 2011). Like Bay-Cheng et al., Parker-Starbuck is interested in committing the entire body of work to specifically computational performances. In this volume she theorizes a 'cyborg theatre matrix' (Parker-Starbuck 2011: 41), which consists in a subjective flux modulated by the interrelational dynamics of three possible states of the performer's body – abject, object and subject – and the technological subject. She advocates the need to view technological 'apparatuses performatively on stage as agents for form and content, not merely as the systems through which ideas are imparted, but as ideas, subjects, themselves' (Parker-Starbuck 2011: 40). In concurrence with the aforementioned authors, she is not interested in performances that simply incorporate video and media devices to signal their contemporaneity; technology must play a central, *subjective* role in the performance event. This book agrees with Parker-Starbuck's stance and aims to synthesize it with resonant perspectives that advocate scenographic thinking as inseparable and antecedent to the performance event (Brejzek 2011; Lotker and Gough 2013; Baugh 2014; McKinney and Palmer 2017).

The body – the crucial site of Parker-Starbuck's theory – is an important point of contention between scenographic and cybernetic theory. Where does one draw the limits of the field of scenographic enquiry? Questions concerning the body, embodiment and disembodiment are central to media scholarship; whereas, scenographic discourse has traditionally focused on spatial practice and performer–audience relations thereof. However, recently expanded scenographic theorizations delineate 'the bodily dimension of the perception of scenography' (McKinney 2013: 65). McKinney propounds that a psychosomatic condition of 'kinesthetic empathy … operates in relation to the scenographic spectacle' (McKinney 2013), provoking an 'embodied response' in the audience. McKinney's theorizations are in relation to experiencing the passing of giant carnival sets in an urban setting, but her reflections exhibit salient parallels with contemporaneous polemics around embodied–disembodied experience in digital culture. This book attempts to draw out these parallels using the hybrid theoretical lens of digital scenography. Media and cybernetic theorists have done much work on the augmented, obsolesced and evolved body, while scenographic theorists have covered much ground on the relations of the body to tangible, physical, architectural, lived space and the mise-en-scène of performance therein. However, there remain incommensurable gaps in scholarship at the intersection of these two discourses, which are central to the overarching themes of this book and which repeatedly arise in each chapter in varying but analogous manifestations.

Developments in computational technologies have propelled advancements in telecommunications and reticulated intersubjectivity (explored in Chapter 1 in the context of Troika Ranch), biological sciences and genetics (explored in Chapter 2 in the context of Stelarc), physiological quantification and human–computer interaction (explored in Chapters 3 and 4 in the context of Klaus Obermaier and Chunky Move), responsive environments and urban augmentation (explored in Chapter 5 in the context of OnionLab) and ubiquitous computing and psychological profiling (explored in Chapter 6 in the context of Blast Theory). Each of these chapters explicates how the intersection of these evolved disciplines with artistic ingenuity opens new uncharted epistemic territory. Each artwork demonstrates the pivotal role that artistic innovation plays in opening big research questions and influencing the direction of scientific exploration. They expose a scenario in which the creative human can invent new types of identity, formulate new systems of intersubjectivity and dream new futures.

Epochal Rupture of Digital Technology and Global Interconnectivity

The invention of the internet should be understood as a profound innovation that has occasioned the 'Third Industrial Revolution' (Rifkin 2013) because it has brought about a cultural shift equal in measure to the agricultural and industrial revolutions. The watershed in global connectivity has accelerated idea generation, productivity and the democratization of, and accessibility to, digital technology. Its gargantuan cultural impact has been described as an 'epokhal technological shock' (Stiegler 2016: 12). This is a technologically invigorated disruption that fundamentally alters socioculture, economics and politics, bringing about a new epoch of intersubjectivity and identity. This technological shock constitutes the conceptual basis of this book, holding that it is the mainspring of a new genre of hybrid visual and performing arts practice. Artists have responded to the new cultural conditions by evolving new methodologies of scenography and design-led performance. There are types of artistic events created during this period, and are still emerging, the likes of which have never before been possible. This book charts some key works, to establish a 'genealogy of the sensible' (Stiegler 2011b: 14), spanning from the earliest avant-garde forays in this new domain (in the early 1990s) to the most topical contemporary manifestations. The goal of this genealogy is to help explicate a conceptualization of scenographic knowledge as an evolving dialogue of material and immaterial traces, arising from individual and collective intersubjectivity across a mutable material milieu of tools, traces, texts and artefacts. A historical mapping of digital innovations in performance can open important questions about the ontology of theatre, the role of the artist/spectator, and broader socio-political crises and successes.

Charting a genealogy of digital innovations in performance can reveal how they operate as a modulator of human subjectivity and identity, thereby defining how we experience reality. An artistic innovation is an intellectual *invention*. It is a recombination, rewiring or repurposing of knowledge that reveals an original intellectual or epistemic discovery – a sort of *re*-invention. Early forms of intellectual inventions are alphabets and numeric symbols (which are effectively a reinvention of drawing and mark-making). These opened the way for expanded scientific and social knowledge and became increasingly refined and specialized over the course of many centuries. More contemporaneously are innovations in the fields of applied mathematics and software development, which constitute a major pillar of the knowledge economy, founded on the basis of patentable intellectual property. This is more characteristic of Tim Berners Lee's discovery that materialized as the World Wide Web.[7]

While artists may not frequently *invent* new physical materials or tools, they do often *discover* new processes by reconfiguring and repurposing – as in hot-wiring – scientific knowledge in unforeseen ways. Artistic innovations are no less profound in their ability to modify the conditions of intersubjectivity, identity and human life, generally. Specifically, in terms of the performing arts, innovating involves developing new ways of combining biophysical gesture and articulation with (now digital) material means of expression. Through distributive paradigms, like memes, artistic inventions travel faster than scientific ones because they are not held up by bureaucracy, intellectual patenting rights and monetization processes. Therefore, they create bigger *bangs* (sociocultural ruptures) because they maintain the capacity to alter entire groups and communities, and ultimately the course of human culture; they contribute to 'the invention of a people' (Deleuze 2005: 209). Through this genealogy of selected digital artworks this book aims to, on one hand, examine how technology has altered the course of performance art over the last thirty years, by offering new means of articulation and new possibilities for critiquing politics and ideology and, on other hand, show how artists have altered the direction of culture and techno-scientific development, by rewiring the circuits of knowledge, reorganizing working processes, inventing new techniques and giving unforeseen creative expression to technological applications.

Methodology

The preceding sections of this Introduction provide reviews of existing scholarly fields that either employ a scenographic theoretical lens, conduct media theory readings, or use aesthetic or avant-garde theory to analyse technologically engaged performances. There is currently no singular work that synthesizes and consolidates these analytical domains. That is what this book aims to do, thereby developing a new grammar for conceptualizing and theorizing digital scenography and scaffolding a robust and enriching methodology. Pivotal to the recentralization of performance design in performance studies, and the co-emergence of a rich discourse, is its inherent connection with the rapid evolution, miniaturization and mutability of digital technologies. The performing arts' openness to interdisciplinarity, and its deep, immanent relations to new technologies, positions scenography as an important player in the fertile digital-cultural domain overlapping with computer science. This book holds that the scenographic, design-led approach produces the most innovative and engaging work. Therefore, only performances that attempt to elicit the new specificities of digital interactive technology, bring forth new art ideas and push the boundaries of possibility are examined; works that simply employ digital techniques to transmit traditional ideas via new media do not feature.

Of pertinence to this book are the new tools of creative expression that have emerged following the *shock of the digital*. In recent years, digital means of expression have soared in popularity and are now deeply embedded in the fabric of what it means to be human. The objects examined in this research can be divided into two genera: technological inventions (the tools) and cultural artefacts (the artistic by-products resulting from the permeation of these tools into the hands of performing arts practitioners). In terms of tools, those discussed are the scientific techniques of telecommunications, computer-vision, biometric sensing, real-time data analysis, signal processing, digital audio-visualization, genetic engineering and plastic surgery, and so on. In terms of artefacts, the projects analysed are a cross-section of digital and quasi-medical cultural events, all of which involve the exploratory fabrication of bespoke technologies for the transmission of art ideas. Established principles of new media that distinguish it from analogue and mechanical precursors are: 'numerical representation, modularity, automation, variability, transcoding' (Manovich 2001), control (Norbert Wiener 1965) and interactivity (Nichols 1988). As this genealogy progresses it expands this taxonomy to include recent developments like deep learning and artificial intelligence – fields that demonstrate the new profound efficacy of the digital. The goal is that the genealogy of periodic progressions in digital scenographic innovation will provide a critical, historical document of how evolutionary developments in the technical milieu incrementally push the limits of how reality is created and experienced.

This book draws on anthropological, ontological, postmodern and contemporary technological-philosophical theories that emphasize a shift away from anthropocentricism. While technological inventions are indeed the fruits of human ingenuity, they should not be straightforwardly interpreted as (objective) means to an end, separate from and dualistically opposed to the human body (Heidegger 1977). This book's overarching position on technē (making art or craft) is that technology is evolving organically with humans and defines the very essence of what it means to be human (Stiegler 1998). Technologies thus conceived are prostheses of the human body that occur because of a demand for specialized tasks in the external, material world. This operation is reciprocated internally, whereby the humans embody the technologies that they use (Leroi-Gourhan 1993). Technologies are not only conceived and shaped by humans, but so too are they assimilated to the psychosomatic operations of the body and mind, thereby continually redefining human nature. Therefore, the theoretical position of the book is one that gives credence to the notion that technologies (which are now at a digital stage of their ontology) hold a fundamental *efficacy*, or *performativity*, or *agency* (Simondon 2017a), which continues to redefine how artists make work and how art-going publics think about and engage with the art event.

Technicity, a philosophical concept that considers technology 'in its efficacy or operative functioning' (Hoel and van der Tuin 2013: 187), is a dominant theme in this book. It describes technology's influential properties and its ability to reorganize human activity. In the context of scenography, digital technology occasions the emergence of new forms of performance practice. The production pipeline that scaffolds the digital scenographic mode of expression can be broadly broken into four main stages: (1) audio-visual capture; (2) data processing, post-production and special effects (which can now be executed in real-time using computers and software); (3) audio-visualization (like digital lighting, screens/projectors, head-mounted displays (HMDs), digital sound design and spatial audio configurations); and (4) telecommunications for dissemination and/or telematic audience participation and so on. This book examines a cross-section of digital-cultural performances that involve some or all of the stages in this pipeline – that is, for the capture, processing, display and distribution of content – to embellish, examine or challenge the space of performance and/or the perceptual space of the spectator. The methodology concerns harnessing a discussion on *technicity* to cogitate how various technological devices and innovations condition the practitioner (maker) and the spectator (interpreter). How do artistic processes and techniques evolve in relation to the emergence of new technologies? How do technological manufacturers respond to the demands placed by ever-innovating artistic practitioners? How does the arrival of digital technologies reorganize the various strata of performance practice and discourse, and what are the effects of this reorganization on other non-technical specializations? And, what does the elevation of process-driven, design-led performance mean for the performing arts in general? These are some of the questions that are broached via the described techno-philosophical methodology.

Through-Lines

There have been a lot of ideas and explanations of rationale articulated in the Introduction thus far. Therefore, for the benefit of the reader and in concluding this introduction, I will attempt to summarize and draw-out these main, cross-cutting concerns that recur throughout the book and highlight the chapters where they are dealt with in most detail.

Each chapter discusses the work of a single artist or collective that reveals a new, original scenographic cultural artefact. The works are chosen on the basis that the artists mobilize technologies to interrogate space and challenge performance practice. Some artists (like Troika Ranch, Obermaier and Chunky Move) augment conventional theatrical spaces to immerse the audience in the spectacle, others (like Stelarc, OnionLab and Blast Theory) expand the performance arena beyond the physical architecture and challenge notions of artist–audience engagement. Notwithstanding their scenographic preferences, each artist was selected for their avant-garde tendency to disrupt theatre conventions through careful process-driven, design-led methodologies, towards experimental spatial practice. Therefore, it must be stressed that this is *not* simply a discussion of digital performance because there are many existing books about performance and digital technology/culture. Nearly every contemporary performance is somehow 'digital performance' because digital audio-visual technologies are the new normal for sonic and visual embellishment, and while often of high quality they are mostly not innovative. This genealogy only selects innovative, influential projects where there is a measured, methodological attempt to elicit the specificities of digital technologies, challenge the space of performance, rupture the landscape of theatre and the perception of the audience, evoke new topical digital-cultural subjectivities, and push the boundaries of possibility in performance.

This book does not purport that the discussed performances are fundamentally new; on the contrary, it delineates how the practitioners draw on a rich heritage of avant-garde, practice-based experimentation and combine their skills to engage materials in innovative, provocative ways. This experimental tradition extends back through the entire history of art, but it experienced an exceptional burgeoning since the Industrial Revolution and now receives renewed vigour in the digital age – the Third Industrial Revolution (Rifkin 2013). Therefore, the book holds on to the position of the reviewed authors who maintain there is an inherent avant-garde, experimental quality to digital media performances. However, these authors do not synthesize digital culture, scenography and avant-garde theories for decoding and discussing performances. This book seeks to close this gap in scholarship by providing an original, hybrid theoretical discourse.

The avant-garde qualities of digital scenography do not just refer to an engagement with cutting-edge technologies. At the heart of this discussion are the provocative and subversive qualities of the avant-garde, evident in their non-conformance to narrative tradition. This aesthetic mentality, which stretches back through Brecht to German expressionism, consists in the will to antagonize, provoke or even destroy the incumbency of the linear, pyramidal dramatic arc (Freytag 1863), which was, and continues to be, the dominant narrative schematic for Western modes of storytelling. A typical characteristic of digital avant-garde performances is that they often use unconventional, non-linear narrative formats. They are not neatly packaged sequential narratives with seamless scenic transitions that would position them as appealing for the conventional expectations of popular commodification; innovative artistic techniques are usually reapplied to conventional formats by the culture industry after they become more established and the experimental terrain, hence, becomes colonized and monetized. Attempts to breach the linear narrative hierarchy often entail spatial strategies to break out of the performer-versus-audience format, consolidated by the proscenium. This demands an engagement with the audience, whose passivity is challenged, and transports the mode of storytelling to the domain of discovery and dialogue. Therefore, it is hardly surprising that digital technologies have been engaged with such enthusiasm by artists seeking to diverge from narrative tradition, since interactivity and dialogue are central to their mode of operation. From motion-detection and electronic sensing techniques deployed for sophisticated immersive audio-visualizations (analysed in Chapters 1, 3 and 4) to site-specific and mobile technologies used to break out of the auditorium into the greater city (documented in Chapters 5 and 6), this book examines a range of innovative scenographic techniques that have revealed new approaches to performance practice via the specificities of digital technologies.

While this book is primarily concerned with experimental performances that break new ground, attention is also given to the evolution of certain digital scenographic techniques over the breath of the genealogy. An important underlying theme is an emphasis on the evolution of techniques, from an embryonic avant-garde stage (in the work of Troika Ranch and Obermaier), through high-quality employments (by Chunky Move and OnionLab), to their broad deployment in commercial cinematic commodities (evinced by *Blade Runner 2049*). A critical theory approach to the genealogy opens the discourse onto important socio-political and economic issues and highlights how quickly cultural innovations become assimilated to mass culture and advertising. This infuses digital scenographic practice with the inevitability of becoming stylistically homogenized by the mainstreaming of ground-breaking, experimental work. Furthermore, the techniques that were used to impress niche audiences in underground venues and experimental research labs are appropriated to market products in ways that question the limits of privacy. Chapters 5 and 6 provide an in-depth analysis of how digital scenography techniques are transforming not only the public landscape of cities, but also the private domains of perception, cognition, interpretation and the very thought processes that constitute how identities are constructed and represented in the new digitalized world. As such, this book is not simply a historical document that charts the development of digital scenography over the last thirty years, but it is also a critical document that applies philosophical and biopolitical scholarship to the selected performances and deeply considers the socio-political, economic impacts of the advancements when employed for symbolic commodification in mass culture. In this regard, the analytical methodology for the book is triangulated between performance analysis, technological philosophy and critical theory.

The deeply experimental nature of digital scenography insists that the vision for projects is often in flux and the outcome unpredictable; there is an uncertainty around how the performance can be presented as a complete product. Accordingly, the artwork often manifests as a series of experimental workshops, concluded by a public demonstration and open discussion. These characteristics, inherently advocated in schools of performing arts, correspond to PaR methodologies championed by Allegue et al. (2009), and are best understood in the context of the inclusive atmosphere surrounding Troika Ranch's creative exploits (in Chapter 1). Of central importance to these processes of discovery is the need for collaboration between various fields of expertise, especially between the arts and sciences. The complexity of digital technology demands that performers, artists and designers work closely with technical experts, like electronic engineers and computer scientists. This genealogy consists of a specially selected sample of projects that demand input from both the artistic and scientific sectors, thereby synergistically expanding knowledge in both domains; no project in this book was created by an individual in isolation.

There is continual pressure in the creative sector to produce original, innovative work; therefore, there is a tendency for artists to gravitate towards the most cutting-edge tools and techniques. Operating cutting-edge scientific tools/processes demands deep technical knowledge because the processes are not neatly packaged and user-friendly; they are simply not ready for uptake by *casual creatives*.[8] Innovative scenographies usually involve building custom technology; so artists must collaborate with technical experts and get access to expensive hardware. This makes these projects deeply expensive in terms of knowledge and equipment; indeed, they are only achievable through philanthropic grants, the support of large institutes (like universities or media corporations) or altruistic contributions from engineers/scientists. Analogously, the sciences need input from creative practitioners because they are under pressure to develop innovative technologies and patent or commercialize products. Therefore, research groups increasingly focus on evermore minute details, like more efficient algorithms or innovative pipelines. The scramble for minute, specialized intellectual property can often obfuscate the big picture. Input from the creative sector is needed to test technologies, identify niches, discern applications, invent over-arching narratives and conceptualize projects that will open new research questions. The clarity of creative applications drives the successes or failures of scientific inventions in the global economy; therefore, artists are needed to *show what they can do*. Furthermore, quantitative research data have limits to how much they can inform research development, before there is a demand to apply the findings and migrate technological research to the commercial sector. The qualitative knowledge of creative practitioners is invaluable for formulating an expanded view of how technologies might operate in quotidian cultural contexts. These internal tensions and complementarities between the arts and sciences surface in each chapter of this book.

Given the mutual interests of the arts and sciences in innovatively augmenting audio-visual perception and aesthetic experience, the inherently collaborative, experimental nature of theatre – the original spectacular forum – makes it an ideal domain for exploring the possibilities of how this technological ecology might evolve. There are deep interests in sustaining a strong and lasting dialogue between the arts and sciences, and scenography is in a privileged position to arbitrate this symbiosis.

1

Avant-Garde and Invention in Early Digital Scenography: Troika Ranch

What in the hell is new media? ... What's new in new media is you! Whoever you are, touching it, you are the newest thing about it, to touch it and influence it with your generation's thinking ... New media is our ever-increasing ability to manipulate space and time. It's not an object, it's not a piece of technology; it's a concept.
(DAWN STOPPIELLO 2018)

Introduction

Troika Ranch was a performing arts company, founded by Dawn Stoppiello and Mark Coniglio, which specialized in design-led digital media performances. In the context of the cultural rupture that generated the digital scenographic revolution (the internet), their work is positioned at ground zero. The period of their research that this chapter covers is their first five years (1989–94). This phase is understood as their avant-garde moment – a pioneering, experimental exploration of the unknown that challenges the institution of art. As discussed, there is criticism about the overuse of comparisons between digital media performance and the avant-garde, but in the case of Troika Ranch this comparison is unavoidable.

During this period, they moved through a series of practice-as-research (PaR) experiments in which they worked with Coniglio's bespoke *MidiDancer* technology – consisting of biophysical sensors and a radio transmitter – to track bio-mechanical movement. The works analysed are *The Need* (1989),

Tactile Diaries (1990) and *In Plane* (1994). This chapter does not give an in-depth analysis of all these works; instead, it focuses primarily on *Tactile Diaries* and uses the others to contextualize their PaR endeavours as a series of avant-garde experiments. A cross-sectional view of their oeuvre during this period permits the understanding that Troika Ranch produced a pioneering series of performance experiments wherein they position themselves as innovators, prioritizing methodological process over concrete outcome. Stoppiello declares:

> In 1989, when Mark and I first started working with the Midi Dancer, we both agreed we were gonna work with this device for at least 10 years. We're not gonna give up on it before 10 years, because we couldn't possibly know anything about it any sooner than that.
>
> (Thompson 2002)

This insightful reflection shows that they understood, not just the significance of their physical invention, but also the time and effort that it takes to learn the technology, harness it expertly, elicit its specificities and identify the unique and innovative qualities that it can bring to the stage.

The goal of this chapter is to emphasize the significance of this sub-genealogy of their oeuvre within the context of the overall genealogy that compromises this book. This first half-decade of their practice influentially contributes to the overall redefinition of scenography as a field that includes the invention of experimental set-ups, in which gestures and audio-visuals are both the instruments and the results of the experiment, that is, both the cause and effect of technology. Indeed, it is fair to say that *Troika Ranch* re-ignites the conception of performing arts as *experimental scenographic thinking*, in the digital age. This is crucial for the genealogical mapping of the book.

Background

Stoppiello and Coniglio attended the California Institute of the Arts (CalArts, 1985–9), Stoppiello with a view to studying with former members of the Bella Lewitzky Dance Company and Coniglio with the objective of becoming a film composer. During her studies there, Stoppiello's mind was opened to the exciting possibilities of how dance could be a stand-alone fine art. She was encouraged to explore 'the far reaches of *what dance was*' (Stoppiello 2018) and redefine the field, which was a radical conceptual departure from her high school tuition. At the time, CalArts was quite small yet many disciplines were represented, so there was a deep sense of collegiality and collaboration. She says: 'It was a very fertile time for me to understand all of the things that were going on in this gigantic artworld, that I didn't know about' (Stoppiello 2018). During their sophomore year, they were required to do a composition class where composers and choreographers were, amazingly, 'randomly paired' (Stoppiello 2018) to work on a practice-based exercise. Henceforth, began a collaboration that burgeoned into one of the great, productive partnerships of contemporary performance. From the outset, they had an affinity in terms of aesthetics and compositional interest; the intersection of Stoppiello's interest in pushing the boundaries of modern dance and Coniglio's pursuit of inventing electronic instruments created a fruitful complementarity.

The success of their sophomore exercise encouraged them to further collaborate on their final-year project. Coniglio was already a proficient computer programmer before coming to CalArts, which armed him with an 'unusual', inventive and timely skillset. His mentor, Morton Subotnick (an electronic music composer and founding member of CalArts), had already commissioned him to code an automated 'score-following' programme that played along with live musicians. The programme was used in a vocal performance, entitled *Hungers* (1987), directed by experimental filmmaker and illustrator Ed Emshwiller and featuring extended vocals[1] by Joan La Barbara. In the performance, she used *AirDrums* (MIDI-based maracas rigged with accelerometers) (Davies 1986), to playback vocal samples while she was singing; therefore, she could kinaesthetically improvise with her own voice. Following his exposure to this avant-garde collaboration, Coniglio was inspired to pursue his own ideas that involved wiring-up a dancer with similar Midi-sensing technology, so that the kinaesthetic movements could be tracked, fed-back, mapped and musicalized in a live setting – Stoppiello would be the pilot. She enthusiastically engaged with Coniglio on this venture into unknown territories of art making, and so began a period of PaR experiments that ultimately culminated in, perhaps, the first live *digital* interactive dance performance, *The Need*.[2]

The Need (1989)

The Need was a big final-year project, consisting of collaborations from various students,[3] that used video, live and recorded music, choreography, spoken word and scenic elements. It was the outcome of the artists' ambitions to make an impression on the artworld at the cusp of their graduation and a manifestation of the collaborative atmosphere nurtured by CalArts. In order to create an immersive ambience, the seating was removed from the theatre and it was performed in the round. The production was mainly composed of formal, predefined choreography and music; Stoppiello and Coniglio's interactive choreography was exclusive to the final scene, which lasted for about three and a half minutes.

Broadly speaking, the system functioned on the basis that bend sensors were wired up with radio transmitters and mounted on the elbows, knees or hips of the performers (see Figure 1.1). The messages – which, at this point, were binary (on–off) messages – were transmitted wirelessly to a receiver connected to an Apple Mac computer, which converted the data to MIDI messages and used them to trigger simple sounds on a MIDI synthesizer. Given the complexity of working with the technology at that time, it was an extraordinary achievement to get this all working in a live performance setting. Stoppiello reminisces on how experimental the PaR really was: 'We were amazed that it was even working …. It was like, "Oh my god, it works! It's amazing!" It totally felt magic, but it failed often' (Stoppiello 2018). They did not really know what they were doing, beyond an immanent curiosity and a passionate drive to discover new performance techniques. Analogously, Coniglio recalls that only a couple of days before the performance the whole system stopped working and he was literally reduced to tears. However, passion and perseverance drove him to resolve the problems (Coniglio 2019). Working on a Mac Plus, Coniglio had to boot the operating system from a floppy disk, then switch disks to run the performance programme (*Interactor*),[4] which he wrote from scratch. Both practitioners openly admit that their main

FIGURE 1.1 *Photo: Steve Gunther.* Tactile Diaries, *Dawn Stoppiello donning the* MidiDancer *(courtesy of Troika Ranch).*

concern was to get through the performance without the technology failing, which they achieved. While the nuances of the choreography were dubious, the significance of the working concept was historically monumental. Referring to the devising process, Stoppiello declares:

> After creating material separately, we came together to work with the dancers and quickly realized that this one-to-one relationship, one gesture producing one (and only one) sound, did not make for the richest composition musically or choreographically. We came to call this technique the 'bleep-bloop' method, as this is all that the first attempt ended up being – a series of bleeps in conjunction with the robotic choreography required to trigger the system.
>
> (Stoppiello and Coniglio 2003: 443)

Despite the shortfall in choreographic finesse, what must be acknowledged is their prodigious contribution to the new field of responsive scenography. The PaR that comprised the weeks preceding their graduation show, which culminated in the short interactive digital dance performance, was the genesis of an art idea that would become the focus of their artistic endeavours over the next decade, and would help stimulate an entirely new field of theoretical and practical discourse. While *The Need* can be understood as the germ of this aesthetic rupture, it is their subsequent performance, *Tactile Diaries*, that is of most interest to this chapter because, thematically and technically speaking, it is more sophisticated. Not only does it use the responsive *MidiDancer* techniques, but so too does it employ other quintessentially cybercultural techniques, such as video-conferencing, decentralized broadcasting and real-time global dissemination.

Tactile Diaries (1990)

It was the following year, after they entered into a collaboration with the founders of Electronic Cafe International (ECI),[5] Kit Galloway and Sherrie Rabinowitz, that they started calling themselves Troika Ranch.[6] The goal was to produce an experimental performance piece that employed the Panasonic WG-R2 slow-scan videophone, a cutting-edge piece of real-time televisual communications hardware. The concept concerned performing 'simultaneously at The Electronic Cafe in Los Angeles and The NYU Television Studios, New York City' ('Tactile Diaries (1990) | Troika Ranch' n.d.), by transmitting images from the former (local) site to the latter (remote) site, in real time. They named the piece

Tactile Diaries. ECI championed the democratization of telecommunications and broadcasting capabilities, which were previously only within the ambit of wealthy media corporations and government institutions. The slow-scan videophone transmitted video images over a regular phone line, thereby placing the capacity for (decentralized) broadcasting in the hands of artists and amateurs operating on low budgets. The internet did not exist at the time, so these slow-scan broadcasts were revolutionary.[7]

Theoretical notions of telematics, telepresence and the disembodied self, afforded by hypertexts and electronic networks, were yet to be teased out. However, there were many video surveillance cameras appearing in public and private spaces, and this compelled them to consider themes of access. Who are the privileged and who are the marginalized? The conversations that evolved during the conceptual development of the project were about writing and inscription – inscribing oneself on the world. Such processes were increasingly taking place through mechanical and digital technologies of inscription. Stoppiello explains: 'This is why, at the beginning of the piece, we were literally writing' (Stoppiello 2018). However, these were not overt themes that they set out to convey; these were techno-subjectivities that broadly influenced the way the artists thought about themselves and society. Coming from a performing arts schooling, Stoppiello was acutely aware of camera techniques and screen placement for live performance, and the power of the mediated gaze. Their intention was to take these quintessentially postmodern performance devices and marry them with the new potentialities offered by the slow-scan videophone.

Beyond the functions of democratized broadcasting and real-time image transmission, the slow-scan videophone introduced another deeper concept to the work: the possibility of visual (disembodied) dialogue across large geospatial divides, which later came to be described as teleconferencing or videoconferencing. Whereas ideas of videoconferencing may have existed in Hollywood films and science fiction literature, the ability for common users to transmit videos of themselves over a phoneline in real time was technically new, and it opened a new world of ideas. Troika Ranch was interested in how this new means of projecting oneself to the world would affect notions of identity and the self.

While the decentralized broadcasts with the videophone already constituted a significant artistic innovation, Coniglio, Stoppiello, Galloway and Rabinowitz's enthusiasm for creative invention drove them to push the technological and conceptual basis of the work to the limit. They fused the *MidiDancer* and slow-scan technologies to concoct an original, hybrid interactive digital scenographic device. Wired-up with bend sensors on her elbows, Stoppiello used the shape of her body to kinaesthetically trigger the videophone, thereby determining when and under what conditions the images would be sent to New York. As such, there are two major aesthetic concepts at work at the heart of this production: the democratization of video broadcasting and teleconferencing techniques, and the electronic prosthesis of the dancers' body that allowed her to alter local and remote scenographies.

Mise-en-scène

The work opens with two performers sitting in two retro chairs at a cheap laminated café table in front of an old piano (see Figure 1.2). Aside from the concrete floor, the setting is like something out of Richard Forman's living room: busy, cramped, cluttered, cosy, raw, rough and ready. There are numerous cathode-ray tube televisions placed around the performance area, which is a corner of the café. The TVs sit on rudimentary stands, shelves, drawer units and makeshift piles of pallets. One wall hosts a large video projection, while the other walls are covered in black-and-white photos, seemingly the captured images of other slow-scan videophone performances, staged there by Rabinowitz and Galloway. Power cables, plugboards and audio-visual cables

FIGURE 1.2 *Photo: Steve Gunther.* Tactile Diaries, *Scene 1, Writing. Performers: Dawn Stoppiello and Ilaan Egeland (courtesy of Troika Ranch).*

are dripping from the walls and ceiling, taped or tacked-up hastily with little concern for discretion.

The performers scrawl notes on scraps of paper, swapping them and examining each other's scribblings. Meanwhile the background soundtrack mainly consists of ominous and ambient electronic rumblings interspersed with electronically generated harpsichord-like sounds with an Eastern tonality. A videographer (Galloway) encircles them, with the slow-scan videophone, capturing images of them and their notes. The videophone images appear on some of the local screens and are sent to the remote venue in New York. There are other videographers capturing standard video feeds, which are only screened in the local space. At one side of the performance space there is a string duet (a violinist and cellist) dressed in formal orchestral attire. After about five minutes they take the lead from the electronic ambient sounds. The cello opens with a prolonged, ominous, deep monotone and the violin suddenly interrupts with a frenetic series of high-pitched squeaks and scratches, bringing discordant, dissonant and distinctly avant-gardist qualities to the soundscape. This is the cue for the dancers to engage in a choreography consisting of counterpoint-shifts and weight transferals that increase in intensity, finally erupting into an expressionistic crescendo of banging, dragging chairs and positional swapping, evoking conflict. Both dancers demonstrate excellent dexterity and, considering the tight space that they are required to move in, the choreography is loaded with dynamism. In the excitement, the written notes get scattered around the stage area, advancing the thematics to that of search, retrieval and the re-sharing of the written traces. The refocusing on the scraps of paper shifts the tempo from dynamism to stillness and the theme from conflict to resolution, furnishing a dramaturgical counterpoint to the preceding frenzy.

The narrative is structured as an expressionistic station drama [*Stationendramen*], in the sense that there are several (in this case, three) disjunct, loosely linked scenes. The second one is composed mainly of text, consisting in a seated actor, again scribbling notes, and a chorus (of three vocalists), repeating punctuated dialogue of deconstructed words, in a sonically hyperbolized tone, evoking a sort of malfunctioning robot or automaton. They are kept in rhythm by the amplified ticking of a metronome, sitting on the round laminated table. The repetitive and disconcerting chorus leads up to a monologue consisting of a visceral and neurotic self-examination of the phenomenology of hands.

The final scene is the most pertinent to the scenographic thematic of this book. Herein, Stoppiello wears the *MidiDancer* and kinaesthetically affects the electronic musical composition, while also triggering one of the videophones into scanning images, which are screened in the local space and sent to the remote NYC audience. The kinaesthetic technique was limited to the final scene of the performance because Troika Ranch maintained that there should be 'no technology before need' (Stoppiello 2018); that is, each performative element should be given its own space, and allowed to 'breath' as an independent entity. Her choreography is slow, still, robotic and, when compared with the duet, lacking in dynamism. However, it also presents a necessary respite from the intensity of the preceding textual scene, in which the audience were bombarded with repetitive, broken, monosyllabic utterances followed by the disturbing monologue. The *MidiDancer* and its electronic musical soundscape transmit a certain stillness, despite its technical complexity and underlying thematics of a cyborg dancer (literally) wired to the hilt. The slow movement qualities are imposed on the choreography by the *MidiDancer* and videophone technologies because they require a specific measured 'robotic choreography … to trigger the system' (Stoppiello and Coniglio 2003: 444), and these feed into the audio-visual mise-en-scène. As the videograms 'would be the only representation of the dance that the New York audience would see' (Stoppiello and Coniglio 2003: 445), Stoppiello was obliged to modify the choreography in consideration of the technological constraints; thus, the (local) narrative and mise-en-scène become determined by the technology and the remote audience. The constraints and affordances of technology comprise a dominant and recurrent theme in this genealogy.

Technical Description

The slow-scan videophone worked like a fax machine; it would progressively scan down through the image. The pixels were written sequentially to the screen line by line, like a printer. When the send function was triggered it would erase the current picture, reset the screen to black and start the next picture. It took five seconds to scan one picture and send it off to the remote location.[8] However, they had to be left on the screen for much longer, because the remote audience needed time to absorb and contemplate what they were seeing. Therefore, the staging problem consisted in a sort of dualistic mise-en-scène, where the local (embodied) audience in L.A. would see one thing and the remote (disembodied) audience in NYC would see another. The latter regarded a series of unique, ephemeral images that were displayed and then overwritten by the next one. Stoppiello wanted to compose a choreography for the videophone that was distinct from what the live audience in L.A. observed. She writes:

> I became very interested in selecting body shapes that, when seen in sequence in New York, would create a different narrative experience from the one that the live audience would have in Los Angeles. It seemed essential

to find a way to have the choppy, low-bandwidth video express something different than the full-bandwidth (live) dancer could provide. What was important about this approach was that it emphasized what was distinctive about the technology and provided a different way of seeing the dance.

(Stoppiello and Coniglio 2003: 444)

From the outset, there was an acknowledgement that the remote audience were neither seeing the live performance nor watching a recording; they were seeing something else. Stoppiello describes it as custom live 'stop-motion performance', made especially for the New Yorkers (Stoppiello 2018).

The videophone was an innovative piece of technology in and of itself. For the hybrid concept to work, Coniglio had to hack the device so that they could integrate a remote-control trigger. 'Galloway was brave and generous enough' to allow Coniglio to cut open one of the bespoke videophones and modify it towards this end (Coniglio 2019). He integrated a custom switch closure, which allowed him to use MIDI messages to trigger the videophone. In order for the technology to function, Stoppiello designed a solo which had a specific machine-readable choreographic vocabulary built into it. When she struck the correct posture, the *MidiDancer* would sense it and send a message to the videophone to snap an image; the preassigned posture symbolically controlled the videophone. Therefore, the choreography had to be very precisely composed because the technology was listening for very specific quantitative biometric data.

> MIDI was no longer just an acronym for Musical Instrument Digital Interface or simply a word in the name of our device but now represented to me a pathway that would allow my gestures to control basically any media device.

(Stoppiello and Coniglio 2003: 444)

MidiDancer functioned by analysing the stream of quantitative biometric data that was being sent by the bend sensors. The software listened for a particular set of statistical figures that indicated Stoppiello had produced the agreed-upon kinaesthetic vocabulary (body-shape), which would activate the trigger and send the videogram to New York. The choreography had to be slow and measured in order for the software to recognize the data sets; a series of rapid movements would produce excessive, spurious data, overwhelming the system and preventing recognition of numeric patterns. This need for a machine-readable (quantitative) choreographic vocabulary meant that a tension arose between the formal and improvisational approaches to the mis-en-scène. On one hand, there was a need to define a clear biophysical language that would allow the software to recognize the activating gestures, and on the other hand, there was a will to keep the choreography open and spontaneous enough to signal the conversational qualities, which would complement the liveness at the heart of video-based broadcasting.

Project Background and Avant-Garde Tendencies

At the time, Stoppiello and Coniglio were taking performance classes, with theatre practitioner Scott Kelman, at The 18th Street Arts Complex (Santa Monica), which housed ECI. Kelman learned his trade in the New York theatre scene of the 1960s where he was particularly influenced by Joseph Chaikin (Open Theater[9]) and the Becks (Living Theatre[10]) ('Scott Kelman Biography' n.d.), all of whom practised experimental, improvisational methods and were staunch champions of an activist avant-garde mentality, regarding 'the stage as a force for revelation and an antidote to bourgeois existence' (Blumenthal 2003). Kelman's classes influenced Troika Ranch to take an open, experimental approach to their practice. They were encouraged to trust their intuition and not get bogged down in formal stage-crafting. The performance development model was based on inhabiting a sort of sandbox – a safe place, where blue-sky experimentation was possible. For Troika Ranch this was a methodological leap because, coming from CalArts, they were schooled into the more conventional mindset of rigorously composing precise pieces. Their methodological shift towards an experimental dramaturgical approach realigned them with the aesthetic dogma of the avant-garde, which cherishes experimentalism and improvisation. Galloway and Rabinowitz were also major proponents of spontaneity and, given their collaborative agency, *Tactile Diaries* took on strong avant-garde dramaturgical and scenographic characteristics. Coniglio notes: 'For sure they were right, this kind of work does not mean anything if it is scripted and fore-scored, because, if you do that, there's no actual reason that the connection makes any sense' (Coniglio 2019). To pre-compose it would strip the work of its meaning and live, conversational qualities because one could, alternatively, pre-record a dance video and get the same result. This begs the question: What's wrong with using pre-recorded video? Artists were already doing it for decades, with relative notoriety and success. Nam June Paik and Wolf Vostell were experimenting with video performance techniques since the 1960s, and 'the introduction of Sony's Portapak video system in 1965 initiated the widespread practice of video art' (Causey 2006: 35). More contemporaneously, theatre innovators like The Wooster Group, Georges Coates Performance Works and Robert Lepage's Ex Machina had firmly established scenographic practices involving video screens and projections. Given that the televisual was already a dominant theatrical device to the point that it simply signalled the contemporaneity of a work (Josette Feral and Bermingham 1987), what distinguished its use in *Tactile Diaries* from preceding and contemporaneous creative deployments of the technology? More pertinently, what is it about this particular employment of video that makes it specifically digital, thus avoiding the pitfall of using new technologies in the capacity of old ones? The real-time, trans-continental video transmissions on the basis of a deregulated, decentralized broadcast represent a pioneering exploration of teleconferencing and teleacting. Therefore, it subverts the government-controlled, hierarchical system of symbolic dissemination and, by projecting a mediatized representation of the self to a physically remote location, it helps pave the way towards the idea of telepresence.

Teleacting and Democratization of Video Broadcasting

The notion of teleconferencing is constituted on the basis of transmitting an audio-visual representation of the dialogists in real time. It is not a phenomenon that is unique to digital technologies; rather, it is something that slowly emerged during the development of analogue technologies. Walter Benjamin's *The Work of Art in the Age of Mechanical Reproducibility* is the go-to text for this epoch, and his emphasis on the relations between optics and distance is pertinent to videoconferencing.

For Benjamin, mechanically reproducible film represents a fundamentally new cultural artefact that disrupts 'familiar patterns of human perception' (Manovich 2001: 158), transforming the way humans engage the world. He proposes there is an 'aura' immanent to art and nature that fosters aesthetic experience, and he asserts that it arises out of the 'unique phenomenon of a distance' (Benjamin 1999: 216), which he compares to gazing upon 'a mountain range on the horizon' (Benjamin 1999). For Benjamin, the conditions of aura are significantly challenged by mechanical technologies because image reproduction and global dissemination establish a new type of mediated distance that undermines 'natural distance' (Benjamin 1999: 227). However, he argues neither for nor against either strain; he is more concerned with the mutation of the relationship between artist, object and audience.

The respect for distance, observed by traditional modes of representation (like painting), is subverted by the new technologies of inscription because the artist and the subject can be anywhere at any time. Objects can be fallaciously supplanted to different spatial–temporal contexts through montage and its time-based language of symbolic juxtaposition, fundamentally facilitating a misleading construction of reality. Thus, the notion of natural distance as well as the unique spatio–temporal location of the object must be discarded.

Of further significance, for Benjamin, is the 'desire of contemporary masses to bring things "closer" spatially and humanly' (Benjamin 1999: 217). He is not perplexed by this inclination; it is a natural instinct that is constituted by a fundamental curiosity, which is a good characteristic that engenders epistemic progress, and mechano-optical technology effectively furnishes this desire. What he *is* concerned with is the 'ardent bent' of masses 'toward overcoming the uniqueness of every reality by accepting its reproduction' (Benjamin 1999), that is, their willingness to unquestioningly accept messages relayed over a medium that is fundamentally truth altering. Techniques of mechanical symbolic reproduction and mass-distribution ultimately coerce audiences into forgoing the uniqueness of embodied encounters – and the truth that can arise out of genuine dialogue – for altered representations of reality. Until the digital epoch, these were always a product of a top-down, unidirectional system of communication from wealthy institutions, with vested monetary or political interests, towards vulnerable and isolated individuals. In terms of Galloway and Rabinowitz's videophone performances, they were levelling a challenge at the hierarchy of access to, and control over, the means of symbolic distribution.

Lev Manovich acknowledges Paul Virilio for his advancement of Benjamin's thesis and cogitating the further reorganization of human sense perception in the digital age (Manovich 2001: 158–61). Benjamin's assertion that technology causes a *withering* of distance provides the mainspring for Virilio's synthesis, which maintains that the mutation of perception worsens under digital technologies. He claims this is a result of the total submission of physical distance to 'the *light-speed* of information carrier waves' (Virilio 1997: 38), which leads to a further destabilization of politics and culture. He employs the terms 'small-scale optics' and 'large-scale optics' to delineate the magnitude of this change (Virilio 1997: 35). The former describes all that is distinguishable to the human eye in 'geometric' space, 'which in the end only covers man's immediate proximity' (Virilio 1997);[11] the latter describes 'active-optics', which is the real-time transmission of information over global electronic networks, a process that occurs at the speed of light and 'disregards the traditional notion of a horizon' (Virilio 1997).

Despite some latency, active optics theoretically facilitate the real-time transmission of audio-visual information from any given global location to another, without significant depreciation in quality. The digitalized world collapses separate locations into the singular space of a message-in-circuit, negating perspectival notions of distance and its referents of *close by* or *far away*, and the time needed to close the gap. These are the conditions that constitute the basis of videoconferencing and its related concept: telepresence. Although there are various definitions of telepresence, it is broadly understood as 'the perception of presence within a physically remote or simulated site' and requires sensual (optical or haptic) feedback (Draper, Kaber and Usher 1998: 354). This statement refers to the *actor* in the system. In terms of *Tactile Diaries*, it is a conceptual stretch to describe Stoppiello's experience via the videophone as telepresent; however, she does execute a type of *teleacting*. This happens at the remote level, in the sense of *acting* for a trans-global audience, and at the local level because she kinaesthetically triggers the videophone, executing *tele-actions* within close range. The latter aspect raises the argument that the *MidiDancer* affords *tele-haptic* gesticulations, that is, the ability to touch over distance. This is deeply linked with the prosthetic potential of digital technology (discussed in detail in the next chapter).

In performing live for a distant audience, Stoppiello does not make the claim that she experienced the sensation of being present in a physically remote location, but it can be argued that the audience and collaborators at the remote (NYC) location *did* experience her mediated, live presence in their local space. This itself is nothing new; it can be argued that news-readers and weather-forecasters have occupied domestic households all over the world, in real time, for decades preceding ECI's transmissions. However, non-corporate and non-governmental transcontinental televisual broadcasts definitely were new. In addition to the affordance of visual dialogue with physically remote sites, the videophone also places the power of televisual broadcasting in the hands of independent arts organizations. ECI pioneered some of the first forays into the new aesthetic and epistemic territory of videoconferencing, teleacting and telepresence, before the theoretical concepts were thrashed out. While this phenomenon is taken for granted nowadays, with the likes of Skype and YouTube's live streaming capabilities, it took a huge effort to get the technology working in the early 1990s. The impact that these techno-cultural innovations have had on the socio-political and economic landscape should not be underestimated. Such impacts are central to both Benjamin's and Virilio's arguments.

Virilio holds that the facility for the live transmission of audio-visual symbols coerces an even more precarious socio-political situation than that envisaged by Benjamin. For Benjamin, mechanical technologies can displace objects from their original location and alter reality; for Virilio, cyber-electronic technologies predominantly eliminate perceptions of distance and space, obliterating reality and precipitating a new mediated world bereft of depth or coordinates. As large-scale optics replace the small-scale types, the distinctive times and locations that constitute orientation and critical judgement are diminished, advancing the sensation of claustrophobia on a global scale. Virilio writes:

> Prospective **telepresence** – and shared **tele-existence** with it – not only eliminate the 'line' of the visible horizon … They also once again undermine the very notion of **relief**, with touch and **tactile telepresence at a distance** now seriously muddying not only the distinction between the 'real' and the 'virtual' … but also the very reality of the

near and the *far*, thus casting doubt on our presence *here and now* and so dismantling the necessary conditions for sensory experience.

(Virilio 1997: 45)

Virilio laments digital technology's ability to dissolve distance and bypass vast natural spaces, which he believes are necessary conditions for critical reflection and correct decision-making. Despite his useful advancement of Benjamin's theory and some insightful hypotheses on politics and speed, Virilio's texts are shot through with nostalgic pessimism that compels an endemic criticism of technology. On the contrary, despite having been forced into exile by the Nazis, Benjamin is not totally despairing about developments in the technologies of perception; rather, he is wary of *how* they are deployed, especially for the ends of aestheticizing politics, an endeavour that he attributes to fascism. Virilio's apprehension forecloses possibilities of appreciating the beneficial aspects of real-time digital image transmissions. However, Bernard Stiegler's more recent philosophizing does not take such a polemical position against technological developments. Stiegler asserts that every technological development should be viewed with the understanding that there are always positive and negative aspects to it. He describes this as a *pharmakon*,[12] that is, something which is both *a poison and a cure*. For Stiegler, all technologies are bound to the fundamental condition of pharmacology.

Rupture and the Pharmacology of Digital Telecommunications

Stiegler regards twentieth-century Western culture as having wholly engaged in a top-down model of cultural production and dissemination, facilitated by analogue technologies of representation and broadcasting. Televisual culture was unidirectional and positioned masses as passive, submissive consumers of content. This was an outright dismissal of the potential for audiences to contribute to cultural production and a characteristic folly of the period following the 'first mechanical turn of sensibility' (Stiegler 2011b: 4). This describes, as per Benjamin and Virilio, a reorganization of the conditions of perception and intersubjectivity as a result of the historical rupture of the industrial revolution – the beginning of automatic processes. These advancements in the technical sphere exerted a deep influence over artist–audience relations and the role of art. The role of the masses shifted from producers to consumers of cultural content, precipitating a situation whereby both artists *and* art were generally 'proletarianized' – they were devalued and put to work in the service of capitalism. In summary, socio-economic, political and aesthetic processes were fundamentally altered by a technological subjectivity, whereby techniques of object production became automated and industrialized resulting in a transferral of the mystery paramount to aesthetic experience from maker to machine – an erosion of anthropocentrism.

A rupture that causes a transformation of perception only occurs very rarely and can only be brought about by a *fundamentally new* discovery (see Introduction, page 17). According to Stiegler, human consciousness is constituted through a technicized perceptual, or 'spiritual,' prosthesis that is *always* 'pharmacological', and which operates towards the industrialization of both techniques and time – techniques in the sense that productive processes are replaced by automata, and time in the sense of capturing one's *attention*, which is a question of giving up one's time (Stiegler 2011a). Since the seizure of cinematic technologies for marketing and PR in the early twentieth century, the attentional faculties of the masses have been seized, held and re-programmed by a spectacular, stupefacient industrial cultural model that coerces a loss of knowledge – of our 'savoir-faire' [knowing what to do] and 'savoir-vivre' [knowing how to live] (Stiegler 2010c: 7). This is not to purport that cinematic technologies are malignant in themselves, quite the opposite; cinematic technologies 'were, until now, industrial functions that were hegemonically controlled by ... the *psychopower* of marketing and the culture industries' (Stiegler 2011b: 4). For most of the twentieth century, only highly capitalized production houses and government-controlled institutions had access to cinematic technologies and global dissemination techniques, which they deployed with a view to manipulating and exploiting human emotions towards amassing profit and political persuasion. Henceforth the establishment of a hegemonic libidinal economy based on the 'proletarianization of sensibility' (Stiegler 2011b), that is, the putting-to-work of drive and desire.[13]

On the basis of his pharmacological analysis, Stiegler maintains that digital technologies, which constitute the 'second mechanical turn of sensibility' (Stiegler 2011b: 4), have the potential to be the antidote to their mechanical precursors. This second perceptual turn refers to the widely supported perspective that, when mobilized ethically and responsibly, digital systems could reinvigorate mass-intersubjectivity with positivity and equality because, theoretically, all participants in the system can be afforded a voice to contribute to socio-political dialogue and participate in the creation of culture (Haraway 1991b; Hayles 1999; Ascott 2003). Digital microelectronics and the emergence of computer-assisted calculation have permitted the *hyper-acceleration* of automatic processes, which now operate at light-speed. In Benjamin's lifetime cyclical automation (like film reel) was perceptible, occurring at 'the dynamite of the tenth of a second' (Benjamin 1999: 229). In the digital age electronic cyclical automata now occur as electrical pulses (infra-circuit) at an imperceptible speed, approximately a hundred million times faster than that of mechanical technology; indeed, time itself is now measured in an unimaginable unit of measurement: nanoseconds.[14] The main difference between the two epochs is a question of speed and scale. The electronic microprocessor affords the placement of automatic processes within automatic processes. This layering of automata constitutes cybernetics, a fundamentally new invention, the advent of which has occasioned an epochal technological shock that harbours new possibilities.

During the nascent period of cybernetic technological development, theoreticians highlighted their pharmacological qualities. Co-founding cyberneticist Norbert Weiner published ethical reports that reflected on the socio-political impact of his scientific practices on the mind, body and community (1989). He understood how the technology had the potential to either open 'seemingly limitless amounts of instrumental power and complex control ... that could be made subject to human direction', or exacerbate 'human beings' abilities to kill and enslave one another' (Biro 2009: 3). This pharmacological characteristic of cybernetic technology is pivotal to understanding the dualistic potential of contemporary digital culture, and it is central to the overarching aesthetics of this book. With every techno-evolutionary surge there is the potential for a positive or negative impact on society, so employments ultimately involve an ethical dichotomy. Thus, while embracing evolving cultural specificities we also need to continually examine them. There is a pressing need to foster the positive aspects of digital technologies – a 'positive pharmakon' (Desmond et al. 2015: 77).

That every technological development is pharmacological is also true in economic terms because, although increases of automata in industry lead to the replacement of human labour, they also lead to a reduction in production costs. This means non-professional masses get access to, not just the previously unaffordable cinematic hardware and software that facilitate audio-visual capture and postproduction, but also new equipment, unique to the digital age, like computers, electronic sensing technologies, distribution networks, social media promotional channels and software that permits the modification of data in previously unconceived ways. The availability of these new technologies to theatre practitioners helps stimulate a redefinition of artist–audience relations, engendering the emergence of a second scenographic turn, where independent artists and amateurs are re-afforded an active, critical and productive capacity to contribute to and shape culture. Troika Ranch's work is an excellent example of this 'recapacitation' (Stiegler 2016: 181) afforded by the digital revolution.

Experimentalism, Invention and Procedure

It is easy to take for granted the availability of digital technologies nowadays, given the speed with which they have become pervasive in mass culture.

However, this was not the case for Troika Ranch and ECI, at the outset of this genealogy. Although the early 1990s was a turning-point in the mass availability of the components needed to make the project work (e.g. desktop computers, Midi controllers, bend sensors and radio transmitters), the success of the project was completely dependent on the artists' inventive capacity; there were no mass-produced devices for tracking gestures, kinaesthetically triggering video recorders or decentralized broadcasting, and there was no software for getting them all cooperating. Coniglio recalls: 'Back then I was building all this stuff because it didn't exist otherwise. Nothing like this existed. The only way to have it was to make it yourself. Luckily I was good enough at that kind of thing to do it' (Coniglio 2019).

The artists demonstrate a penchant for inventiveness by developing a bespoke hybrid technology, and an original choreography based on the principle of a new human–computer readable choreographic syntax. As such, *Tactile Diaries* is constituted by two types of invention: the physical technological innovation (the *MidiDancer*-cum-videophone) and the choreographic innovation (a computer readable gestural grammar). The fusion of these two innovations within a singular work makes it a seminal contribution to the field that opens new possibilities in the performing arts, on the basis of computer agency.

Videoconferencing and teleacting were already central themes of *Tactile Diaries*; therefore, impulse, intersubjectivity and liveness were crucial to the conceptual underpinnings of the work. Stoppiello and Coniglio wanted to use the *MidiDancer* technology in tandem with the videophone but they were still only beginning to understand the potential of their own technology; therefore, they were uncertain about the justification for mixing the technologies. They invested much energy in questioning and reconciling what it meant to perform with the two devices. The concept evolved into the idea that the *MidiDancer* would be used as an electronic prosthesis that allowed Stoppiello to kinaesthetically trigger the videophone into scanning and sending the messages. *Tactile Diaries* is essentially underpinned by a curiosity; the slow scan technology was brand new at the time and Troika Ranch wanted to challenge it, push it to the limit and discover what was possible. This evinces that their practice was essentially founded on experimentalism, a quintessential quality of the avant-garde underpinned by the will to explore new epistemic territories and open up new fields of enquiry. 'When impulse can no longer find preestablished security in forms or content, productive artists are objectively compelled to experiment' (Adorno 2002: 23). This experimental drive to challenge predominant norms (established by the institute of art) is representative of a general demand for originality and newness in contemporary art determined by late capitalist socio-economics, and a need to respond to the evolving technological and sociocultural conditions. Analogous to the way that photographic technology destabilized the function of the visual artist as a producer of naturalistic pictorial documents, audio-visual recording techniques impelled the evolution of live performance; faced with its redundancy, theatre had to innovate and offer something more than film.[15] Hence, the birth of modern avant-garde theatre. Theatre's strongest counter position to film is in its ability to, on one hand, embrace embodied presence, by staging live actors, and, on the other hand, establish itself as a hybrid space that can accommodate both the present actor and the mediated (pre-recorded) actor.[16] The increased use of technology on the live stage has also afforded theatre its reclassification as a sandbox, a space for experimentation, investigating not just human to human (mediatized) interaction but also human–machine interaction.

The tendency towards experimentalism impels the artistic subject to employ 'methods whose objective results cannot be foreseen' (Adorno 2002: 24); the final outcome is cast into the realm of indeterminacy, and this impels a methodology that celebrates the flux of process over a final, fixed product (already explicated as PaR). The emphasis on process in PaR occasions a paradigm shift that destabilizes the artist, as authoritarian messenger, and positions the performance as a living, breathing, mutable system of constellating things in which the artist must define rules and organize the elements. *Tactile Diaries* exemplifies this functional shift of the artist, as *a singular, authoritative, subjective modifier of material, towards that of a designer, engineer or inventor of a rule-based system*, which, in turn, modifies the performance event through its own contingency. The role of technology, as an agent in this process, cannot be understated. In *Tactile Diaries*, the relational complexities unearthed by new technologies and indeterminacy open a tension between the *MidiDancer*'s demand for a formal, structured machine-readable choreographic syntax, and the improvisatory dramaturgy impelled by the conversational qualities of the videophone. Between the quantitative, techno-scientific repurposing of the technologies, by Coniglio, and the qualitative, artistic reinterpretation of the choreographic discipline, by Stoppiello, there is an oscillation between formalism and expressionism, between rigour and improvisation, that shifts the conceptual focus from a fixed product towards an open-ended performance system with an unpredictable and mutable outcome.

Systems Art

This indeterminate, open-ended art arrangement is rooted in the discipline of systems art, an artistic movement beginning in the late 1950s with John Cage and extending through the Fluxes Movement and E.A.T. (Experiments in Art and Technology) to postmodernism,[17] and continues to receive acclaim from practitioners and critics (Stott 2015). It was influenced by cybernetics and systems theory. Under its open-ended strategy, a rule-based system is established and the art product, which varies from iteration to iteration, is allowed to emerge; the conceptual emphasis switches from the product to the process. *Tactile Diaries* operates along this strategy. The difference between this and, for example, Cage's magic-square (mathematical chart) compositions is that the system is more sophisticated; the algorithms for generating the indeterminate musical composition and capturing and sending images are more complex. However, the overarching pipeline is similar: (1) human gestural input, (2) systematic calculation based on human input and (3) numerical output. In Cage's compositions, the variable numerical output determined the selection of certain instruments and qualitative properties such as note, pitch, duration, timbre and so on (Pritchett 1988); in *Tactile Diaries*, the numerical output of the bend-sensors similarly affects the musical properties – now altered in real time – and determines how and when a videogram is captured and telecommunicated. In the latter, the affective quality of the number becomes more deeply embedded in the infrastructural fabric of the system, but the overarching strategy remains the same. The genealogical progression from the former to the latter is symptomatic of the broader metanarrative of technical evolution: numbers are becoming more deeply tied to the ontology of work, accumulating layers of technical abstraction that erect an increasing opacity around operational processes and contribute to an inability to perceive the system in its totality (Hui 2016). In this regard, there are increasing levels of agency and responsibility deferred to the microprocessor and its automated technical processes that, on one hand, augment the spectacular sophistication of the work and, on the other hand, cast doubt over the involvement of human performers. This aporia consistently raises its head throughout this book. It is crucial to understanding the socio-political critique inherent in the various works, and the general impact of technical evolution on contemporary culture.

Technological Transformations of Methods

The indeterminate, experimental and hybrid nature of *Tactile Diaries* confirms that Troika Ranch's aesthetics and methodologies were closely bound up with the category of the possible, which is immanently intertwined with *invention*, or *discovery*. By doing so, it firmly situates the work within the avant-garde. On a more discreet level, it also connotes a mischievous, provocative message about Western culture generally: human activity is increasingly determined by an evolving agency in the technological domain. This raises one of the central tenets of this book, which is a discussion of the affordances and limitations that digital technologies bring to scenographic practice. As in all contemporary professions, developments in technology exert a pressure on the various expert domains of performance – acting, directing, choreographing, lighting, costume, sound and stage design. As technology evolves, it demands that work and working processes also evolve.

Digital technologies have transformed all areas of socio-economics, culture and politics as profoundly as the agricultural and industrial revolutions (Rifkin 2013), because they penetrate every area of work. The ubiquity of the digital in contemporary productivity and intersubjectivity is quite inescapable. In the performing arts this is visible at the macro level, by the spectacle's 'tendency to expand and share its effects with ever-greater bodies of spectators' (Baugh 2017: 23), and at the local level, through the use of sensors, computers, microcontrollers, etc., combined in a system 'that responds to the embodied participation of [human interactors] in real time' (Stern 2013: 6). *Tactile Diaries* exploited both genera. It mobilized the new hyper-automatic specificities of the second mechanical turn to influence the artistic outcome, revealing a computationally affected and globally distributable choreography that was inconceivable in the context of pre-existing technologies and performance methods. The Troika Ranch/ECI collective exposed new possibilities for technical processes that reflect an increase in the agency, responsibility and intention of machines in the arts and society generally. They used these interactive digital specificities to explore new non-anthropocentric possibilities for choreography and dramaturgy at the intersection of human and software, establishing an epochal milestone in the legacy of scenography and a rupture to the discursive economy around performance and technology.

Towards *In Plane*

Although this chapter is primarily focused on *Tactile Diaries*, it is important, in terms of a genealogy, to give an outing to *In Plane* (1994). While *Tactile Diaries* may be understood as a profoundly avant-gardist gesture, *In Plane* should be viewed as a milestone in the refinement of Troika Ranch's theoretical and methodological processes, and the maturation of their understanding of how to stage the new choreographic and dramaturgical qualities afforded by the *MidiDancer* technology. Stoppiello writes:

> *In Plane* ... was a seminal work for us. It was not only our most technologically complicated piece but it became the cauldron in which we synthesized the theoretical paths that we had been on for the past four years.
>
> (Stoppiello and Coniglio 2003: 445)

For Stoppiello and Coniglio, the period from 1989 to 1994 constituted a continuous PaR enquiry, which was not only powered by their ardent passion for the subject but so too was it nurtured by inspirational discussions that took place in the rich digital-cultural research space of the Centre for Experiments in Art, Information and Technology (CEAIT), founded by Morton Subotnick using a philanthropic research fund acquired from AT&T. The two-year funding strand provided full-time employment for Coniglio and furnished him with institutional and infrastructural support to experiment with various ideas that were both directly and indirectly linked to Troika Ranch. Coniglio recalls:

> I was making work there. It wasn't my work that was being shown, but I was creating stuff, and we were deeply into the question of, what does this all mean? ... We were constantly thinking about, debating and figuring out what these materials were, and how we work with them, and what works, and what doesn't work.
>
> (Coniglio 2019)

From 1991 to 1993, the centre presented experimental work to the public by holding ten major events, where they brought some of the most exciting contemporary digital arts practitioners to ECI.[18] New ideas were being explored and new questions were being asked about the field. Even though she was not directly employed by the centre, Stoppiello was attending all the events and was a central figure in the open discussions that conceptualized what it meant to make art with digital technologies. The importance of the establishment of this forum cannot be understated; it was a visionary move by Subotnick and it demonstrates his understanding of the importance of creating open, friendly, creative and interrogative conversations. A forum for discussing, reflecting upon and theorizing praxis is a paradigm that has been firmly in place since the beginning of Western civilization. *Logos* is the Greek word for discourse (or reasoning) and it forms the basis of that familiar word, *dialogue* [dia | logos], that is, discussion between two or more people. Logos, as a process of rationalization and persuasion through logical argumentation, is understood as the basis of Western philosophy and aesthetics for about 2,500 years. The individuals of a collective conversation affect and influence each other through the disclosure and absorption of knowledge, thereby contributing to the development (the *becoming*) of each participant and reshaping the overall group. 'As knowledge is transferred from one being to another (or from a group to an individual etc.), each transaction is interpreted and embodied in an individual way – depending on the already acquired experiences of the receiver – and so undergoes differentiation in its re-usage' (O'Dwyer and Johnson 2019: 7–8). Every subject is mutable and all transactions, whether oral, gestural or written (symbolic), are irreversible. This principle, known as *individuation*, is rooted at the foundation of continental philosophy.

Individuation and Influences on Troika Ranch

Individuation is a philosophical principle that describes how individual things can be differentiated from, and understood as distinct and unique from, other things of the same category. The concept is particularly useful when applied to organic species, like the animals of a herd. It becomes complex when applied to humans because of the multiple layers of human subjectivity and identity, constituted by internal and external factors, such as socio-culture, traditions, experience, language and so on. The principle is founded on the basis that individuals are identified as distinct from other individuals and the groups they comprise. Stiegler explains it succinctly when he writes:

> The *I*, as *psychic individual*, cannot be thought except to the extent that it belongs to a *we*, which is a *collective individual*: the *I* constitutes itself through the adoption of a collective history, which it inherits and with which a plurality of *I*s identify.
>
> (Stiegler 2014: 50)

The principle has provided a rich, nuanced conceptual terrain for various theorists over the centuries, from the very early hypothesis of Aristotle, moving through Thomas Aquinas, Duns Scotus and Francisco Suárez, to the modern period in its adoption by Henri Bergson, Friedrich Nietzsche and Carl Jung. It was revived in modernity/postmodernity by Gilbert Simondon (1989) and Gilles Deleuze and Felix Guattari (1980) and now plays an important role in the technological philosophizing of Stiegler. It is this last surge in interest – from Simondon to Stiegler – that is most pertinent to this book because their non-anthropocentric perspectives shift the theoretical focus towards the influence of technology on human processes.

Simondon's contribution to the theoretical discourse is quite radical because he posits a non-anthropocentric view that contradicts the incumbent Aristotelean substantialist, metaphysical schema upon which a whole host of theories are based, thus challenging the basis of continental philosophy. Substantialist theories are grounded in the supposition that the individual and the collective exist as already individuated entities, or substances. Simondon argues that individuation is a fluid and mutable process through which the individual and the group co-constitute each other, continually redefining their identities. Simondon's philosophy inverts the dominant metaphysical strategy and pursues knowledge by considering individuation as 'the "primordial" operation through which the individual *becomes*, and of which individuals are "modalities"' (Scott 2014: 6). That is, being is a process of becoming; becoming withholds being within the nature of its operations. Being does not condition becoming; being is conditioned by becoming.[19] The individual is thus conceptualized as a temporal and relative state of reality in the broader unfolding of multiple affective realities.

Stiegler sides with Simondon's inversion of the substantialist, metaphysical schema towards a relational view. He writes: 'An *I* is essentially a *process* and not a state, and this process is an *in-dividuation* (this is the process of psychic individuation) in that it is a *tendency* to becoming-one, which is to say *in-divisible*' (Stiegler 2014: 50). This process of becoming takes place through dialogues and interactions between individuals and their interacting milieus. Human individuation is a constantly developing process; it is always in flux – never in a fixed state. The process '*never comes to a conclusion* because it encounters a *counter-tendency* with which it enters into a *metastable equilibrium*' (Stiegler 2014: 51). Analogously, the *We*, as a collection of individuals on a trajectory towards establishing a collective identity, is also an entity undergoing a continual change. The individuation of the *I* is 'always inscribed in that of the *we*, while, inversely, the individuation of the *we* only takes place through the conflicting individuations of the *Is* that compose it' (Stiegler 2014: 51). The individual and collective are not straightforward binary opposites; they exist within each other, determining each other through processes of consensus and dissensus, which are also fluid and subject to economies of scale. When this concept is expanded to a digitally networked global culture, processes of individuation become deeply reorganized by technological means of interaction.

Considering individuation in the context of Troika Ranch and their participation in the artistic dialogues at CEAIT, we can surmise that they were influencing and influenced by the other practitioners. They were beginning their careers and establishing their practice in the context of a dynamic community composed of experienced practitioners who were modifying their work based on critical feedback from the young duo. The hub of activity provided by CEAIT and the various events experienced by the audience–practitioners in attendance were crucial elements that impacted Troika Ranch's digital media performance practice and the entire legacy of digital scenography.

Of further significance to their development was the patronage that Coniglio and Stoppiello received from Subotnick, under the research fund. In reciprocity for their dedication to the CEAIT community – developing bespoke applications and contributing to the dialogues – Subotnick generously funded

Troika Ranch to do residencies in Santa Fe and the Atlantic Centre (Florida). The goal was that Coniglio and Stoppiello would participate in a performance event, in which Subotnick, Woody and Steina Vasulka, and Troika Ranch would exhibit a digital media work. It was a very generous offer by Subotnick because Troika Ranch was granted the time, resources and freedom to truly explore the mise-en-scène and dramaturgical potential of the *MidiDancer* technology and they would be billed with highly established, acclaimed artists. They were furthermore afforded the privilege of rehearsing and conversing with experienced, high-profile artists towards the unitary goal of a performance trilogy. Coniglio remarks:

> We suddenly had residencies for the first time, where we could be completely focused ... We had never before, at any point, except when we were students, had dedicated time to work on these things. So, that was a super-important moment – to be helped. So, all this information is building and filtering into our process, but now we have real time to think about it.
>
> (Coniglio 2019)

Stoppiello acknowledged the influence that the Vasulkas had on their work by introducing them to the possibilities of working with digitized video footage (Stoppiello 2018). Steina was experienced at using a Midi violin to manipulate LaserDisc video footage. In the spirit of individuation and knowledge transmission, the Vasulkas generously taught Troika Ranch to work with the technique and introduced them to their professional network, so that they could get their own LaserDisc pressed for *In Plane*, their contribution to the trilogy.

In Plane

In Plane premiered at the Walker Art Centre in Minneapolis in 1994. It was the performance that really made a name for Troika Ranch. Their acclaim was also catalysed by Coniglio's connection to the electronic music community. The work was exhibited widely at art festivals and electronic music conferences over the following decade. They brought it to IDAT '99 (International Dance and Technology 1999),[20] where it received critical praise. It was the first piece in which they thematically and technically consolidated the vision of the kind of work they aspired to. In terms of operating the show, the objective was to automate everything so that Coniglio only had to trigger a few scene changes and Stoppiello would primarily manipulate the audio-visuals through her gestures. They used a refined version of the *MidiDancer* system, which

FIGURE 1.3 *Photo: Mark Coniglio.* In Plane. *Performer: Dawn Stoppiello (courtesy of Troika Ranch).*

included 'a costume embedded with eight Flex sensors at the elbows, wrists, hips and knees' (Stoppiello and Coniglio n.d.). The mise-en-scène consisted of a completely open stage with a single large projection screen positioned upstage. The video projections were recordings of Stoppiello wearing an identical shiny, futuristic lycra *MidiDancer* costume, establishing a dualism (see Figure 1.3); the stage was inhabited by the present, embodied dancer and the screen was inhabited by her digital duplicate. Stoppiello succinctly explains the thematics:

> The piece was to be a competition between the corpus and its electronic Doppelganger, a body that bleeds, sweats, gets tired, and feels pain versus a body made of light that is not bound by time, space, or gravity. I became the fleshy presence, while my video image, stored on the laser disc, was my electronic counterpart. Which was the more powerful and beautiful presence? The flesh-and-blood woman exerting herself to an exquisite extreme with the potential of physical failure at any moment? Or the ethereal video body who flies so gracefully through space, can freeze in midair, and never tires?
>
> (Stoppiello and Coniglio 2003: 445)

The thematics work on two levels: firstly, there is the *digital double*, the projection of a reorganized and mediatized self (a public mask), and, secondly, there is the idea of *technology as a performance counterpart*. The former concept evokes the fluidity of the contemporary subject, moving between the tangible body and the virtual body, and the discourse around the limitations of the embodied self compared with the infinite potential of the disembodied digital other. The latter concept deals with the notion of *technological agency*, a central theme of this book; that is, when established as a performance partner, technology affects the choreographic and dramaturgical outcome of the work. Instead of discussing these topics in the context of Troika Ranch's work – for their oeuvre could easily comprise this entire book – these subjects are discussed in the following chapters, in relation to Stelarc, Klaus Obermaier and Chunky Move. We will instead move directly to a brief conclusion on Troika's Ranch's scenographic legacy.

A Final Thought on Troika Ranch

This five-year sub-genealogy of Troika Ranch's corpus represents a prodigious contribution to the field of digital scenography. There was a constellation of several factors that afforded their PaR: the availability of the new technology, which demanded speculation and experimentation on new artistic and cultural questions; the collaborations with ECI and CEAIT, which provided venues for the staging of inspirational and pioneering work and a forum for the development of and reflection on practice; and the patronage that facilitated residencies and afforded the time, space and dialogue needed to develop nuanced work. Troika Ranch was henceforth enabled to develop a clear and strong conceptual basis for their PaR and a technically eloquent deployment of digital specificities in a performance context.

Stoppiello and Coniglio have become increasingly expert in engaging the conceptual problems of (dis)embodiment and interactivity. The goal of this chapter was to recognize and pay tribute to the pure innovation at the outset of their investigations. Although electronic sensing techniques were already established in electronic engineering circles, their deployment in cultural contexts was quite rare – usage was reserved for hi-tech industrial and security applications. Troika Ranch's work represents a profound cultural innovation – an alchemical merger of (quantitative) technical knowledge with (qualitative) cultural know-how. Their original synthesis of choreography and electronic sensing should be understood as a performance art *Event*. That is, its originality opens a unique 'truth procedure' that proposes an absolutely novel philosophical position (Badiou 2005b), a new plane of thought that occasions epistemological, techno-historical and socio-political reflections. Their use of the responsive technologies for choreographic expression heralds a new storytelling paradigm particular to digital technologies. It shows a will to experiment, re-invent cultural paradigms and challenge the dominant views and tastes administered by cultural institutions. The artists do not make egotistical claims that they intended to rupture history; nevertheless, their deployment of digital sensing techniques in a cultural context impels a *surprise* 'in the sense that, suddenly, it jumps out at us ... affects us, and gets us hooked, to the extent that it directs us towards a mystery' (Stiegler 2011b: 6). Their inventive fusion of audio-visuals and choreography on stage creates a *shock* that catalyses a cultural rupture. The importance of their pioneering contribution to the field cannot be understated, and their legacy lives and breathes in every performing arts project that engages specifically digital subjectivities in a live context.

Their ingenuity in developing new modes of creative expression deeply resonates with contemporaneous cybercultural theories, actuated by the emergence of the electronic microchip and networked society. There was a consensus among theorists in the 1990s that cybernetic systems afford the new ability to invent an alternative version of the *self*, and to present in online communities (aka chatrooms, at that time) as another figure (an avatar), constituted by different psychosomatic subjectivities to those assigned at birth. Influential scholars advocated the positive potential for this new intersubjective paradigm, holding that, as a new world-space bereft of preconceptions and prejudices, 'cyberspace' offered an opportunity for democratization. By starting afresh there was a chance to diminish, perhaps even negate, dominant oppressive, patriarchal and capitalist ideologies (Haraway 1991b; Hayles 1999; Ascott 2003). These theories, which focused on the utopian potential of diminishing embodiment from subjectivity, did not suddenly emerge with the arrival of the internet; they were already well-established in postmodern theories that were formulated on the basis of information exchange in late capitalism. But the arrival of hypertexts and mass interconnectivity gave concrete validity to the theories. By examining the work of Stelarc, the next chapter traces this theoretical narrative, which stretches from postmodernism through to cyberculture, with a view to understanding the resultant theoretical and physical arrival of the cyborg, in both cultural theory and the performing arts.

2

Scenography of the Cyborg: Stelarc's *Extra Ear*

Introduction

The story of Troika Ranch's work brings the genealogy up to the mid-1990s. By examining the work of cyberculture artist, Stelarc, who was practising rich, provocative and ground-breaking work during this period, this chapter continues from approximately the same point. Because of the emergence of the internet, online communities, virtual reality technologies and so on, the mid- to late-1990s was a bountiful period for cybercultural theory and praxis. There are numerous media artists from this period – Char Davies, Jeffry Shaw, Laurie Anderson, David Rockeby, Guillermo Gomez-Peña, Rafael Lozano-Hemmer, to mention a few – whose work could comprise a rich discussion of early cyberculture. This chapter focuses on the work of Stelarc because of his commitment to the concept of the cyborg, in the purest sense of prosthetically augmenting the body through technology. By entangling his body with technology, Stelarc explores corporeal, visceral internal space as opposed to environments encompassing the body. He turns the focus inwards and presents the body as the canvas of spatial exploration.

Developments in computational technologies and robotics have propelled advancements in biological sciences, genetics and medicine. This chapter discusses *Extra Ear* (1996), a project classifiable under the then nascent field of *bio art*, which emerged at the intersection of biological technologies and artistic invention. Rather than embarking on a full-blown discussion of the genre, the analysis concentrates on a singular performative surgery, wherein the artist literally *embodies scenography*. By putting himself *under the knife*, experimenting with living tissue and inserting technology into his body, Stelarc validates the invasive scenographic idea apprehended by Stephen Di Benedetto (2013) in a short, personal provocation. Embodying scenography under surgical conditions demands further expansion; Stelarc's *cyborg scenography* in *Extra Ear* provides a ripe landscape for further cogitating this scheme. By placing his body on the line for the purposes of ontological and epistemological enquiry, Stelarc exposes a scenario where the human can invent new types of identity, formulate new systems of intersubjectivity and dream new futures. Furthermore, he demonstrates how artistic innovation can open up new research questions and influence the direction of techno-scientific scholarship and exploration.

Locating Stelarc's work within the timeline of this genealogy was tricky because, due to its logistical complexity, *Extra Ear* developed over many years. It was first conceived in 1996, yet the first surgical procedures were in 2006 and it was not fully completed until 2008. By then it had evolved into something different and was suitably retitled, *Ear on Arm*. Notwithstanding the slow execution date, 1996 is used for placing the project within the genealogy because this was when the thematic conceptualization occurred, and it is representative of bio art's burgeoning during that period.[1] The project is also very different from the other (mainly digital audio-visual) performances in this genealogy. However, it is important to have a representation of work that employs surgical transformation techniques towards corporeal enhancement because, despite the technical differences, these themes are inherently aligned with cyberculture and design-led performance.

Themes and Concepts

Stelarc is another artist with prolific breadth to his corpus that has constituted an entire book (Smith 2007). Spanning beyond the thirty-year genealogy of this book, his portfolio is thematically preoccupied with questions about the body and evolution. The concerns of his art practice oscillate between the physiological, the machinic and the virtual. In an early article, he articulates his frustrations at the limits of the corporeal self and advocates the potential for moving beyond current biological, physical and subjective shortcomings, pre-assigned at birth, by modifying the body using innovative bio-techniques:

> It is time to question whether a bipedal, breathing body with binocular vision and a 1,400-cc brain is an adequate biological form. It cannot cope with the quantity, complexity and quality of information it has accumulated ... It malfunctions often and fatigues quickly; its performance is determined by its age. It is susceptible to disease and is doomed to a certain and early death ... For it is only when the body becomes aware of its present predicament that it can map its postevolutionary

strategies. It is no longer a matter of perpetuating the human species by REPRODUCTION, but of enhancing the individual by REDESIGNING.

(Stelarc 1991: 591)

This statement is symptomatic of many postmodern and cybercultural perspectives that conceive humans as networked beings on a trajectory towards becoming increasingly entangled with technology in every aspect of existence (Lyotard 1984; Deleuze and Guattari 1987; Baudrillard 1994). Some of the ideas in Stelarc's article can come across as dated transhumanist Utopianism. He wrote it at the dawn of the cybercultural revolution, a period characterized by positive reactions against the pessimism rife in postmodernity, so his zealous enthusiasm can be excused. Whether supportive of his appeal for merging human biological organisms with technology, what must be acknowledged are the questions and provocations opened by his artworks, which are irrefutable manifestations of cyborg aesthetics.

The field of sociological and philosophical enquiry borne out of the discourse around intersubjectivity in digital culture was originally known as cyberculture, but the phrase has become less fashionable of late; many authors prefer the terms *digital*, *postdigital* or *posthuman*. However, when Stelarc established his practice *cyber*-terminology was very fashionable, as were tendencies to deride the organic body and invest Utopian hope in the potential of cybernetics as a site for psychosomatic and communal augmentation. Feminist theorists like Haraway, and later Hayles in the context of posthumanism (1999), were early innovators in mobilizing the positive potential of cyberspace towards their influential agendas. In this new world space, Haraway famously depicts the individual subject as a 'cyborg'.[2] While she did not coin this term, she is largely responsible for its assimilation to humanities discourse through the publication of her impactful and widely read *Cyborg Manifesto* (1985).

Haraway's essay is a feminist critique of subjectivity and identity in the digital age and its impression on late twentieth-century humanities scholarship is arguably unsurpassed. Following the thought of Luce Irigaray, in *Speculum of the Other Woman* (1985a [1974]) and *This Sex Which Is Not One* (1985b [1977]), Haraway's work attempts to discredit *phallocentric* principles, categories and values by insisting that language is saturated with an inherent grammar of patriarchal domination. She contends that writing – as the original technology – is 'preeminently the technology of cyborgs' (Haraway 1991b: 57), and cybernetics (hypertexts), which are essentially textual technologies, represent an opportune domain for reconstructing ideology anew, free from patriarchal encumbrances. Haraway conceives the cyborg as a hybrid feminist political figure who critiques 'the central dogma of phallogocentrism' (Haraway 1991b: 57) and colonial hegemony, and champions a more equal, non-essentialist future. Her strategy for transforming dominant patriarchal linguistic constructs consists of embracing multifarious perspectives and re-imagining human relations with 'nature' as something 'genuinely social and actively relational' [mutable], while preserving the inhomogeneity of the various 'partners' – language, ethics, science, politics, technology and epistemology (Haraway 1991a: 3). For Haraway, the cyborg represents a hybridized sociocultural, technoscientific assemblage 'of wholes and parts' where 'there is an intimate experience of boundaries, their construction and deconstruction' (Haraway 1991b: 66). Fundamentally, she rejects the essentialist view that vital and social characteristics like gender, identity, behaviour and ideology are fixed, pre-established and codified prior to existence. Haraway appeals for a non-deterministic, social-constructionist world-view towards the configuration of diverse coalitions based on affinity. She supports the postmodernist (pre-Socratic) scheme of hybridity and flux, where things are constantly transforming, intersecting, mutating and fusing to create new categories between various organisms, including human and machine, animal and machine, human and animal, and so on.

Haraway's theories are detectable in Stelarc's graphic account of the body as obsolete and his call for its re-designing under the auspices of cyber-technological innovations. His inclination to deride basic carnal functions and drives, like sexual reproduction, articulates his identification with feminist ideologies, and the hopes invested in the technological milieu as a site for dismantling misogynistic normativity. His modus operandi for engaging these themes is undeniably performative; however, it is much more in the vein of performance art than theatre. 'Through his performing body, the subjectivity of all bodies is brought into question. His projects work as a rupture to normative renderings and interpretations of the "subject"' (Baraibar 1999: 165). Stelarc's artistic investigations are inextricably linked to the physiological and subjective impact of digital technologies on the human body, that is, questions arising from the scholarly discourse of cyberculture. In fusing cybercultural hopes and anxieties with technology-driven performances in the space of his own body, his oeuvre represents a monumental aesthetic gesture that concretizes the original, innovative field of cyborg scenography.

His performances, such as *Third Hand* (1980), involve developing bespoke hardware in collaboration with robotics research institutes. Originally conceived as a semi-permanent robotic prosthesis, the artist was forced to re-classify it as a performance device 'because of the skin irritation of using the gel for the EMG electrodes and the heavier than expected weight (initially it was to be constructed using carbon fibre but at the time it was less expensive to use aluminium, duralumin, stainless steel and acrylic)' (Stelarc 2020). Having performed with the object in many countries all over the world (1980–98), the *Third Hand* has become Stelarc's most known performance device. He writes:

The Third Hand has come to stand for a body of work that explored intimate interface[s] of technology and prosthetic augmentation – not as a replacement but rather as an addition to the body. A prosthesis not as a sign of lack, but rather a symptom of excess.

(Stelarc n.d.)

While this might seem like the obvious work to discuss in the context of cyborg scenography, this chapter analyses his lesser known but equally provocative work, *Extra Ear*. Doing so highlights the controversial genre of body-modification-as-performance through surgical intervention, which is a derivative of cyberculture that evokes the grotesque hybrid beings of William Gibson's *Neuromancer* (1984).

The theme that characterizes Stelarc's corpus is that of adding technology to the body as an act of prosthetic augmentation. 'Rather than replacing a missing or malfunctioning part of the body, these interfaces and devices augment or amplify the body's form and functions' (Stelarc 1996). Contrasting the project to its predecessors, which use 'hard materials and technologies' (Stelarc 1996), the artist frames *Extra Ear* as a 'soft prosthesis' (Stelarc 1996) because the fabricated organ is built from his body's native 'soft tissue and flexible cartilage' (Stelarc 1996). His goal was to prosthesize in a permanent, sustainable way, not to simply make a wearable, removable artificial limb.

Extra Ear: Description

The initial concept for the project consisted in having a third ear fabricated and surgically installed on the side of his face, beside his original ear. Despite initial expressions of interest from medical practitioners, Stelarc ran into ethical issues around the apprehension that the act consisted in more than simple cosmetic surgery. It was perceived more as a 'monstrous pursuit of constructing an additional feature that conjures up either some congenital defect, an extreme body modification or even perhaps a radical genetic intervention' (Stelarc 1996). Although the adjustment, embellishment or modification of existing anatomical features is socially sanctioned, the addition of extra features is not. He researched the necessary steps for the surgical implant and drew up a plan of action; however, health and safety factors determined that alterations be made to the initial concept. The prosthetic ear had to be moved away from the face because the originally envisioned placement would detrimentally interfere with the facial nerves and jawbone. The final designated construction site was on his forearm; this would be the easiest and least (surgically) invasive option. The skin there is more elastic

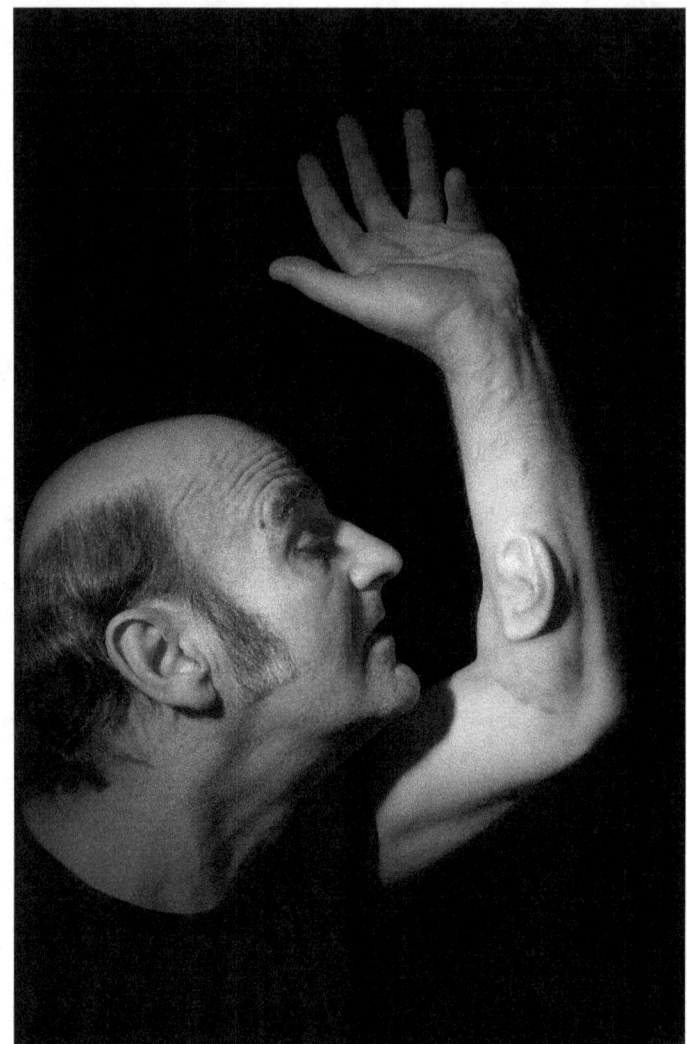

FIGURE 2.1 *Photo: Nina Sellars. Stelarc –* Ear on Arm, *2006 (courtesy of Nina Sellars and Stelarc).*

and capable of accommodating the meta-corporeal structure; henceforth, he renamed the project, *Ear on Arm* (see Figure 2.1).

Embracing the medically determined relocation of the Ear to his appendage, Stelarc 'experimented with alternative anatomical architectures' (Stelarc 2020); for example, assigning it directional sonic capabilities, for pointing at various sound sources (like a rifle microphone), or inverting its functionality so that it would emit sound, by also implanting a 'sound chip and a proximity sensor' (Stelarc 1996). The prosthetic aural organ would, therefore, interact with its *exosomatic*[3] environment as well as the native (endosomatic) organs of its host body, giving it more artistic validity. Furthermore, he conceptualized networking it by connecting it to a wearable computer, so it could broadcast transmitted 'sounds to augment the local sounds that the actual ears hear' (Stelarc 1996). Thus conceived, the *Extra Ear* becomes a sort of telematic[4] antenna that augments the body's acoustic experience. Stelarc also stresses that these evolved utilitarian ideas were not core concepts of the project. Reminding us of the ear's beauty and complexity that also provide the implicit essential function of balance, his justification for adding another one was to open new dialogue around technologically catalysed corporeal possibilities beyond visual or anatomical excess (Stelarc 1996).

Surgically constructing the extra ear on Stelarc's arm was not a simple procedure; the process was composed of several stages that were highly invasive to the artist's body. Months of recovery time were required after each surgical intervention, in which the bio-artist, just as his contemporaries like Orlan, put his body on the line for the sake of ontological and epistemological enquiry. The artist and physicians encountered some serious complications during the process. They had to create excess skin by injecting saline solution into an implanted skin expander, in order to create a pocket that would accommodate the quasi-corporeal organ. However, 'a necrosis during the skin expansion process necessitated excising it and rotating the position of the ear around the arm' (Stelarc 2008). Ironically, the new position (inner forearm) ended up being anatomically preferable, in terms of safety and ergonomics. Stelarc elaborates on detailed accounts of the surgical processes and the materials used, including: structural fabrication using cartilage grown from his own tissues, encouragement of 'fibrovascular ingrowth' (Stelarc 2008) and its integration with his own tissue using *MEDPOR* – a bio-compatible synthetic polymer that is omnidirectionally porous in structure ('MEDPOR | Stryker' n.d.) (see Figures 2.2a and 2.2b) – and, for the earlobe, cultivation of mature adipocytes and adipose-derived stem cells (Stelarc 2008).[5]

Aside from the surgical procedures and biological techniques, there was also an electronic aspect to the implanted ear, which is pertinent to *digital* scenography. The second surgery involved inserting a miniature microphone 'to test the plausibility of transmitting sound wirelessly' (Stelarc 2020), which was successfully tested at the end of the surgery. The artist described how the surgeon's voice was successfully transmitted wirelessly and heard clearly at a remote receiver. It was planned to leave the microphone in-situ for several weeks but, after about ten days, it had to be removed because it caused a serious infection that compromised the structure of the ear, the vitality of the project and, indeed, the artist's life. Stelarc recalls: 'I almost lost an arm for an ear. I was hospitalised for a week and was on industrial strength antibiotics for 6 months. Fortunately, the ear was saved' (Stelarc 2020). Despite its

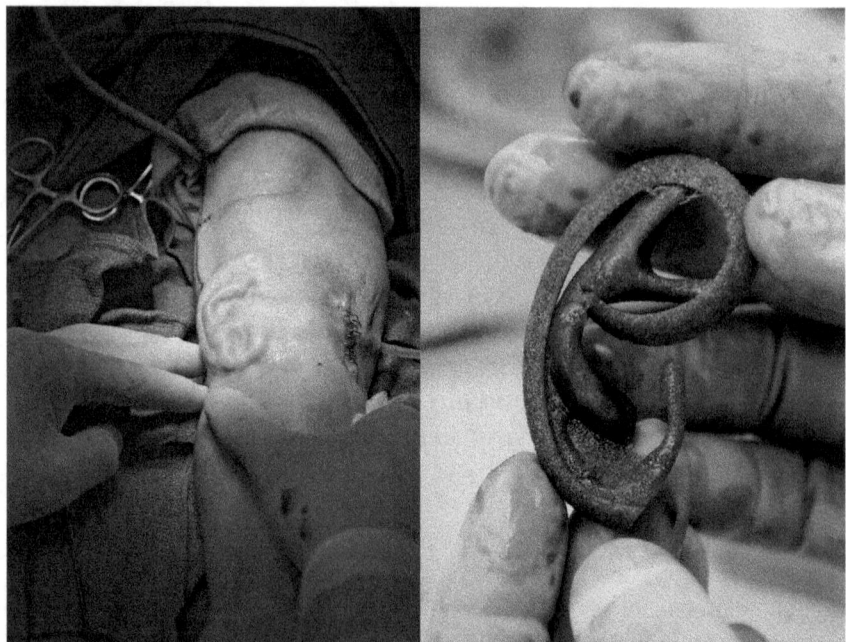

FIGURE 2.2 *(a) Photo (left): Nina Sellars. Stelarc Extra Ear surgery – surgical implantation procedure, 2006 (courtesy of Nina Sellars and Stelarc). (b) Photo (right): Nina Sellars. Medpor scaffold, just prior to its insertion, 2006 (courtesy of Nina Sellars and Stelarc)*

short operational lifespan, the gesture was an epistemically ground-breaking moment because a surgically implanted digital, quasi-corporeal organ was afforded extra-human communicative functionality. It was a brave and pioneering investigation into unknown epistemic terrain because the artist put his personal health and safety at risk.

In terms of ambition and scope, the technical process is fascinating and ahead of its time, but it is the philosophical and conceptual nature of the performance that is so central to the overarching narrative of this book. The artist's bio-aesthetic gesture – constituted by attempts to construct an electronically enabled, quasi-biological organ out of biological matter and bio-compatible synthetic materials – epitomizes practice-as-research (PaR) in performance. His gesture is a performance Event constituted by the notion of *performativity*, as opposed to the traditional (mimetic) performance paradigm; that is, it is lived experience enacted as performance, and vice versa. The theory of *performativity* is derived from J.L. Austin's linguistic definition of a *performative utterance* as a statement that commits an action (1975). Performativity describes words and actions that have real-life consequences that impact the subject above and beyond the immediate spatiotemporal context wherein it is committed. This concept has gained strong currency for articulating the significance of aesthetic gestures in performance art. Stelarc's *Extra Ear* is not a performance that ends when the surgery does; it stays with him, becomes him, and irrevocably and irreversibly alters the nature of his being. It is 'postevolutionary' (Stelarc 1991), to gather the artist's terminology. By positing this metaphor, Stelarc is reframing the human body as an object to be 'monitored', 'redesigned' and 'modified' through bio-technological interventions, with a view to subverting dominant philosophical, epistemological and physiological schema (Stelarc 1991). Stelarc's consolidation of the performance act to lived experience not only opens new discourses around human ontology in the context of sophisticated technological innovations, but also asks new questions that catalyse further bio-medical, scientific developments. While the latter fields are beyond the remit of this book, the discourse on a technologically altered ontology is very much central.

In the context of contemporary theory, there are arguments for dismissing Stelarc's thesis on postevolution as transhumanist–accelerationist rhetoric.[6] However, it must be acknowledged that he was leading the field since the early 1970s through his artistic praxis,[7] that is, through making-as-thinking. While this book takes a circumspect stance against transhumanism and accelerationism, to silence the camp would be totalitarian and therefore equally misguided. The subject of evolution has recently gained significant currency in technological philosophy. There are many measured, responsible syntheses with anthropology and sociology, extending from Leroi-Gourhan to Stiegler, that clarify our contemporary historical–material position and essentialize the relations between human and technology, which is not at all really a relation so much as an immanence. Indeed, Stelarc himself signals the essence of the argument when he writes: 'The significant event in our evolutionary history was a change in the mode of locomotion' (Stelarc 1991: 592). He is referring to the evolutionary phenomenon that marks the quintessence of humanity: the transition from quadrupedal to bipedal mobility.

Leroi-Gourhan, Evolution and the Technical Tendency

In *Gesture and Speech*, André Leroi-Gourhan (1964) proposes the convincing paleoanthropological argument that there is a fundamental and continuous evolutionary trajectory, from the biological to the sociological, mediated via technology. Therefore, all technologies, including those that facilitate the most advanced forms of intersubjectivity, are always reducible to the biological. Leroi-Gourhan explicates a two-tiered evolutionary phenomenon arising from the transitioning of humans to the upright posture. Firstly, the mouth is freed from grasping and focused on tasks of communication and language and, secondly, the hands are freed from the duty of mobility, allowing them to also become part of processes of 'exteriorization'.[8] Ever since this evolutionary development, exteriorization has been transferred from the zoological milieu to the technical, and the 'history of "hominisation" is a direct result of the use of tools to manage our environment' (Howells and Moore 2013: 22). Henceforth, the human body becomes less specialized in relation to the fulfilment of any one particular task; instead, specializations occur through recombinations and deployments of technical knowledge in the material domain. Analogously, the relation operates in the inverse as a process of interiorization, whereby humans embody the technologies that they use. This simultaneous reciprocation of interior and exterior is a process that fundamentally defines the nature of what it means to be human. It is continually in flux and is vectorized by the co-constitution of human and technology.

Leroi-Gourhan's paleoanthropological thesis provides an important mainspring for philosophers, like Simondon and Stiegler, to establish a non-metaphysical basis for theorizing human nature. Leroi-Gourhan's systematic materialist approach to defining the human provides a rationalized foundation for bringing latent ideas into clear consciousness. He formulates his methodology on the basis of 'questioning what he considered to be the intellectualist bias of the anthropology deriving from the sociological tradition of Durkheim and Mauss, in which the role attributed to technology in the study of human society was normally a subordinate one' (Howells and Moore 2013: 35). This attitude drove him to develop his pivotal concept of the *technical tendency* [*tendence technique*], a concept that continues to influence a contemporary canon of technological philosophers. The technical tendency describes how a technological determinism occasions humans to interact with their exterior environment in an expected and increasingly refined manner. Importantly, this provides a counter argument against the dominant heliocentric view of diffusionism, which is 'the conviction that all cultures originated from one culture center' ('Diffusionism and Acculturation' 2017). The point is not to debunk the fact that technical innovations spread through processes of exchange and communication between socio-ethnic groups; rather, it is to show that innovations arise independently in geographically non-contiguous *culture-circles* and transmit contingently and arbitrarily (Winthrop 1991: 83–4). According to Leroi-Gourhan, technological determinism occurs at a level above ethnics and geography. That is, the technical tendency describes a normative factor in the relation between humans and their environment that impels them to communicate, fabricate and innovate in a manner that is common across mutually exclusive socio-ethnic groupings. This constitutes the basis of interethnic exchange and social development generally. Leroi-

Gourhan's inclination to focus on an epi-phenomenon in the human–habitat relation provides contemporary techno-philosophy with a foundation for conceptualizing that the efficacious, deterministic and influential qualities of the techno-material domain essentially modify our experience of reality. This is defined as *technicity* in more recent scholarly discourse.

Technicity

The concept of technicity is central to this book because it refers 'to technology considered in its efficacy or operative functioning' (Hoel and van der Tuin 2013: 187); that is, technicity describes an ontological force that modulates the relationship between humans and the exterior world of objects. Technicity is something material and historical. Without it we would be unable to experience the past or select the technical objects – artefacts, knowledge, tools, information and so on – that facilitate the invention of possible futures; without technicity we would exist in the animal, biological state of an unending present, without any means of transcending it. This predicate moves Stiegler to assert that technicity is the constitutive transcendental horizon of the human that conditions the temporal, the social and the cultural.

The concept of technicity provides a conceptual basis for a techno-philosophical lineage from Gilbert Simondon to Stiegler. It prompts Simondon to consider 'symbolic production, language and meaning included, as partially subordinate to technics as a constructive relationship between the human being and the world' (Bardin and Rodriguez 2018: 58). He does this by situating the 'tense relations' between the relatively stable, predictable patterns of biological evolution and the relatively open, indeterminate ones of technical evolution within the framework of psycho-social individuation (Bardin and Rodriguez 2018: 58). For Simondon, technicity affords the understanding that humans exist within a dynamic, efficacious temporal–material system where there is a fluid 'relation of equilibrium and of reciprocal tensions' (Simondon 2011: 407). Stiegler goes further than Simondon and makes a complete break from anthropocentricism, theorizing the 'autonomy of technical development in relation to the human' (Howells and Moore 2013: 36). Stiegler mobilizes this thought towards explaining existence as a co-constitution of technology and humans, where they share an inseparable horizon of meaning, action and evolution. Stiegler places technicity at the root of what it means to be human, thereby assigning quasi-biological characteristics to the technological milieu. Under the aegis of technicity, there is a fundamental intertwining of the technical and the human that has important ramifications for how that relationship is perceived. Technology is not something outside of, or separate from, the body; conversely, it is something inherent and mutable, which resides at the very source of our humanity. Therefore, when humans design and build technological systems, we are designing not only the type of humans we are, or want to be, but also the type of social system we want to inhabit and the reality that we want future generations to experience.

Although Stelarc does not cite these theorists or their terminology, it is clear the artist's praxis sits comfortably with such theories. However, despite their non-anthropocentric arguments, neither the theorists nor the artist advocate the notion of relinquishing responsibility to technical systems. Stelarc clearly articulates this in his reflections on practice, which elucidate thematic preoccupations with survival, prolongation of the human race, concern and accepting accountability for the future of the species. His conceptions of the body as an 'object for designing' (Stelarc 1991: 591), his assertion that 'utopian dreams become postevolutionary imperatives' (Stelarc 1991: 593), and his aspirations for enhancing human adaptability to hostile 'extraterrestrial environments' (Stelarc 1991: 592) facilitating 'planetary escape' (Stelarc 1991: 591), all show an overarching rationale based on care, concern, responsibility and developing a deeper understanding of the cosmos. Stelarc's praxis concurs with the principle that not only is technology a determinant of human life, but so too do humans maintain the power to design a good reality for future generations. Stelarc responds to the evolving conditions of the techno-material milieu by intervening with his own body, thus displaying an area of agreement with theories of technicity. Reading his praxis in the context of individuation, as per Simondon and Stiegler, permits an understanding of the sociohistorical significance of his work.

Towards Technical Individuation

It was established (in Chapter 1) that individuation is a fluid socio-political process through which the individual and the group continuously co-constitute each other's identities; however, the transhistorical nature of the process has not yet been clarified. In *L'individuation Psychique et Collective* (1989), Simondon makes two major contributions to the discourse. First is the (aforementioned) non-substantialist re-casting of individuation as a fluid process and second is his (not yet discussed) non-anthropocentric, historical-materialist position that individuation is profoundly influenced by and takes place across external, non-human environmental factors and material artefacts. Simondon's contributions are quite radical because they contradict the traditional discourse around the question of the individual, which was originally dominated by substantialist metaphysics and the philosophical theory of hylomorphism, developed by Aristotle. The hylomorphist schema presupposes being (i.e. the coming into being of an individual) as a compound merger of form and matter, which is the basis for numerous speculative metaphysical theories. For Simondon, the hylomorphic schema is overly anthropocentric because it 'places the principle of individuation anterior to individuation' (Scott 2014: 4); that is, Simondon insists there is a pre-existing principle of individuation that precedes and vectorizes the operation of individuation, causing the 'individual to appear' (Scott 2014: 5). For Simondon, the human individual is neither the sole cause nor outcome of the process; the individual is one component produced by the amalgamation. This dethroning of the Anthropos (Scott 2014: 7) allows Simondon to conceive what he calls a 'pre-individual milieu' (Simondon 2007), which is a fund of knowledge – composed of skills, tradition, heritage, etc. – accumulated over time by various socio-ethnic collectives. The transactions and processes that constitute individuation are mediated through this epistemological, historical-material manifestation, hence the importance of Leroi-Gourhan's technical tendency to his antithesis. This knowledge-fund, which constitutes technicity, consists in a collection of reified, tangible artefacts (texts, objects, audio-visual documents, etc.), tools (technologies) that facilitate their coming into being and methodological information (techniques). The accumulated repertoire is *transhistorical*; it is shared by, and connects, generations. It acts as a sort of bank that holds, safeguards and transmits knowledge from one generation to the next. Its survival is dependent on it being continually reactivated through its '*intergenerational transmission (synchrony)* ... and its *individual adoption (diachrony)*' (Stiegler and Rossouw 2011: 53). Every generation adopts the pre-individual fund in a singular and mutable way, keeping certain elements and discarding others, depending on what is useful, relevant and necessary. Similarly, the individuals of each generation *individuate* themselves against their interacting milieus on the basis of the evolving knowledge fund.

In addition to Simondon's relational conceptualization of individuation, Stiegler also agrees on the existence of the pre-individual fund and its mutable, influential properties. Stiegler writes: 'The *I* and the *we* are bound in individuation by the *preindividual milieu*, with its positive conditions of effectiveness coming from what I have called *retentional apparatuses*' (Stiegler 2014: 51).[9] Retentional apparatuses refer to artefacts that embody and *retain* (epistemological and technical) memory. They comprise the pre-individual fund and afford intergenerational knowledge transmission. In the stasis of their finality they withhold the possibilities of the past, whilst challenging forth new ways of thinking about the future. For Stiegler, these artefactual concretizations are made possible by the existential precondition of technicity (or *technical tendency* per Leroi-Gourhan), which not only facilitates (or vectorizes) the exchange between the psychic individual and the collective, but so too does it assert its own organizational logic: '*individuation of the technical system*' (Stiegler 2014: 51). Just as the technical system supports the fundamental possibility of retentional apparatuses, so too do those retentional apparatuses 'condition the organization of the individuation of the *I* with the individuation of the *we* in a single process of *psychic, collective and technical* individuation' (Stiegler 2014: 51); that is, the technical system can and does individuate. Technical individuations are reciprocally constituted by indeterminate individual–collective human contingencies (human reinterpretations of processes) and their own internal mechanistic mutations.

A General Organology

It is precisely on the topic of technical individuation that Stiegler's philosophy bifurcates with Simondon's. Simondon maintains that only living beings can individuate, whereas Stiegler argues that technical objects – as 'inorganic organized beings' (Stiegler 1998: 17) – not only mediate and influence human individuation, but so too do they themselves individuate. In *Note Complémentaire* (1958),[10] Simondon argues against Wiener's society-machine model, concerning the concept of regulation as a dynamic stability (Simondon 2017b). Simondon holds that an automaton's requirement to internally regulate, based on information exchanged with the changing outside milieu, is always 'predetermined by a fixed code' (Bardin 2015: 115), and this precludes any possibility of meaning-making ['signification'] (Bardin 2015:116). However, Simondon wrote his thesis before the emergence of second-order cybernetics;[11] the technology was not yet mature. The emergence of big data, deep learning and 'black box' phenomena allow Stiegler to assert 'the cybernetic object is capable of individuating itself' (Stiegler et al. 2012: 166) because, under these architectures, the system does indeed engage with and respond to the infidelities of the human milieu, which, as per biological philosopher George Canguilhem, is the basis for life. Synthesizing these scientific philosophies Stiegler deftly explicates how life is no longer the exclusive domain of organic beings, but of 'organological' beings (Canguilhem 1992: 129–64) and individuation is actually a three-way dynamic process that modulates the relationship between the psychic individual (the endosomatic cerebral *organ*), the collective (social *organ*-izations) *and* the technical (prosthetic or exosomatic *organs*). Henceforth, his call for a *general organology*, which describes a methodology for understanding all human activity in the context of 'triple individuation' (Stiegler et al. 2012: 166). Endosomatic sense-organs and social organizations are modulated by the agency of exosomatic organs which reciprocally reorganize in response to their contingencies. His thesis aims 'not to differentiate technology from the body', but to fuse them and affirm that technological organs are subjected to evolutionary processes, just as biological organs are (O'Dwyer 2015b: 55).

The point of this theoretical digression is *not* to make the claim that the ear evolved on Stelarc's arm; he obviously put it there. Considering Stelarc's project in the context of a general organology delineates how the appearance of an ear on his arm should be understood as a constellation of various subjective, environmental and socio-technical factors, including:

1. The artist's idea and his impulse to follow through on the concept.
2. Socio-political and aesthetic topics arising from cybercultural theory and practice, which afford new concepts for the mental and physical augmentation of the human.
3. The availability of new technologies and bio-compatible materials.
4. The recognized professional practice of plastic surgery and a legacy of medical knowledge, which permit safe body modifications.
5. The social normalization of plastic surgery, in terms of its moral and ethical acceptance.
6. The ability of the artist to justify this type of artistic output as valid, topical and relevant to philanthropic funding sources, without which such a complex, expensive bio-art project could not proceed.

The emergence of an ear on Stelarc's arm is the result of an unpredictable convergence of human and non-human forces; it is an organological development. This is evinced by the series of dialogues with the surgical team that resulted in its compromised relocation, due to the physiological complications of inserting a bio-compatible scaffold into the face. Furthermore, by integrating the artefact into the infra-dermal space, it 'becomes a living part of the artist's arm through tissue ingrowth and vascularisation' (Stelarc 2020), thereby reifying the notions that human evolution takes place through technical progressions (Leroi-Gourhan 1964) and technology needs to be conceptualized in terms of biological organisms (Canguilhem 1992). The double-helix bind of the human and the technical means they are co-evolutionary and always already bound up in one another. Technology is not something alien that we can choose to eliminate; it is fundamentally encoded into the genetic make-up of the human phenotype.[12] Thus, technology becomes the domain that provides impetus for some of the most essential questions about what it means to be human, and its mutability ensures that these questions continue to be asked afresh in innovative ways, as Stelarc does.

The genealogy of technological philosophy – from Leroi-Gourhan, through Simondon and Canguilhem, to Stiegler – explains how the human and technology co-constitute each other. The human is compelled to design and reshape the world, consistently developing new tools to facilitate this process, then those tools become embodied by the human and feedback into the processes of fabrication, continually modifying existential experience. The tool invents the human every bit as much as the human invents the tool because humans consistently re-invent themselves by developing new tools in a progressive feedback loop that is a co-constitution of interior and exterior. Although Leroi-Gourhan's paleo-anthropological analysis is the mainspring for this meta-narrative and the protracted timespan of his study is useful for philosophizing the history of humanity, it does not suffice to explain the singular techno-evolutionary leap of Stelarc's *Extra Ear*, in the contemporary digital epoch. Notwithstanding the failure to integrate the microphone and wireless transmitter into the ear (long-term), Stelarc's intention was to assign it acoustic functionality; thematically speaking, the ear was to be an artificially functional endosomatic organ with exosomatic capabilities, fabricated from bio-compatible materials and synthetically grown tissues. Therefore, the project justifies analysis under more contemporary theoretical advancements of technical evolution.

Technical Evolution

In discussing technical evolution or, more precisely, the *phylogenesis*[13] of artificial organs, one might assume the process follows the organic model. However, the evolution of technical organs differs from the biological order, because they do not necessarily follow a progressive lineage. 'The reproducibility of the technical machine differs from that of living beings, in that it is not based on sequential codes perfectly circumscribed in a territorialised genome' (Guattari 1995: 42). Biological organisms can only get a new genetic characteristic by 'inheriting it from a previous generation, or by evolving it in the present one' (Vaccari and Barnet 2009: 4); however, 'in technical evolution, machines are not entirely dependent on the previous generation. They can borrow innovations from generations in the past (retroactivation) or they can borrow from entirely different branches of the evolutionary tree (horizontal transmission)' (Vaccari and Barnet 2009: 4). Furthermore, it has been demonstrated that technical objects have an intrinsic dependence on 'the biology of human bodies and the variations of natural milieu' (Bardin and Rodriguez 2018: 58). Topological shifts in socio-economics and culture affect relations between individuals and groups, which occasion changes in the material (pre-individual) milieu that are uncertain. 'As technological organs evolve they can metastasise and give way to entirely new types of artificial organs that are employed in different social contexts for previously unforeseen ends' (O'Dwyer and Johnson 2019). Evolutionary surges in the technological domain manifest in various non-contiguous branches of the human evolutionary tree. In terms of Stelarc's work, this is apparent in the use of biomedical and electronic techniques towards the genesis of an artificial organ with exosomatic capabilities.

Importantly, the artificial organ is not tied to the artist's genotype; the trait cannot be organically passed on to biologically linked progeny. Despite the fact that we are talking about the development of a feature of an organism, it is not a phylogenetic development because phylogenesis implies that the feature is adopted by the species. It is an *ontogenetic*,[14] or, perhaps, an *epi*-ontogenetic, surge. This shift shows an area of agreement with the Nietzschean concept of evolution, which consists in *individual*, intellectual and creative surges beyond the bounds of a largely inactive, equalized human genotype; that is, Nietzsche locates potential for human evolution in ontogenetic leaps that have no real impact on phylogeny – the species as a whole (Moore 2002: 34–5).[15] However, the question of phylogenesis should not be entirely discarded because Nietzsche fails to consider the evolution of the material milieu. The thematics of Stelarc's project become even more nuanced when considering the implications for the phenotype arising from interactions between the (human) organism and environmental (non-human) factors.

Preindividual Milieu and Epiphylogenesis

For Simondon and Stiegler, the transhistorical nature of the pre-individual milieu is constituted by its immanent bind to the material domain. Therefore, it should be thought, as Leroi-Gourhan conceived, in terms of evolution and the originary human departure from pure endosomatic functionality. The beginning of tool-use is conceived as an extracorporeal, non-genetic influence on human gene expression, which Leroi-Gourhan describes as an *epigenetic layer*. Stiegler advances this supposition by insisting that the manifestation of the epigenetic layer was not a singular prehistoric event (i.e. the transition to the bi-pedal, upright posture); conversely, it is continually vectorized by an evolving primordial memory that is sedimented, preserved and passed down through technical exteriorizations. He calls this *epiphylogenesis*, defining it as 'that store of memory that is particular to a unique life form – the human – and that is also the "life of the spirit". It is a matter of memory retained in things' (Stiegler 2014: 33). It describes the preservation, intergenerational transmission and reactivation of knowledge. The *memory* originally organically programmed into the genotype – which was a biological determinant of development, diversification and environmental adaptability – has, since the beginning of hominization (anthropogenesis), been gradually transferred to the exteriorized realm of technical artefacts and processes, which now hold that memory instead. These extend from the most basic primordial exteriorizations – tool fabrication, cave paintings, symbolic carvings, logograms, hieroglyphics, etc. – to materially advanced automatic processes and telecommunications that shape contemporary ways of being. Epiphylogenesis represents a break with pure, organic life and confers exosomatic characteristics upon the human, which constitutes our mode of existence as conscious, cognizant beings.

In summary, Leroi-Gourhan describes the phenomenological-anthropological transition of human evolutionary processes from the biological to the technical milieu, gradually predicating the stasis of organic phylogenesis. Henceforth, the conditions of human evolution and environmental adaptability become manifested in the technical milieu, which Stiegler articulates as *epiphylogenesis*. Said differently, the calming of genotypic advancement gives way to an exaltation of the phenotype. This is an important notion for this book as a whole because it helps provide traction for the hypothesis insisting on an increasing technological efficacy in scenography, visibly manifesting itself here in the artistic, performative will of Stelarc to surgically implant an ear on his arm.

Stelarc's *Extra Ear*, Post-evolution and Organ Functions

Extra Ear is a new type of artificial organ, but the profundity of its functionality may not have been precisely aligned with Stelarc's original vision. Although his ambition for long-term formal (digital) functionality was not fully realized, due to health and safety complications, the significance of its meta-functionality (its sociocultural impact) is admirable. For Stiegler, epiphylogenesis is inherently tied to memory and constitutes the basis of the preindividual milieu. Epiphylogenesis is a metaphor for an artefactual fabrication that embodies cultural and technical knowledge. It describes both the object and the process; it refers to the functional artefacts, tools/processes and the articulations thereof. Therefore, all fabrications are functional because they embody knowledge. As an art object, there is an aesthetic functionality conferred upon the ear by its non-functioning. Since Kant, we know that the most engaging and (dis)interesting thing about art is its purposelessness (Kant 2000); indeed, *Extra Ear's* malfunctioning may have given it a stronger aesthetic impact. What began as a project based on simulation ended as one rooted in the domain of representation. In this context, the ear's functionality is to mimic the body through a sort of hyper-surrealism, pretending to be native through a *soft prosthesis*. The audio transmission of the surgeon's voice testifies to the artist achieving his objective of having functional digital technology implanted into his body; however, the non-functioning aspect of the surgical experiment is just as interesting. Although stripped of its long-term claim to simulation, the ear's uncanny resemblance to the original bodily organ and the pretence of its apparent belonging there, on the arm, give it an air of monstrosity. Enduring functionality is irrelevant because the interpreting audience can join the proverbial dots. Thus, Stelarc opens the thought of a 'technological chimera ... by emphasizing the view of the body as technologically organized matter' (Caygill 1997: 51), which is intensified by its non-functioning and its delivery to realm of pure representation, pure artifice. If there is a functionality, it is one closer to Stiegler's epiphylogenesis, by its contribution to artistic–scientific discourse and as a document of post-human, cyborg cultural identity.

The performativity of Stelarc's gesture means that the circulation of audio-visual documentation is crucial to its validation. The representations of the performance are disseminated via the internet and displayed far beyond the local site of the event. Because of their shocking nature, Stelarc is widely recognized for his aesthetic provocation. 'These impressive images serve to decentre and continue the performance beyond the stage' (Baraibar 1999: 160), thereby acting as a sort of reticulated, ephemeral, digital memorial of his work. The photograph is an especially impactful exosomatized memory that can embed itself in the epiphylogenetic fabric of the technical genome and lie dormant there for several generations, before being retroactivated under the auspices of a technical advancement that can ensure the idea's successful implementation (i.e. a functional *Extra Ear*), albeit in a different context. Therefore, the photographs of Stelarc's work are more than simple documents; they are 'life-giving part[s] of a greater whole' (Baraibar 1999: 160) because they contribute to the digital pre-individual knowledge fund that challenges the boundaries of the body, which is transmitted globally and intergenerationally.[16]

Subversion and Rupture

By employing existing scientific knowledge towards unforeseen cultural ends, Stelarc *changes the rules* of how certain types of knowledge are engaged. His artistic gesture subverts the status quo and ruptures dominant modes of thinking, not only in art but also in the sciences and society generally. This subversion lies not straightforwardly in the fact that the body was carved open and modified through surgical techniques for the sake of art – although the disruptive capabilities of this act are commendable. The subversion resides in Stelarc's submission of scientific, medical knowledge to a process of defunctionalization and refunctionalization; he strips it of its intended use and repurposes towards a goal that was previously unforeseen, staking a claim in pure innovation. Stelarc's body-based art experiments, thus, generate new types of artefacts, information, methods and so on; he drives knowledge progression in the collaborating scientific research areas. This is witnessed by, on one level, the innovative stem cell and bio-plastic fabrication methods for growing cartilage and, on another level, the attempt to integrate operational digital hardware into the infra-dermal substance of the human body. Thus, Stelarc *changes the rules* concerning how scientific research is applied, thereby altering the ethical conventions of performing the body. By putting himself under the knife for epistemological discovery, he is rerouting rational, quantitative techniques towards generating irrational, qualitative artifice, creating new, unconventional configurations of the various epistemic fields. Analogously, he reconfigures performer–audience relations, pushing them away from the more conventional paradigm of the spectacular, towards that of the grotesque (the hi-tech freakshow). Thus, the audience endure shameful self-judgement by the realization that their curiosity is peaked by violence and monstrosity.

The event of Stelarc's performance can be described as a singular *artefactual ontogenesis* that subverts prevalent conceptions of artistic and scientific situation. It reveals new possibilities and understandings of contemporary reality through its inventive recombination of subject, form and matter. By communicating a new art idea, it irreversibly changes audiences' acceptances and expectations of what constitutes humanness in the contemporary digital-cultural epoch. An individual epi-ontogenetic surge impacts on the phylogenesis of the herd.

Sociocultural Impact

Stelarc advocates the need for humans to amplify, accelerate and adapt the body to extreme conditions, by merging with technology. This can deliver his thematics to transhumanist speculation; however, his conjectures about telepresence, telehaptics and teleautomation have been validated by the forty to fifty years that close the gap between his early practice-based explorations and the contemporary, postdigital sociocultural situation. Many of the cutting-edge technologies he was exploring in the 1980s and 1990s are now widely deployed in society, especially his projects concerning 'hard prostheses' and reticulated intersubjectivity; however, the same cannot, *yet*, be said of his 'soft prosthesis' experiments. While plastic surgery, synthetic implantation, bio-material and stem cell cultivation techniques have undoubtedly improved, there are not many bio-art experiments that explore them with a view to developing infradermal apparatuses to be surgically implanted.[17] Electronic circuitry is still quite primitive and immoveable in this respect because circuit manufacturing is still dominated by biologically incompatible materials, like silicon and conductive metals. Stelarc's experiment demonstrated that the physiological reflex of the body is to reject these materials, when they are placed below the skin. There is research into fabricating circuitry out of biological matter, but it is very primitive compared with conductors and semiconductors.[18] Socioculture is *technologically* not ready to appropriate Stelarc's avant-garde gesture, but Adorno's logic of the culture industry insists that it will happen.[19] Notwithstanding the practicalities of appropriating his ideas, developing workable solutions and consolidating them with the tastes and fashions of mass culture, the themes of Stelarc's praxis are undeniably pertinent to contemporary socio-political and scholarly discourse. These themes concern exosomatic prostheses of the mind and body that have manifested as portable telecommunications technologies, the biopolitics of surveillance and control of individuals through informational systems of governance, and demystifying dominant (patriarchal) ideologies that impose normativity on identity, with regard to subjectivities like gender, taste, race, creed and so on.

Stelarc's performative practice oscillates between two genealogies of the discursive economy – from Irigaray to Haraway and from Leroi-Gourhan, through Simondon and Canguilhem, to Stiegler – that chart the theoretical development from postmodernism to digital culture. Both genealogies intersect and agree on the need for debunking essentialist ideas of the individual as a fixed entity and promote the view that the human is constituted by multifarious external social and environmental contingencies. The proximity of Stelarc's praxis to these philosophies is salient in his own writing:

> The body now performs beyond the boundaries of its skin and beyond the local space that it occupies. It can project its physical presence elsewhere. So the notion of single agency is undermined, or at least made more problematic. The body becomes a nexus or a node of collaborating agents that are not simply separated or excluded because of the boundary of our skin, or of having to be in proximity. So we can experience remote bodies, and we can have these remote bodies invading, inhabiting and emanating from the architecture of our bodies, expressed by the movements and sounds prompted by remote agents.
>
> (Stelarc 2008)

Stelarc's singular PaR methodology celebrates heterogeneity and emphasizes the relations between the individual, technology and environment. He performs a discursive praxis which concurs with the explicated theories of the cyborg and individuation, which espouse an understanding of the individual as an incomplete, temporal, relational amalgamation of material and intersubjective influences, existing in a fluid social paradigm and on a continual trajectory towards completion. Individuals are subjected to a series of outside forces which necessarily affect their development and integration as a valuable agent in a greater cohesive unit (the community). The encounters which impact on the individual, either subjectively or tangibly, are the causes which shape, augment or curtail it. In the context of Stelarc's practice, the technical teams that Stelarc engages employ technologies and materials to actuate prostheses that function as important reconfigurations towards the artist pursuing a sense of completion. 'The body and technology must be framed together as an interrelated, inter-sustaining chain of evolutionary systems which must be continually reinterpreted in order to effectively propel an understanding of both forward' (Baraibar 1999: 160). Conceptualizing the body–technology–society relationship as a fluid, interdependent evolutionary ecosystem affirms Stelarc's oeuvre as an apt articulation of the genealogical cross-section of the postmodern and cybernetic theories outlined above.

Stelarc's performances reveal a cyborg scenography that affirms the body as a site for the performance event, to regain agency over the body, expanding its limits and existential possibilities. By searching for alternative ways to experience his body, Stelarc's work demonstrates thematics of corporeal exploration, which abstractly expose the limits and potentialities of all bodies in contemporary socioculture. Through his theatrical reframing of the body, Stelarc enacts a new way of presenting the body, levelling critical questions concerning what the body is and its socio-political role. By delineating the limits of the body and reframing it under 'his evolutionary strategy of awareness' (Stelarc 1991: 161), Stelarc locates the body as a site of political action where it can be repurposed as the ground-zero for reconstructing a new identity politics and a new reality. He expounds the provocative argument that the purely organic human is obsolete and advocates a reorganized understanding of being-in-the-world that acknowledges the entanglement of the technological and the biological. Although the goals of his post-evolutionary project were somewhat narrowly framed in terms of quality, strength, adaptability and an avoidance of death (Stelarc 1991: 593), the important aspect that must be acknowledged is his agreement with the cyborg and techno-philosophical theories discrediting essentialist views of the human as purely organic, and simplistic binarisms falsely edifying technology as inorganic, cold, hard mechanics. Such attitudes are insufficient to explain the intersubjective nuances of contemporary human life. Technology is the epi-milieu where individual and collective human phylogeny can be reshaped to ensure responsible, fair and sustainable development.

An undergirding theme in Stelarc's work is the question of control. Organic evolution operates on the basis of chance and the ability of the individual organism to respond to environmental factors; however, arbitrariness has no place in hyper-modernized societies where all aspects of life are subjected to increasing degrees of rationalization. For Stelarc, digital technology's exquisite capacity for control represents the domain where an evolved architecture of the body can be designed, pursued and realized. He identifies the issues of human contact and intercommunication as key areas for improving individual and community well-being in the 'hyperindustrial epoch' (Stiegler 2014); hence, his inclination to furnish *Extra Ear* with telecommunication functionality. By improving intersubjectivity, technology affords the development of 'healthier realities' (Baraibar 1999: 162). The extra-corporeal aural organ is assigned material functionality, thereby contributing to an aesthetics constituted on the basis of prosthesis for social good, that is, making bodies more 'useful' and apt to the environmental conditions of hypermodernity. This positive engagement contributes towards his project of 'extended life-span (whether [it be] the individual, the species, or other kinds of artificial and intelligent life)' (Stelarc 2020). By adding technological organs that augment and complement the functions of his pre-existing biological organs, he embraces the avant-garde conceptualization of the artist as social guide via activistic provocation. He is not suggesting that everyone should have an extra ear grafted on to their body, or that such an act would add any social value, resilience or longevity; rather, the aim is to incite people to question the role, meaning and significance of all bodies in the context of digital culture. Technology is essentially constituted by a condition of prosthesis. But that fact becomes increasingly abstruse in highly industrialized environments that are progressively fabricated, artificial and unnatural. Stelarc's aesthetic gestures aim to foreground these conditions by following the thought to its chimeric limit.

Stelarc is acting in the tradition of interpretative performance art or, more accurately, *Body Art*, a related subgenre that more specifically takes 'place through an enactment of the artist's body' (Jones 1998: 13). Body art opens up 'the interpretive relation and its active solicitation of spectatorial desire ... [and] provides the possibility for radical engagements that can transform the way we think about meaning and subjectivity' (Jones 1998: 14). The political potential of Stelarc's performative gesture lies in an aesthetics of suggestion, that is, in the interpretative responsibility of the audience. The meaning pivots on the exchange between artist and audience, although the performance is not dependent on the presence of the latter because the performativity is so effective in transmitting the art idea. The migration of the performance event to a sterile operating theatre, where it is inappropriate and unsafe to house an audience, makes the documentation equally important to the event itself, such that it can be disseminated and 'experienced subsequently' through various media (Jones 1998: 13). This is what it means to embody scenography and to enact a scenography of the cyborg: to bravely spatialize performance within the vulnerable fabric of the body as chimeric self-portraiture and to electronically disseminate the documented results as an activistic catalyst that implicates the subjectivity of all bodies. *Extra Ear* represents a groundbreaking rupture that challenges forth questions about the normative effects of socio-politically imposed subjectivities. The perception that the body is a rigidly defined, fixed, self-bounded entity is an ideological mythology purveyed and maintained by incumbent socio-political actors, who champion 'an all too narrow economy of socially acceptable body projects' (Baraibar 1999: 164). Stelarc's praxis of embodied scenography aims to debunk this.

Extra Ear, amongst Stelarc's other performances, confidently illustrates and validates postmodern, cybercultural and digital theory because it advocates that the rigid, essentialist modalities of the individual (e.g. gender, race, ethnicity, creed and so on) be revised, perhaps even eradicated. Analogously, he views the culturally transformative capabilities of technology as an opportunity, not an impediment. His work energizes a positive interpretation that potentializes not just the reconfiguration of the individual body, but also the relations of multiple bodies, rupturing the social base and speculating on alternative realities. Through performative surgeries (soft prostheses) and technological augmentations (hard prostheses), Stelarc demonstrates a scenography of the cyborg that is extra-human in ambition but utterly human in purview. However, the human conditions of lacking and weakness are equally emphasized in the thematic impetus that drives the artist to commit his body to such grave acts of exploration. By manipulating and modifying the body under the auspices of technology, it can be quantified and reconceptualized in diverse ways. Stelarc aims not to save the human body but to theorize it alternatively, so that individuals can relate to themselves and to others in new, inventive ways in a rapidly changing world.

The importance of Stelarc's work lies in his advancement of future realities. By innovatively repurposing scientific knowledge and tools, he shows original, inventive ways to engage self-expression and self-realization, which provide the basis for an expanded visionary model of socio-political and economic functioning. Through the performative implantation of the *Extra Ear*, Stelarc reconfigures his body as an exploratory vector that ruptures artistic, biological, technological and sociological thinking. He challenges known limits of various fields by folding them together in the fabric of his corporeal self, thereby establishing an embodied scenography that reifies 'the body not as a site for the psyche nor for social inscription, but rather as a site for a sculpture. The body as a host for an internal work of art' (Stelarc 2020). Thus, he selflessly offers up his body as a prototype for possible futures, thrusting it ahead with technological advancement and bringing those futures closer, making them palpable. Pushing the boundaries of knowledge towards the invention of new worlds through technological agencies that modify the human body is precisely the task that is taken up again, in the next chapter, in a discussion of Klaus Obermaier's projection-mappings.

3

Innovations in Motion-Tracking and Projection-Mapping: Klaus Obermaier

Klaus Obermaier is a critically acclaimed digital media artist from Austria. He has been practising digital media arts since the mid-1990s and is applauded for his innovative, pioneering work in the areas of performance, music and installation. He is yet another artist whose prolific oeuvre could constitute an entire book on digital scenography, so it is a challenge to do him justice in a single book chapter. This study focuses on a selection of his early works – *D.A.V.E.* (1999), *Vivisector* (2002) and *Apparition* (2004) – that specifically deal with digital media projections and the live performer, and proposes them as an avant-garde, pioneering investigation of digital projections as scenography.[1] This is not the first book chapter on his work nor will it be the last. Klich and Scheer use Obermaier's work to contextualize their theoretical framework at the beginning of their book, emphasizing him as a pivotal figure in the genre (2011: 1), Scott deLahunta gives him an important outing in his pithy overview of the field (2008) and *Apparition* was analysed in relation to its dialectical tensions with the culture industry (O'Dwyer 2015a). Obermaier is widely recognized as one of the major innovators exploring the performing body and human–computer interfaces, (dis-)embodiment, interdisciplinarity and the impact of information technologies on audiences and arts practitioners. Taking account of his six-year exploratory trajectory, from *D.A.V.E.* through *Vivisector* to *Apparition*, this chapter recognizes the research trilogy as another exemplary gesture of practice-as-research (PaR) in performance and contends that Obermaier's innovative repurposing of digital projection and computer vision software technologies creates an aesthetic rupture. His work challenges the status quo of filmic, cinematic and theatrical paradigms, by showing that 'video projection, physical presence and acoustic environment [... can] blend into a symbiosis and create their own new reality' (Obermaier and Haring 1999). This inclination to frame the work as a symbiosis is a key discussion point in this chapter and the book generally. It would be erroneous to reduce Obermaier's work to digital mergers of audio-visuals and the performing body because his central philosophy concerns a conceptualization of the computer *itself* as a performer. He states:

> When I work with performers and an interactive system they are always equal partners for me ... Treating the machine as performance partner and equally is the only way that makes sense. If not, you may miss the real opportunities and probably run into the danger that the digital part becomes just a decoration.
>
> (Obermaier 2019)

With this in mind, this chapter traces the development of this idea over the said six-year period of Obermaier's practice, revealing a sub-narrative of the larger genealogy that charts the increasing agency of computers in digital scenography.

D.A.V.E.

On 26 March 1999, at dietheater Kunstlerhaus, Vienna, Klaus Obermaier and Chris Haring (performer/choreographer) staged an innovative performance work, entitled *D.A.V.E (Digital Amplified Video Engine)*, consisting of a 'concentration of projections on the body in motion' (Obermaier and Haring 1999). It built upon the aesthetics of Robert Brownjohn,[2] on one hand, and Merce Cunningham and Alwin Nikolais,[3] on the other. The unique advancement that Obermaier and Haring brought to the genre is that they employed interactive digital computer-vision and projection-mapping techniques for a live performance scenario. The work is acclaimed for its innovation and toured for about twelve years.

The performance opens with Haring, who has a shaven head and dons only a pair of beige combat trousers, revolving slowly on the spot. A projected video image of a man similarly turning is brought up and precisely fits Haring's body-shape. The rate of revolutions gradually increases until they become inhumanly fast, as if he were a 'human spinning top' (Lavender 2006: 58). In fact, the embodied performer stops spinning and his stationary body forms the projection surface for his super-human cyborg other. This opening visual metaphor establishes a ludic digital scenography that constitutes the performance: the mise-en-scène of perceptual illusions or mind games. As the projected digital double slows and stops, it becomes apparent he has hair, a feature emphasized by Haring's positioning with his back to the audience. The contrast between the (projected) hirsute avatar and the (embodied) bald character founds the overarching theme of the performance: the 'potential future removal of limitations on the body' (Obermaier and Haring 1999). The performance speculates on the possibility that in digital culture people could construct public facades and identities above and beyond the restricted set inherited through genotypical reality, thereby mischievously exposing an unnerving dualism between the fixed materiality of the flesh-and-blood body and the mutable immateriality of the mediated self.

Dramaturgically, the remainder of the performance consists in flipping between segments of gymnastic choreography and sections where various visual metaphors are projected on to Haring's relatively stationary body. Through the malleability of digital media, D.A.V.E. undergoes a series of visual transformations that question notions of gender, sexuality, ageing and corporeal limitations. Visualizations iterate through various imagery superimposed onto Haring's body-canvas, positioned in a range of carefully considered poses, giving the illusion of impossible bodily manoeuvres and contortions. Early on, Haring faces the audience (hands over his eyes, palms facing out) with the projections mapped precisely to the combined shape. Upon his hands are projected massively enlarged eyeballs that convey the symbolism to that of an insect, or alien-like, disembodied head, floating in the blackened stage space. Then his mouth and ears are enlarged and distorted in a similar manner, establishing preparatory manipulations for a series of scenographic assemblages that become increasingly biologically fantastic. In a later scene Haring kneels with his back to the audience. The forward-facing digital persona is projected onto his back and head, while its lower half honours the performer's physical orientation, resulting in an overall digital–physical hybrid that is twisted through 180 degrees at the midriff (see Figure 3.1). The stomach is simultaneously pulled into an incredibly skinny hourglass-shape, while the head is squeezed to half of its original width. The expression on the face is one of pain, as if enduring a torturous process in moulding the body into something original and alternatively fashionable. Thus, Obermaier reengages the cybercultural thematics – evocative of Stelarc's Chimeric body-enhancement surgeries and Haraway's theories – that celebrate fluid modalities of the self, where people are enabled to conduct somatic alterations towards self-fulfilment and a radical identity politics.

The 'body scenography' (DeLahunta 2008: 226) becomes progressively more weird. Haring stands apparently facing the audience with his hands covering his chest and groin whereupon an androgynous naked torso – full breasts, ostensibly pregnant yet hirsute – is projected onto the upper half

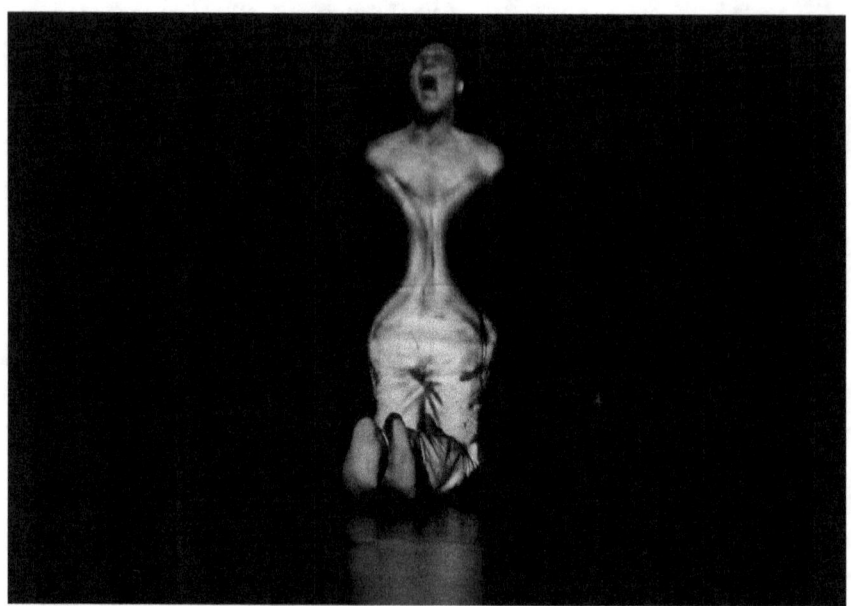

FIGURE 3.1 *Photo: Felix Noebauer. D.A.V.E., Deformation (courtesy of Felix Noebauer and Klaus Obermaier).*

of his body. Is *D.A.V.E.* pregnant, or at least fantasizing about it ... living the experience through a digital avatar? The digital image is pictured from the side whereas Haring is facing forwards, and the lower half is again twisted, though, this time, only through 90 degrees. These impossible distortions and intersexual conditions continue to offer the audience a perspective of the body that is evolved, mutated and uncanny. Further on, he is positioned in a prostrate squat with his posterior facing towards the audience. There is a mouth projected onto the buttocks that is mainly engaged in hyperbolic articulations of o-sounds, affording the lips a predominantly o-shaped orifice. On one level this image comically denotes the notion of a talking anus, or talking *through* one's anus (depending on the interpretation); on another level, it connotes the libidinal desire for heightened control over the bodily organs towards the augmentation of sexual pleasure. In another scene, *D.A.V.E.*'s head transforms into a glowing bright red orb, which he playfully removes and, by means of juggling choreography, moves it around his body as a mime-artist performs with a crystal ball. The contours of Haring's body are simultaneously highlighted with fluorescent white lines against a topology of oversized blue pixels, portraying him as a sort of lo-fi computer game character (see Figure 3.2). These imaginings all contribute to the overarching theme of interrogating the possibilities of bodily augmentation through digital media.

The audience are challenged to ponder who is the *real D.A.V.E.* Is he the tangible, present performer on the stage, who embodies the

FIGURE 3.2 Photo: Marianne Weiss. D.A.V.E., Red Orb (courtesy of Klaus Obermaier).

projection screen and, by doing so, manifests as a host for the digitally projected flux? Or, as Lavender eloquently suggests, is he the mediated, binarized 'video body, placed parasitically on the flesh that it simultaneously obliterates? ... D.A.V.E. is teasingly bi-textual' (Lavender 2006: 59). He exists in the tangible performance space and digital mediatized space in equal measure. By questioning the liminality between embodied performer and video projection, blurring the threshold of where they begin and end, Obermaier and Haring's scenographic metaphors foreground the ambiguity of D.A.V.E.'s materiality. This establishes the aesthetic reality that precisely summarizes the major ontological concern of the digital era: as a container for (linguistic, textual, visual or aural) symbols that constitute the basis of how people construct identities and represent themselves to the world, the modular digital self has the potential to overtake the corporeal, embodied self.

Digital and cybernetic technologies have obliged philosophical, sociological, anthropological, socio-economic and political discourses to reconsider thresholds of the body and mind. By interrogating the body's relation to its digital double, the imagery and thematics of D.A.V.E. are appropriately chosen to complement topical, contemporaneous subjects. The project description explains that the goal is to engage the possibility of a potential future where, 'thanks to futuristic technologies and implantation, mankind will be in a position to eliminate the restrictions upon the natural body'

(Obermaier and Haring 1999). These body-alteration metaphors are limited to the digitally projected image; they are not explored organically through embodied representational formats like choreography and dramaturgy. It initially seems they champion the potential of mediated existence over embodied existence; however, although theoretical stances predominately supported the potential of interactive media in the mid-to-late 1990s, there were also plenty of cyberculture sceptics cautioning against the new conditions of intersubjectivity. The utopian cyborg-vision was short lived in the wake of, firstly, the dot-com bust in 1999 and, secondly, the global economic collapse of 2008, explained as arising from an over-confidence in the ability of financial algorithms to manage the global economy (Greenspan 2008). The scenographic oscillation between the digitally enhanced body and Haring's comparatively energetic *unmediated* movement seems to acknowledge this inherent jeopardy of digital technology. Despite the apparent advocation of the digitally enhanced body as more elastic, configurable, malleable and sublimely grotesque, the scenes using digital projections are lacking in corporeal dynamism in comparison to those composed solely of Haring's acrobatic choreography. Curiously, *D.A.V.E.*'s embodied persona is valorized through the lithe movement that comprises the scenes allocated to its staging, ironically assigning it a greater sense of liberation. Knowing what we know now, two decades after its release, the overall performance appears to advocate the (widely supported) theme that *the less one is immersed in digital media, the more free one really is*. The polemics of time spent in front of screens, *plugged-in*, is raging now more than ever.[4] However, these connotations of liberation arising from the juxtaposition of mediated and non-mediated scenes are a consequence of scholarly hindsight, rather than the express intention of the artist-makers.

Technical Determinacy in *D.A.V.E.*

The mise-en-scène of the mediated persona consists in passages of slow, measured poses because of a technical determination. The claim that the performance involves 'projections on the body in motion' (Obermaier and Haring 1999) is slightly misleading because the images do not strictly follow the performer in real time; Haring has to remain relatively still during the moments when projections are mapped onto his body. Although dynamic, interactive projection-mapping is the trajectory of Obermaier's research during the six-year period that culminates in *Apparition*, the mappings in *D.A.V.E.* do not involve locational calculations that track the dancer's movement. *D.A.V.E* is more precisely the embryonic stage of the idea. As deLahunta states,

'Obermaier intended only that the relationship between body and projected image would successfully drive the linear narrative of the piece on stage' (DeLahunta 2008: 226). This is not to reprimand the work; there should be no mistake that *D.A.V.E* brings something fundamentally new to the field of projected digital scenography.

The performance is composed of a series of short gymnastic dance sequences punctuated with moments of corporeal stillness, at which point the dynamics of movement are deferred to the performing projections of the cyborg other. This dramaturgy highlights the core questioning of this book: what affordances and limitations are brought to the stage by digital technology and the artists' will to push the limits of the field? Their ardent experimental fusion affects epistemic development of the performance spectacle's mise-en-scène and research in the computer sciences more generally. Obermaier and Haring's performance experiment exposes a key theme of this book: the emergence of a new art idea conditioned by the arrival of new technologies, and its repercussions thereof. The Event of its revealing can be reiterated in terms of Event Theory, that is, an aesthetic rupture causing a fundamental break with the status quo, in which the taxonomic substrata of culture undergo a tectonic shift, becoming re-stratified. This re-stratification consists of the idea's adoption and refinement, by the artists, and its redistribution to the greater community, as an expanded scenographic trope. The remainder of this chapter is concerned with tracing the first instance, that is, charting how the scenographic idea becomes a research question for the artists that is teased out over several years. This exemplifies PaR processes involving the continual redefinition of dramaturgical and scenographic methods towards integrating technology more seamlessly in performance practice. Ensuing chapters chart the larger (socio-anthropological) phenomenon involving idea (knowledge) dissemination and its uptake by other cultural practitioners across the globe, demonstrating the overall normative trajectory towards the consolidation of digital technologies at the heart of performance design.

What is crucial to this chapter and book is that the affordances of interactive digital technologies exert an influence over how the choreography and dramaturgy are developed. These affordances demand a careful reconsideration of each performer's relationship to one another and to the technology, and they determine how these relations evolve over the life of the performance. In their subsequent project, *Vivisector*, Obermaier and Haring became more ambitious in the number of dancers they staged. Therefore, they had to be mindful of developing a unique dramaturgy, contextualized by a plurality of actors, that does not simply repeat themes explored in *D.A.V.E.* and avoids the pitfall of mere technological exhibitionism.

Vivisector

Vivisector represents a significant leap in their idea development. It is a more ambitious project, in terms of choreography and scenography because the staging concerns several performers, not just one. In this project, the artists contribute to the aesthetic legacy of scenographers like Josef Svoboda and choreographers like Alwin Nikolais because their methods involved incorporating multimedia components, such as strong light and film projection to reveal and secrete performers on a blackened stage, ultimately toying with the audience's perception. In particular, Nikolais' goal was to challenge and destabilize dominant formal, structured choreo-dramaturgical paradigms. In *Vivisector*, Obermaier and Haring contribute to this aesthetic discourse using digital technologies to explore 'a reduced technique of body projection to explore the limitations of perception' (deLahunta 2005). From a technical point of view, *Vivisector* does not significantly advance the projection techniques explored in *D.A.V.E.* but the artists clearly start to integrate aspects of choreographed movement with the mapped projections. In *D.A.V.E.* Haring remains relatively still during the moments of projection; in *Vivisector* the performers do move, albeit in a very prescribed manner. The movement consists in rapid changes of pose and location, which are then held for varying durations, while short, sharp, bright punctuations of digital graphics are projected onto the performer's bodies and/or body parts, constantly drawing the spectator's gaze to varying regions of the stage. When the light illuminates the limb, head or torso of a dancer, the others rapidly relocate or reconfigure their body-shape in the darkness. Although allowing the audience to marvel at the dancers' dexterous movements is the dominant aesthetic and raison d'être for audiences, to do so in this instance would reveal the process and break the perceptual illusion that is central to the dramaturgical and scenographic experiment at the heart of the research. Surgically precise flashes of digitally projected light reveal disembodied limbs that pull the spectator's gaze around the blackened stage, playing on the perceiver's ability to focus and refocus on the object. It is the perception of the spectator that assigns an interactive quality to the projected graphics by imagining the lighting system has a degree of programmed intelligence, which does not actually exist. Neither *D.A.V.E.* nor *Vivisector* uses 'interactive technologies, but [... rely] on a creative and precise combination of set choreography, staging and recorded video' (deLahunta 2005). The dancers follow a strict, time-dependent choreographic routine, moving into preassigned positions that have been carefully calibrated in rehearsal. But the routine is all the more impressive because it is executed in darkness.

Description

The performance opens with the slow revealing of four male performers on a blackened stage using flashing, pixelated graphics that map directly to their body shapes. Right from the outset the audience's perception is tested because the darkened stage and shifting projected light make it difficult to discern how many performers there are, where exactly they are and what postures they strike. The graphics begin as blocky, oversized, diffused pixels but gradually decrease in size and increase in density to the point where the shape of the bodies becomes clear, and they appear as anthropomorphic formations of white noise or swarms of insects (see Figure 3.3). The graphics then consolidate as pure planes of pale whitish-blue, covering the entire bodies of the performers. What value do these flat planes of light add to the mise-en-scène above traditional theatre lighting? Could not carefully pointed spotlights with gels (e.g. techniques used to great effect by Alwin Nikolais and Robert Wilson) give a more atmospheric scenography? The planes of digitally projected light bring their own peculiar aesthetic to the stage. The low, front-on position of the projector and its brilliant beam gives the bodies a harsh, grey flatness that sets the technology apart from the soft tones achieved with electrical lighting. Furthermore, during the period of its exhibiting (2000–7), the resolution of digital projection was very low. In comparison to the smooth, uninterrupted topology of analogue lighting, the discreet pixels of the beamer are discernible even when flat colours are used, covering the bodies with a

FIGURE 3.3 *Photo: Klaus Obermaier.* Vivisector, *pixelated bodies (courtesy of Klaus Obermaier).*

fine mesh and reinforcing the notion that the performers are not fully present, but semi-screened. At this point, the fully illuminated quartet performs synchronized movements that are slow, robotic and devoid of gymnastic energy. As they twist and turn on the spot, the graphics gradually revert back to their retro, oversized, flickering origins, finally disappearing and plunging the scene into blackness again.

As the performance progresses, the musical composition evolves from ambient, granular-synthesis towards the electronic genre, with a strong emphasis on rhythm. As opposed to *D.A.V.E.*, which deals with the interrogation of a singular solipsistic, narcissistic being, *Vivisector* consists of four dancers, so the relations between the performers are instrumental to the choreography. These relations are explored primarily through visual and sonic rhythm. Bands of light sweep up and down their bodies on the blackened stage, as if scanning them, using some futuristic bio-technological surveillance process. They begin in synch but become a-rhythmical in complementarity to the pulsing musical beats. The symbolic device of projecting oversized pixels onto the performer's bodies is used again, reinforcing the sense of mediatized presence. Combined with the vertical scanning, they connote themes of biometric data processing, as if the characters' personas were being inspected and processed – the digital double disappearing into the ether of digital networks. The electronic musical soundtrack continually remains in synch with the flickering pixels and the rhythm of the roving scanlines.

As the scanning continues, it is difficult to discern the exact posture of each performer because spectators can only perceive a narrow cross-section at any given moment. Are they moving or are they static? They slowly shift position as the scanning bands sweep up and down their bodies, creating the impression that they are transforming anthropomorphic creatures that cannot be perceived in their entirety. This is a clever way of exploring the moving body with digital projection without having to execute infra-software calculations in real time, based on the dancers' movements, although this is ultimately where Obermaier brings the research. In *D.A.V.E.* there is very little movement; the performer holds his position quite rigidly while the images are projected onto him. In *Vivisector,* the performers are permitted limited movement through the employment of digital scenographic devices that do not allow the performers to be perceived in their totality at any given moment.

The scanning process continues for a long time, becoming quite repetitious and plunging the audience into a state of hypnosis. However, suddenly a full body is revealed, as if pulled out of a rift in the darkness or teleported into the space. It has an uncanny aspect because the image of another mediated persona is superimposed onto it. This harkens back to the mise-en-scène of *D.A.V.E.*, which establishes a dualism between the real, present, embodied performer and the mediated, ethereal, telepresent digital double.

The fully revealed dancer stands awkwardly, uncomfortable and isolated as the scanning of other bodies continues on either side. The projected imagery on the lone dancer begins to ripple and distort as if the performer is now a reflection of himself, materialized on the turbulent surface of a pool of water. Agitations of the fluid increase steadily as the digital double's image becomes increasingly fragmented, until it degenerates once again into a fabric of discordant, randomized pixels that finally evaporate into the blackened space. This theme of sudden appearance followed by gradual disintegration is explored for each of the characters in various ways, for example, through pixel resolution and particle systems. Each trope is successful in its own way and the visual variety keeps the spectator engaged, avoiding ennui through the simple repetition of graphics for each character. Thematically speaking, the message that prevails through the mis-en-scène of these scenographics is that which was so dominant in the first scene: disappearance of the spiritual, discarnate self into the ether of digital networks. Therefore, the themes of *Vivisector* are related to those first raised in *D.A.V.E.*; however, it takes a different approach by visually and metaphorically exploring them through inter-character relations, as opposed to the voyeuristic spectator paradigm of *D.A.V.E.* where the audience bear witness to his private, fanciful explorations of possible alter-egos.

The artists combine visual rhythm with other types of graphics to explore relationships. Figures are wholly or partially illuminated intermittently using a stroboscopic effect that gives animation to bodies that are actually quite inanimate. It begins as a finely tuned digital spotlight, flashing between fully illuminated bodies twisting on the spot, and then fine-tunes its precision by focusing on singular limbs, amputating heads, legs and torsos, giving the mis-en-scène a Beckettian flavour (see Figure 3.4). The soundtrack initiates without percussive beats; the rhythm is achieved through the visuals alone. However, a soft, deep, heartbeat-like rhythm is slowly introduced, at first very faint but gradually intensifying. This heartbeat soundtrack dictates the timing of the flashes that periodically illuminate the dancers in various positions, sometimes with flat planes of white light, and other times with the superimposition of a digital double. At one point a dancer is lit, and stays lit. He executes movement phrases that are jerky and punctuated, evoking robotic, inhuman characteristics. The spectator's attention is intermittently distracted by flashes of precise, concentrated projection-mappings that concurrently illuminate the discrete limbs of the other dancers – limbs amputated by the razor-sharp precision of the projector's malleable beam. This exercise in rhythm, light and perception tests spectators' abilities to attend to and focus on discordant bodily fragments at varying distances, thrown at them from the blackened space of the theatre. However, this perceptual challenge is brought to an abrupt halt with the simultaneous illumination of all dancers, each overlaid

FIGURE 3.4 Photo: Klaus Obermaier. Vivisector, *disembodied limbs (courtesy of Klaus Obermaier).*

with their digital personas who subject their hosts to more jerky, inorganic movements. However, this time, the movement is wholly inhuman. Whereas the spasmodic movements of the embodied performers in earlier scenes still had some semblance of humanity, the movements of the superimposed avatars are thoroughly machinic and inhuman; that is, they are only possible through the manipulation of discretized video footage. They iterate through various trompe l'oeil scenographic projection devices, giving the illusion that the performers are levitating, twisting and turning inhumanly, or twitching and convulsing repetitively like some malfunctioning, misfiring robot.

In *Vivisector*, a narrative framework is established based on the flipping between two main choreo-scenographic paradigms: firstly, the testing of audience perception via the stroboscopic projection of flat colours onto the performers' bodies, whereby they are permitted a degree of movement and, secondly, the precise mapping of a digital video on to their bodies, whereby they are obliged to stay relatively still and defer movement to their digital other. The final projection sequences continue with this dual methodology. The audience's perception is once again challenged by the stroboscopic device. The performers are dispersed across the width and depth of the stage and their full bodies are illuminated with flat flashing planes of white light. However, this time the flashes occur at fractions of a second, while the performers again engage in controlled, gradual movements. In contrast to the earlier scenes, they all execute the same choreography in synchrony: turning slowly on the spot, raising and lowering their arms, while their legs and torso remain straight and upright. This gives the illusion that a single body is being teleported to various locations of the stage, a trompe-l'oeil compounded by the fact that they all have bleached blonde, cropped hair and don similar trousers. The dancers then slowly move back and forth across the stage, while keeping their legs bolt straight and only shuffling their feet in tiny, almost imperceptible, increments. They pass in front of one another, occluding each other and interfering with the perceivable body-shape of their co-actors. They pass from one stroboscopic zone to another, seemingly splicing their bodies in asynchronized vertical segments. These illusions give the overall impression of watching a life-size zoetrope, a visual reference that is reinforced by the white silhouette punched out of the black background. The choreography does not evolve much in terms of the dancers' physical movements. Apart from the shuffling back and forth, they are relatively stationary for most of the scene; their movements are deferred to the technology and its ability to affect the perception of the onlooker. The dancers come to a halt in synchrony, facing the audience with hands on hips. While the flashing continues, the final video images are introduced: elliptical projections of twitching torsos, precisely mapped to the midriff of each dancer. The imagery is modified with a hard light that accentuates the contours of the chest and abdominal muscles, connoting a visual thematic of perfectly engineered bodies, similar to the visual tropes used in *D.A.V.E.* The visual's movements are repetitious, convulsive and spasmodic, implying gastric and respiratory malfunctioning and delivering themes of viscera and bodily disgust, typical of cyborg theory at the time. The exaggerated gastral movements evoke notions of biomechanical short-circuiting and malfunction. As the stroboscopic flashes on the full bodies become more sporadic and are gradually phased out, only the pulsating topologies of the projection-mapped torsos are left floating in the blackened stage space. The arrangement of these in a row highlights the biological parallels between the distinct individuals. As they continue to pulse, the hard light is ramped up and inverted so that the shadows become thick, white outlines evocative of a disembodied, floating, beating heart or the ultrasound of an embryo – signs of a new life.

The Ambivalences of Digital Scenography

Of all the scenographic passages in *Vivisector*, there is only one brief moment – which hardly qualifies as an entire scene – where some of the dancers can be seen in their totality executing choreography in a classical manner, and an appreciation of their expertise is fully afforded. The timing and execution demanded of the dancers in the scenes where they are largely hidden are probably more onerous than on an illuminated set. The projection system, which is not interactive, operates on an unvarying timeline, requiring their precise placement at the right moment. This is necessary so that the mise-en-scène of the dancers and the digitally projected light can synchronize and harmoniously complement each other, maintaining the illusory method of disclosure that underpins the performance. This technical determination of the choreography is particularly evident in the third scene, where the metronomic heartbeat soundtrack dictates the timing of the flashes. It is not surprising that this performance was greeted with a degree of ambivalence by the dance community and critics. On one hand, it opens exciting questions concerning what is possible on the contemporary digitally equipped stage, and on the other, it does not necessarily push the boundaries of choreographic and movement practice. As such, dance purists greeted the performance with some uncertainty:

> And the result is a great visual show lasting about one hour, which deals with dance only marginally. Human beings move like machines, aiming to increase the technical effect. A frightening vision at the end of a dance festival, fascinating as well as irritating.
>
> (Suchan 2002)

While undoubtedly impressed, Suchan's apprehension concerns the emergence of a performance paradigm where the dancer becomes secondary to the digital projections, that is, where the dancer becomes a vehicle for demonstrating the technology.

Vivisector exposes a central topic of this book, concerning the new affordances and limitations that digital technologies bring to scenography and performance generally. It begs the question as to who, or what, is given the central role in this performance? Notwithstanding their mastery of counting and keeping time with the machine, to a certain degree the dancers take a backseat in this production because the performance system is the thing that is literally pushed to the foreground. The foregrounding of one thing demands the backgrounding of another. The dancers execute most of their phrases in pitch dark, holding their pose until they are pulsed with projected light then shifting position again, always in time with the machine. Although the master–slave paradigm, where music determines choreography, has dominated formal Western dance practice, there is usually a synergy between the two in their staging, so it is alarming when the system overtakes the performer.

In *D.A.V.E.* and *Vivisector* the agency of the projection-mapping system specified that the backgrounded performers be accurate, timely and relatively static in their positioning. The mise-en-scene of projection-mapped video and dancers was designed around this clause. However, Obermaier's ongoing PaR sought to overcome this deterrent to mobility during the projection sequences. Henceforth, the goals of his third project, *Apparition*, in this projection-mapping trilogy were to design a scenographic system that would afford a confluence of the moving body with projection-mapped graphics, and to conceive a choreography that would conceptually and dramaturgically resonate with the technological breakthrough.

Apparition

Apparition is Obermaier's most widely known and critically acclaimed production. It was refined over two main releases, the first involving a collaboration with choreographers Robert Tannion (GB/AU) and Desirée Kongerød (GB/NO), the second involving a collaboration with Desirée Kongerød and Matthew Smith (NZ). In opposition to *D.A.V.E.* and *Vivisector*, which have fixed choreographic directions, *Apparition* engages the concept of technological determinacy in a way that encourages improvisation. It is exemplary of the new possibilities available to the arts by drawing out the new, computational and interactive specificities of digital technologies.

The digital performance system operates on an interactive framework that entails defining a set of rules, tracking the dancers using computer-vision hardware and software, quantizing and analysing the information, and, if certain conditions are met, generating specific audio-visual content in *response* to the given gesture. The interactive stage set is rigged with computer vision technologies that track the dancers' movements. This is afforded by the real-time video analysis technique of *frame differencing*, which compares each current video frame to a first (empty) one, allowing the computer to perceive and locate a body in the space. The biomechanical movement data generated by the tracked dancers are fed into procedural graphics (which depend on a numerical input) that are then projected back onto the set. The mise-en-scène of the projections is played out on two types of projection surface: a large, immobile projection screen positioned upstage, and the mobile, kinetic body-canvases of the dancers themselves. Both types of projection surface are responsive – the dancers' bodies in relation to the motion-tracking system and the screen in relation to the dancers. The performers literally dance with the machine, not simply because the machine responds to the dancers' movement and modifies graphics in response to their kinetic flux, but also in the sense that the scenographed kinetic imagery influences how and where they move. The intention of the performative digital system is to release the dancers from the limitations of prescribed choreography and to propose an innovative, fluid scenographic paradigm. As well as demonstrating new artistic possibilities opened by tracking live performers, the artists make the claim that 'video projection, physical presence and acoustic environment thus blend into a symbiosis and create their own new reality' (Obermaier and Haring 1999).[5] This positioning of the responsive scenography as a symbiotic ecosystem, encompassing human and non-human elements, establishes a strong aesthetic and conceptual basis for Obermaier's research. The remainder of this chapter is dedicated to unpacking this theme, which is considered to be central to the overarching narrative of this book, that is, one that deeply considers the agency of digital technologies in processes of creative expression and intersubjectivity generally.

Responsive Scenography

Responsive environments, defined as 'spaces that interact with the people who use them, pass through them or by them' (Bullivant 2006: 1), are electronically enabled spaces that require the presence of an interlocutor to fulfil their technical and aesthetic potential. Without human presence they lie dormant, awaiting interaction; with the arrival of an interactor they are awakened. The affirmation of physical presence stimulates them into activity, and electrical flux flows through their circuitry as blood does through the veins of a living organism. Their dependence on interaction is not unreciprocated; their audio-visual affirmation of human interlocutors commands curiosity and further action, precisely in the manner of a dialogue. In *Apparition,* the mise-en-scène of human–computer interdependence foregrounds the efficacy of technology in choreo-dramaturgical conceptualization. While perhaps certain successful passages are noted and locked-off for the finished performance, much of the choreography is distinctly improvisational. Furthermore, the rehearsals were a corporeal dialogue with the responsive space towards the development of a dramaturgy. DeLahunta writes:

> [The] interplay between dancer and system and how one begins to understand the properties of the other ... [is] crucial to the conceptual and aesthetic development of the work; helping give shape to the choreography and underpinning its dramaturgy.
>
> (deLahunta 2005)

This exploratory feedback loop characterizes the finalized production, suffusing it with themes of dialogue and discovery. The spectacle evokes a sense of witnessing humans familiarizing themselves with the system, and vice versa – like a sort of courting ritual.

The reactive nature of the system and its demand for co-presence nurture a dialogical choreo-dramaturgy in which improvisation and spontaneity are key characteristics. Analogous to Troika Ranch's work, this gives *Apparition* compositional properties akin to those favoured by the historical avant-garde: improvisation, spontaneity, dynamism and flux. The graphical visualizations do not simply trace the performers' movement and spray visual contrails in relation to their location, like a spotlight following a performer across the stage; the computational models are based on physics libraries that underpin a responsive scenographic environment, simulating organic ecosystems modelled on cause and effect. Herein the dancer is but one element whose actions affect and are affected. The motion-tracking system harvests quantitative biomechanical data – such as direction, acceleration, size and proximity – which is used to simulate collisions in semi-autonomous particle-system and spring-based simulations, that are 'not "controllable" by the performer, but can be influenced by his or her movement' (deLahunta 2005). This establishes a scenographic paradigm that is not fully predictable, thereby encouraging a choreo-dramaturgy whose outcome is, analogously, not fully fixed. While the overall scene progressions *are* generally fixed, there is space in between for the dancers to improvise because there is less demand for them to be at the right place at the right time. This approach is similar to the indeterminate, open-ended performance system adopted by Troika Ranch and is evocative of the aforementioned systems art tradition.

The scenographic decision to suffuse the stage with responsive visuals, which simulate organic movement and abstractly conjure natural phenomena, establishes a rule-based performance system advocating indeterminacy over the execution of a fixed choreography. Therefore, movement becomes more energetic and expressive but less structured, from a formalist viewpoint. The mise-en-scène of the dancers and particle system visualizations projected onto the backdrop engenders a gymnastic choreography that, 'sometimes gives the impression that the dancers are moving through fluids, and at other moments, provides a spectacular sensation of being projected through hyperspace' (O'Dwyer 2015a: 37) (see Figure 3.5). The graphical models respond to and augment the 'kinaesthetic dynamics' (O'Dwyer 2015a: 38) of the dancers, giving the sensation that they inhabit an organic underwater world. The movement of the set is synchronized to that of the dancers by the precision of machine optics and lightning-quick calculations performed by computers. This influences how the dancers interact with each other and the machine; meaning that, under these conditions, the mediated audio-visuals and the embodied dancers do indeed co-exist in a symbiosis. Certain choreographic specificities are introduced by the responsive scenography

FIGURE 3.5 *Photo: Klaus Obermaier.* Apparition, Particles *(courtesy of Klaus Obermaier).*

and its dramaturgical efficacy. The spontaneity that the responsive system commands of the performers is obvious in the gymnastic movement of the dancers whose energetic leaps, when viewed against the lofty expanse of the interactive backdrop, give the impression that they somehow defy gravity. In his description of the mis-en-scène, deLahunta writes:

> The precise synchronisation of projections on the background and the bodies result in the materialization of an overall immersive kinetic space / a virtual architecture that can be simultaneously fluid and rigid, that can expand and contract, ripple, bend and distort in response to or [exert] an influence upon the movement of the performers.
>
> (deLahunta 2005)

This statement not only captures the essence of the scenographic innovation, but so too does it highlight the new synergetic choreographic paradigm afforded by the introduction of responsive digital technologies to performance design. The convergence of body and architecture is permitted through the electronic flux of digitally enabled space. However, the performance is not all dynamism and improvisation; there are moments of slow, measured movement that reinforce how different types of computer-drawn, graphical interfaces consistently influence the movement of the inter-actors.

Projection-Mapping

As well as encouraging improvisational choreography, the bespoke technology furnishes the artists with a performative capacity that distinguishes the work not only from their own similar earlier works, but also from all preceding performances employing projection. This is the innovative ability to accurately map projected imagery onto the performers' moving bodies. This is achieved by lighting the large screen from the rear with infrared (IR) light so the IR motion-tracking camera – that is aligned with the audience's gaze – 'sees' the bodies as two-dimensional silhouettes (Obermaier 2019). Once this information is available, the artist can draw graphics on or around the performer's digitized body-shape using real-time procedural graphics software. Through bespoke hardware and software processes that align the camera with the projector, these graphics are then accurately projected back onto the performer's real body (see Figure 3.6). Therefore, the technology transforms the performers'

FIGURE 3.6 *Photo: Klaus Obermaier.* Apparition, Lines *(courtesy of Klaus Obermaier).*

bodies into mobile receptors for the display of mutable digital costumes, sculpted through the medium of light. Coupled with the ability to perceptually affect the shape and kinetics of the backdrop, the artist is afforded a fundamentally new capacity to dynamically control and manipulate the set and costumes in real time.

In the scenes where the performers' bodies are projection-mapped, the choreography is analogously affected. When projecting onto them, there is a techno-determinant that conditions the speed of their movement: they must move slowly so that the computer system can keep up and the fiction is preserved. The mis-en-scène of bodies and light responds to this by staging a choreo-dramaturgy that is darker and more inauspicious in mood. The dancers perform slow, acrobatic movements, both independently and in unison, involving tumbles, stretches, hand-stands and rolls. When they are separate they are clearly humanoid; when united, they conspire to challenge preconceptions of anthropomorphic form because their amalgamated silhouette takes on an alien appearance when viewed against the projection backdrop. 'Contorted bodies, knotted limbs, and intertwined duets morph in and out of human form, all the while their other-worldly silhouette is punched in and out of perceptive visibility using computer-vision exactitude, coupled with the, hitherto unthinkably accurate, moulding of light' (O'Dwyer 2015a: 38). The assemblage undermines known referents and anthropomorphic categories because the combined silhouettes arouse uncanny, 'grotesque materializations' (O'Dwyer 2015a: 38) that transport the audience to a state of incomprehension. This theme is exacerbated by the use of perception-challenging scenographic tropes that hark back to *Vivisector*, for example, particle-based graphics bouncing randomly around the amalgamated silhouette of the dancers, fragmenting their form and giving the appearance that they are dematerializing on stage.

The methodology of challenging visual perception, which was deployed so effectively in *Vivisector*, is used again in *Apparition* with even more complexity and precision. In the darkened space, the performers' bodies are fragmented and perspectives are distorted through the flashing of minimalist, geometric, abstract shapes and lines. In contrast to *Vivisector*, the body-canvases are in motion and there are often complementary designs concurrently projected onto the backdrop. This is not an option in *Vivisector* because it is performed in a black-box style theatre where inaccuracies are hidden by the light-absorbent black-outs lining the stage. *Apparition* demands extreme accuracy because it is performed against a huge white projection screen; any light-spill would be noticeable to the audience, destroying the spectacular illusion. Therefore, a prevalent theme of *Apparition* is to provoke the audience into questioning what they see and what they believe cognitively possible. However, the dancers and the light projections belong to the tangible, present world of live performance, not the fantastic world of science fiction that is so carefully fabricated through cinema, animation, green-screen capture and hours of exhaustive postproduction processes, in which the actor is alienated from the finished performance product. *Apparition* operates through an intense spatial paradigm that is representative of the various modes of embodied and mediated interaction in contemporary existence. The theatre, dripping with surveillance and biometric-monitoring technologies, is like a laboratory for testing and exposing contemporary modalities of digital intersubjectivity, wherein human somatic qualities are quantified, examined and calculated through the broad and deep observational capacity of digital technologies. Although it does not use psycho-profiling or neurological scanning techniques, metaphorically speaking, *Apparition* challenges its audience to reflect upon the vulnerable condition of the human body and mind actuated by digital surveillance techniques.

Socio-political Metaphors of *Apparition*

In *Apparition*, there are scenes where text is superimposed on to the human body, evoking a 'lexical camouflage' (O'Dwyer 2015a: 39) (see Figure 3.7). This visual rhetoric conjures postmodern theories critiquing the capacity of inscriptive technologies to erode embodiment, presence and logocentrism from Western subjectivity (Derrida 1981), and cybercultural/posthuman concepts, suggesting the carnal body is increasingly overtaken and replaced by its own textual traces and narratives, recasting the individual as an information container (Hayles 1999). That is, the physical, embodied self is preceded by its immaterial, disembodied digital duplicate. Given that the digital duplicate describes the interior, mindful self, or *spirit*, the conferral of the posthuman spirit to a fragmented collection of discretized textual segments and nodes, distributed across a globalized intertextuality, is evident. Both the private articulations and public/private dialogues of contemporary technocratic citizens (whether big or small) predominately happen over electronic networks; therefore, everyone has a traceable digital impression that is at once ineffaceable yet immaterial. The details of interactions are recorded, duplicated and backed up on servers across the five continents, yet reside as discretized bits and abstracted electronic signals on silicon chips and hard drives. Stiegler describes this condition of digital culture as 'the disappearance of the "interior"' (Stiegler 2008: 77). This refers to the ability of various incorporated media conglomerates to access, extract and exploit personal, sensitive and vital information towards the ends of marketing, public relations and financial gain. With the ongoing sophistication of their

FIGURE 3.7 Photo: Klaus Obermaier. Apparition, Text *(courtesy of Klaus Obermaier).*

surveillance and analytical methods, there is an inversely proportional erosion of the private, 'interior' realm, which was less accessible prior to the digital epoch. The interior (spirit) is, henceforth, laid bare as an open, unprotected and *calculable* entity, quantifiably prepared for surveillance and exploitation under the contemporary global economic model of statistical information exchange. Under this economic paradigm, information harvesting is more important than making a sale; the liberal capitalist cash-for-goods (Fordist) economic model and its 'virtuous' (Stiegler 2016: 3) Keynesian framework of wealth redistribution are replaced by the hegemonic profiling agenda of neuro/cognitive capitalism (Moulier Boutang 2011; Griziotti 2019) and psychopower (Stiegler n.d.), which prioritizes harvesting data (relating to taste, social circles, spending patterns, political inclinations, work/leisure interests and so on) over short-term financial gain. These political–economic positions must be read in the aftermath of critical thinkers like Frederic Jameson (1992) and Mark Fisher (2009) who advocate a moderation of polemical attacks against neoliberal socio-economics. They maintain that projects aspiring to imagine an alternative to the time–space organization of capitalism must firstly acknowledge their own epistemological position as a product of it, that is, of a fluid sociocultural flux that consistently reconfigures the limits of human thought and the possibility of going beyond. Sympathetic to this position, Stiegler calls for a pharmacological reading of *capitalism* in the 'hyperindustrial epoch' – an age in which 'more than ever we are experiencing the industrialisation of all things' (Stiegler 2014: 47) – because the antidote resides within the toxin. While computational technologies are a major driving force of neoliberal *hyperindustrialization* that threaten to exacerbate misgivings that capitalism may summon, they also represent the site of innovations that afford the fabrication of a better future. It is for this reason that Stiegler pinpoints the artistic avant-garde (with its inherent embeddedness in technology and politics) as embodying the potential remedy to the disadvantages of hyperindustrialization. In *Apparition*, Obermaier precisely draws out the antidote by mobilizing hyperindustrial (surveillance and biometric) techniques towards aesthetics, showing a different way.

The live biometric monitoring and mapping of the dancers, in *Apparition*, constitute powerful visual metaphors that activate a disclosure of truth about how information technologies facilitate the extraction and exploitation of vital, personal marketing-sensitive data towards the ends of purchasing and political persuasion.[6] The perceptual union of bodies and set represents a new type of spectacle that poses questions about the complexities of the new biopolitical situation, and it exposes new potentialities for non-anthropocentric, symbiotic alliances between human and non-human entities. It challenges the human-centred tradition of performance and the preconception of built space as fixed, static and inert. Indeed, it arms the stage with its own performativity – a techno-performativity. This brings us back to a central thesis of this book: technology maintains an inherent, profound efficacy that, at a local level, underpins the evolution of modes of expression and, at a general level, modifies paradigms of intersubjectivity that constitute the basis of identity, politics and socio-economics.

Symbiosis or Organology?

Apparition is an eloquent treatment of a strong, original scenographic concept and is visionary in its establishment of an interactive/responsive choreography. Predicated on the basis of symbiosis, it uses machine-vision technologies to define a basic gestural language comprehensible to both humans and computers. While it has been established that the artists innovatively explore the idea of establishing symbiotic relations between performers and audio-visuals, they avoid making claims that the computer is artificially intelligent or a co-creator of the work. This is astute conceptual positioning because such claims would erect a deleterious, dualistic human–technology binary that could deliver the praxis to a regressive discourse indulged by technophiles and Luddites.

Symbiosis refers to the interactive co-existence of two *biological* organisms, either from the same or different *species*, through mutualism, commensalism or parasitism. Regardless of whether one believes the interdependence of humans and technology is mutualistic, commensalistic or parasitic, the crux of this enquiry should be more appropriately focused on, as per Stelarc's praxis, the question of evolution and species. Indeed, to advocate technology as a separate organism or species would imbue the praxis with transhumanism, which is an undesirable and quasi-deistic definition of technology. Far from undermining Obermaier's deeply nuanced aesthetic questioning, the goal here is to seriously cogitate on his decision to essentialize his praxis on the basis of organic terminology. If technology is neither a separate biological organism nor a species, how can *Apparition* be taken seriously under the conceptual rubric of symbiosis? In order to reconcile this claim, it is useful to return to the concept of organology explicated in the last chapter, in the context of Stelarc's praxis.

A general organology advances the principle of individuation to a three-way process encompassing psychic organs, social organizations and technical organs. In consideration of this, *Apparition* can be understood as the revealing of reciprocal processes of human and technological becoming. This happens both inside and outside the fictional frame – inside, in terms of staging the cause and effect of the performers' bodies on the digital visualizations and vice versa, and outside, in terms of how the computer determines choreographic, dramaturgical and devising processes. The becoming of the technical milieu manifests in 'the machine-determined imposition of choreographic articulations on the performers' bodies' (O'Dwyer 2015a: 45). *Apparition* thus clarifies the non-dualism of human–technology relations, articulated in the philosophical trajectory from postmodernism to cyberculture. Understood as artificial, exosomatic organs, technologies are subject to evolutionary processes every bit as much as endosomatic (biological) organs. As outlined in the charting of technological theories in the last chapter, human evolution increasingly takes place in the technical milieu, and biological evolution has essentially plateaued. Thus, Obermaier's digitally augmented stage can be interpreted as an extension of the dancers' bodies – an organological coming-into-being of an exosomatic technical organ evolved to enhance their gestural expressive capabilities. Technology is an epigenetic phenomenon, inscribed at the root of the human genotype, that manifests as exosomatic (technological) organs that are intertwined with biological organs under an evolutionary principle most developed in humans. The terms 'symbiosis' and 'evolution' tend towards the purely biological; therefore, they are insufficient for thinking through the developmental nuances of human becoming. As such, a general organology is most useful for understanding Obermaier's aesthetics.

Similar to Stelarc's praxis, Obermaier demonstrates a new acquisition of control over evolutionary processes; while humans are constituted by technological development, they also decide the direction of technological developments. This assigns a pivotal socio-anthropological role to avant-gardists because their political activism and innovative repurposing of quantitative, techno-scientific knowledge towards qualitative cultural outputs change the rules and deviate the direction of organological becoming.

As with all technological developments, there are positive and negative aspects to their uses in sociocultural contexts. What may be considered an ingenious innovation in the context of a singular aesthetic gesture may not be advantageous to pluralities, communities or masses. There are arguments for and against every technological innovation that are often dualistically reduced to the zealous enthusiasm of technophiles and transhumanists, versus the sceptical reservations of the Luddites. Since postmodernism, it is overly reductionist to diminish discourses to simplistic binarisms. Therefore, the important point is that all technological developments harbour agency; they reorganize the relations between the individual, the group and the material world, continually reconfiguring creative articulations and what it means to be human. The next chapter continues the genealogy of digital scenography through the work of Frieder Weiss and Chunky Move with a view to expanding and deepening the socio-political discourse.

4

Responsive Environments and Choreographing Indeterminacy: Chunky Move

Introduction

Mortal Engine (Obarzanek 2008a, b) is a collaborative performance involving Australian dance collective, Chunky Move, and digital media scenographer Frieder Weiss.[1] Similar to Obermaier's work, they employ sophisticated electronic sensing and computer vision techniques to augment choreographic expression via interactive/responsive digital scenography. Despite the technical similarities between the two collectives, their approaches to themes, tone and scenography are notably different, facilitating an intriguing comparison. Chunky Move's work appeared several years after Obermaier's and this timespan marks an important developmental period in the evolution of interactive digital scenography.

A particularly useful concept for thinking about the genealogical development is Stiegler's unique and original contribution to the principle of individuation: *transindividuation*. This is a special type of individuation that operates *trans-epochally* and *trans-globally*, finding its ideal expression in artistic creations. Stiegler holds that artworks are special, powerful and enduring manifestations of knowledge that collapse time and space, allowing them to transmit ideas anywhere, anytime. This characteristic has been intensified by the internet, which, when combined with the atmosphere of cultural excitement surrounding the artworld, occasions distant and rapid idea dissemination. Art provides an epi-ethnic language, allowing individuals and groups to individuate with each other across cultural and linguistic differences. Crucially, artworks summon processes of interpretation and identification, inspiring and motivating audiences into action, that is, into thinking *actively*. 'To see a work by showing *what it makes us do* ... this is what initiates a circuit of *transindividuation* (of the formation of an epoch)' (Stiegler 2010b: 17). Transindividuation does not describe an inclination to reproduce the work of predecessors; it concerns taking up the aesthetic, technical and political questions at the heart of their research. This is evident in Chunky Move's (and Obermaier's) outspoken citations of Merce Cunningham and Alwin Nikolais as inspirational figures in the formation of their performances. These digital reinterpretations of avant-garde performances testify to the transindividual agency of artefacts, which compels the artists into action, to 'show' their *re-*action, establishing themselves as energetic transmitters within the circuit of knowledge regeneration. The concept of transindividuation is crucial to this genealogy of digital scenography because it describes intergenerational and geospatially diverse re-engagements with consistent art ideas.

The main themes of Mortal Engine focus on relationships, interchange and the slippage that individuals undergo in digitally networked societies. Gideon Obarzanek (Director and Choreographer) explains: '*Mortal Engine* looks at relationships, connection and disconnection, isolation and togetherness, in a state of continual flux' (Obarzanek 2008c).[2] The kinaesthetic, interactive digital scenography combined with kinetic bodies provides a powerful means for illustrating these themes. Obarzanek expounds: 'The idea was that the body is really not separated from the space around it, that there is a constant exchange and influence going on' (Collins and Nisbet 2010: 304). Pertinent to the central narrative of this book is the view that these themes are every bit as applicable outside the fictional world of the performance, in terms of technicity, that is, technology's ability to influence making processes and affect the artistic outcome.

Description

As in the case of Obermaier's and Troika Ranch's systems, Chunky Move's performances operate by gathering the dancers' (quantitative) movement data using video surveillance techniques and feeding the data into procedural audio-visual systems that respond to the biometric information. Weiss separates his bespoke scenographic software framework into two parts: the first, called *Eyecon,* is 'mainly used for movement to sound interaction' (Weiss 2019), and the second, named *Kalypso* (see Figure 4.1), uses 'algorithmic transformations of the video image as visual output' (Weiss 2019), which form the basis of real-time abstract interactive visualizations, from 'shadow-like abstraction[s] and outline-based effects to particle systems and more

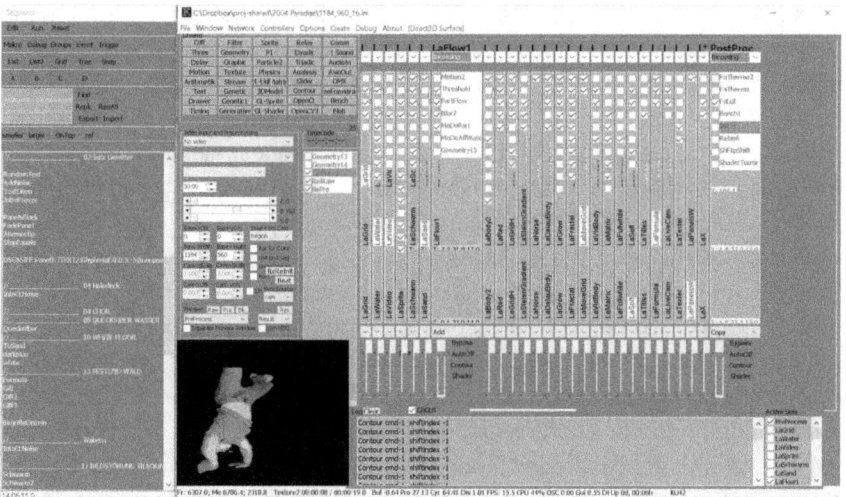

FIGURE 4.1 *Screenshot:* Kalypso *software (courtesy of Frieder Weiss).*

complex transformations' (Weiss 2019). As in the case of *Apparition*, Weiss' frameworks support a responsive stage environment that requires interaction in order to function. Without an interlocutor the audio-visuals are lifeless; with an injection of human presence, they come alive. Obarzanek declares that they make 'it possible for instruments and bodies, that generate light, video, sound and movement, to all share a common language and respond to each other in real-time' (Obarzanek 2008c). Resonating with aesthetics explored by Obermaier, the Obarzanek–Weiss partnership creates a kinetic lightscape where dancers are revealed and secreted using lighting tricks that play on the spectators' perceptions. A three-way dynamic dialogue between lighting, performer and computer system energizes a performance that proceeds on mysterious, magical relations connecting the individual, the group and the environment.

Obarzanek summarizes *Mortal Engine* as 'a dance-video-music-laser performance using movement and sound responsive projections to portray an ever-shifting, shimmering world' (Obarzanek 2008c). 'The use of light as an expressive material in theatre' has a rich history in scenographic practice (Palmer 2015: 31), beginning with the pioneering exploits of Adolphe Appia who advocated 'active light' as a performative force that energizes and brings life to the theatre (Baugh 2014: 133), moving through Joseph Svoboda's acclaimed glistening, incandescent lighting effects obtained through bespoke mechanical inventions, to contemporary practice which frequently employs such techniques, now consolidated in the standard operating mechanisms of the control room. However, Chunky Move's originality resides in the automated interaction between the lighting system and the performers, which affords heightened accuracy and control. Contrary to the technological setup in *Apparition*, *Mortal Engine* adopts a spectator paradigm where the audience look down on the dancers, who primarily perform floor movement; the projector is placed high up on the ceiling, beaming imagery down, on and around the performers. The intention is to move away from the proscenium model, which demands that dancers perform in front of a vertical (upstage) projection, eliminating the perception of there being a top and bottom. The goal was to create a 'sense that something was emanating from within the human body ... of being able to see into someone's imagination ... or the effect that they were having on the space around them and the way space and environment was affecting them' (*Gideon Obarzanek's Digital Moves* 2009). 'The resultant compositions are accumulations and clusters of abstract and expressionistic imagery combined with, and procedurally modified by, the dynamic, sculpturesque, three-dimensional relief of the dancers' bodies in motion' (O'Dwyer 2015b: 45).

This performance model is accomplished through the new affordances of digital technology, that is, the new ability for lighting scenographers to capture, discretize and map the performer, and to respond by modifying the shape, colour, tone and hue of projected light in real time. In genealogical terms, from Appia, through Svoboda, to Obermaier and Obarzanek, the sculpting of light is achieved with increasing degrees of control and precision, and technology becomes increasingly embedded in choreo-dramaturgical heritage.

Grammatization

Grammatization is a term coined by Sylvain Auroux that describes the reductive, logical process of rationalizing spoken language into written form, by discretizing vocal utterances into symbols, letters and letter combinations (*grammes*). As a technical and rational process, 'it is the precondition and structural archetype for all written language, and so also for knowledge in general, including science and mathematics' (Fitzpatrick, O'Dwyer and O'Hara 2021). Stiegler extends this into the spatial field of gesture, by highlighting the ability of mechanical audio and film recording techniques to capture 'temporal sequences of gestures (including the voice) and movements' (Stiegler 2014: 54), affording the grammatization of bodies 'through sound and image' (Stiegler 2014: 54). Gestural grammatization undergoes a paradigmatic shift under digital technologies because electronic automation amplifies and accelerates the processes. Like Obermaier's framework, Weiss' system functions on the basis of total surveillance, through the unremitting capture, analysis and processing of live video footage. Contrary to analogue techniques, the footage is not recorded, stored or played back; instead, they analyse and modify a transient video feed towards creating new types of scenographic worlds and exposing the cultural significance of biometrics.

Under the surveillance model data becomes devalued and ephemeral, due to its overabundance. The captured representations are not actually visualized; instead, they are statisticalized, algorithmically analysed, subjected to metrics, computationally reinterpreted and re-visualized. The concrete production of a naturalistic representation suffers a demise in inverse proportion to the ecstatic elevation of abstract expression and the transaction. This is the symptom of a generalized socio-economic condition intensifying since postmodernity:

> Work becomes a control and manipulation of information ... The availability of information is becoming the only criterion of social importance. Now information is by definition a short-lived element. As soon as it is transmitted and shared, it ceases to be information, it becomes an environmental given, and 'all is said', we 'know'. It is put into the machine memory. The length of time it occupies is, so to speak, instantaneous.
>
> (Lyotard 1992: 105)

By digitally encoding the continuous flow of the performance, the dancer's movements undergo a process of numerical formalization, in which the metrics of their bodies are exposed and logged so that calculations can be performed on them. Thus, the function of the camera's lens shifts from documentation to perception – from capture to computer cognition.

A computer expects numerical data; naturalistic representations mean nothing to a computer. Even when numerically encoded as an MPEG or JPEG symbolic information still makes no sense; the central operating system simply identifies their metadata and allocates a secondary programme to decode and display them. For a computer to make sense of video footage, special programmes must be written that can run analyses on the series of discrete images over time. The computational research field that enables computers to visually perceive phenomena, like organic species do, is known as computer vision. Motion-tracking, the technical area specific to these live performances, is a subset of this field. As in *Apparition*, Weiss uses frame differencing for detecting movement with the video camera. This allows the software to recognize if something has changed in the computer's field of vision, constituted by the camera's lens. The current frame is usually passed through a thresholding filter, so that the object of the gaze (in this case the interfacing dancer) is converted to a silhouette – dubbed a 'blob' in computer vision terminology. Substantial biometrics can be calculated on the basis of the blob's size, position and changes over time, which enable digital scenographers to create audio-visuals in response to the movement using real-time data processing applications.

While the above process elucidates the cutting-edge of gestural grammatization under the aegis of digital surveillance technologies, it also raises the dialectics of its positive and negative deployments – artistic contra socio-economic applications. To grammatize is to reduce something into its discrete constituent elements through rationalization, that is, through *ratio*. Before being primarily given over to calculation in modernity, for a long time, the term and concept of ratio enjoyed liberal deployment in epistemological discourse as a principle for the ordering of knowledge along the lines 'of judgment and discrimination' (Amsler 1989: 206). The problem with rationalizing a cultural artefact under the auspices of statisticalization is that the faculties of judgement and discrimination, upon which the metaphorical poetry relies, are short-circuited in favour of a value system based on numbers.

> In this process qualitative information – that is, the idiomatic language of choreographic expression, which is knowledge passed between instructors, students and peers through rigorous training processes – is translated into quantitative information, such as location, speed, acceleration, direction, intensity and volume, via motion detection and video processing algorithms.
>
> (O'Dwyer 2015b: 52)

This conflict elucidates the new condition of hyper-rationalization, taking place in digital culture, that is characteristic of the 'hyperindustrial epoch' (Stiegler 2014). The crucial aesthetic question that arises in light of this techno-epistemological tension is: how to employ cutting-edge tools and techniques, while retaining the metaphorical and idiomatic qualities of expression that evoke singular subjective interpretations that constitute art? The point of this genealogy of digital scenography is not to make recommendations, but to historicize a cohort of digital performance artists that have elicited the specificities of an evolving technical milieu, while maintaining nuanced metaphors that harken to the legacy of *non-calculable*, expressionistic knowledge. Their creations sustain the heritage of embodied, experiential knowledge that eludes quantitative systems that seek to place a numerical value on everything, while staying central to techno-political discourse. Therefore, the artists stake a claim in the question of the avant-garde by producing art that interrogates techno-subjective forces that increasingly play a pivotal role in the formation of identity in the contemporary (hyperindustrialized) world.

Specificities of Digital Scenography

As per the qualifying criteria established in the introduction, this genealogy is only interested in performances that elicit the specificities of digital technologies. Interactivity and responsivity have been quintessential characteristics of digital media, for the greater part of the digital epoch. Analogue technologies of representation are primarily characterized by their facility for channelling cultural symbols and affecting the consciousness of the viewer/listener; however, those symbols are not modifiable by the consumer. This establishes a one-way flow of information, which, considered in terms of Western philosophy, is a paradigm that is obstructive to dialogue and the emergence of 'wisdom' (Plato 1972: sec. 275). The characteristic of digital technologies that is consistently argued as beneficial by their advocates is interactivity – their facility for dialogue. This includes dialogue between, not just the producers and consumers of content, but also humans and non-human entities (software). Computer systems expect input from users; interfacing is the logic of their operation. Under the interactive paradigm, consumers are able to affect and modify cultural symbols. This can either happen at the local level, using software, or at a metalevel, through comments, indexation and annotation, extending the articulation to the social web and establishing an economy of contribution. Gaming is the cultural phenomenon that most zealously and innovatively embraces interactive modalities, but the genealogical progression from Troika Ranch, through Obermaier, to Chunky Move demonstrates a progressive adoption and refinement of these modalities in the performing arts.

It has been established that technology constitutes a prosthesis of both the mind and body. But as automation becomes more sophisticated this characteristic becomes more nuanced, affording the conceptualization of (cybernetic) technologies as separate entities. Performances that employ analogue technologies for scenography maintain and reinforce the paradigm of prosthesis because they are conditioned by an operation of recording and re-presenting gestural grammes. Apart from a handful of performances that scenographically stage the technology as a narrational agent, for example, *Krapp's Last Tape* (1958) (O'Dwyer forthcoming), they do not offer a dramaturgy based on human–machine interaction. Changes in content are limited to manual cueing by an audio-visual operator. Recordings are frequently stored on external devices (like tapes) and processes of searching, retrieval and playback are slow and labour-intensive, complicating possibilities of staging these operations live. With digital technologies, the content is numerically encoded and stored in a (local or networked) database, where 'every sentence, word, syllable and letter become discretised, and therefore equally and immediately accessible' (O'Dwyer et al. 2018: 7). Furthermore, operating analogue recording technologies involves pressing a button on a relatively simplistic control panel. 'The automation is only one level deep ... When the tape recorder is stopped there is nothing else happening; it is, to a certain extent, lifeless (or at least dormant)' (O'Dwyer 2015b: 57). For digital technologies, however, capture and playback are but a few of the numerous, concurrent tasks performed by a central processing unit. Finally, if using pre-captured material under the analogue format, the content must be shot, postproduced and assembled in advance, or, if using a live video feed, content is limited either to naturalistic representations (mediated objects or performers), or expressionistically distorting the image while keeping the base signal. Under the database framework, programmes can be written to perform automated operations on stored content and live video feeds, such as their immediate retrieval and modification, or they can be used as a basis for generating completely different content. This is possible because of the facility for nesting automatic processes in cybernetics, which allows multiple processes to be run in parallel, affording the implementation of conditions, rules and choices – if one does this, then the machine will do that. All of this contributes to the argument that as machines become more sophisticated, technology's organic (or *organological*) essence becomes more salient. This conceptualization accords with Weiss and Obarzanek's thematics:

> I was always trying to work with the body and the movement. Initially it was just tracking of the body, and now it's more like an encounter with something you influence. It's like another body, like another dancer. Like another performer that is closely related.
>
> (Weiss 2015)

As their working processes and computational systems evolved, they began to perceive the computer as another performer, just as Obermaier did. For performance apparatuses to be perceived as (organic) performance partners and not simply objective props (a means to an end), they must have certain naturalistic attributes, not necessarily in their visual appearance but, more specifically, in the way they move. In this way, the performers can relate to it and generate a dramatic tension. To simulate 'life' there must be something happening even when there is no engagement by an interlocutor, for example, a subtle, slow heaving that might resemble breathing, or a periodic twitch that evokes rapid movements, like blinking. Cyberneticist Hiroshi Ishiguro[3] states:

> A human never stops breathing or eye blinking, because these easily observable kinds of behaviour are driven unconsciously by the autonomic

nervous system ... Thus to increase a geminiod's[4] naturalness, the ... system emulates a human's autonomic nervous system by automatically generating these micro-movements, depending on the state of interaction.

(Stocker and Schöpf 2010: 218)

Parallel, indeterminate movements, known as degrees of freedom in cybernetics,[5] are afforded by the ability to nest processes of automation, a technique indebted to the invention of the electronic transistor and, then, the microelectronic chip, which is ultimately a collection of millions of transistors – each one controlling a cyclical electronic flow. This is why graphical visualizations based on organic phenomena work so well for the mise-en-scène. Once activated, they continue to move, pulse and breath; propagate and grow; or degenerate and die, like organisms. When fed the dancers' movement data they blossom into weirdly beautiful and transient designs that recall patterns found in nature.

Unlike a human or natural organism, this system does not have the capacity to intuitively learn by itself; the rules of its operation have to be pre-programmed depending on what kind of dramatic intention the artists want. Based on the number of performers on stage, what parts of their bodies are tracked, and the sensitivity of the graphical simulations, certain movement phrases trigger various scenographic events. Weiss continues:

Like the particles, that's a good example ... These particles are sort of independent, but they are relating to the performer. That's the tricky issue: what kind of projections and algorithms can you come up with that have a behaviour on their own, but still relate to the performer?

(Weiss 2015)

The digital scenographer sets up a sort of quasi-organic ecosystem that simulates real, physical attributes of a natural environment. While not directly identifiable as representations of specific entities from the natural world, the graphical systems *do* behave like organic matter because they move in natural ways. Weiss' particle systems, which behave on the basis of mass, gravity, elasticity and so on, provide the movement patterns for graphical scenographies that evoke an impression of the performers moving through liquid, gases or foliage (just as in *Apparition*). The system senses the dancer's movements, measures the quality of the movement and calculates how a natural entity might react under the same physical conditions. This allows the systems to visualize a response based on the simulation. While there are no actual forces impacting on the dancers' bodies, they are (especially the choreographer) influenced by the impact of the bodies on the graphics and vice versa. By submitting to the bio-fiction and allowing their bodies to be reciprocally affected by the movement of the graphics, they enter into a feedback loop that typifies the essence of the human–computer contract in general. The impulsive quality of the relationship stipulates that the choreo-dramaturgy is emergent and indeterminate. As Obarzanek says:

> There are no fixed time-lines and the production flexes according to the rhythm of the performers. While the scenes are always in the same order, the work is truly live every night, not completely predictable and ever changing.
>
> (Obarzanek 2008c)

In contrast to performing with mechanical (representational) technologies, such as film, the performers are not spatially or temporally obliged to synchronize with an uncompromising system. The multi-layered automata that comprise the digital audio-visuals permit the fabrication of a simulated responsivity that gives rise to the diametrically opposite template, where there *is* a margin for error and spontaneity *is* encouraged. Similar to Troika Ranch and Obermaier, the collaboration between Chunky Move and Weiss elicits the interactive specificities of digital technology towards developing an improvisational methodology with an indeterminate outcome. This unpredictable, inventive attitude is indicative of activistic avant-garde tendencies and representative of the new epistemic domain arising from the confluence of experimentalism and new technologies. This is crucial to the genealogical trajectory of this book because it shows how the continued folding together of artistic endeavours and techno-scientific knowledge catalyses evolutionary advancements in the technical milieu that afford the emergence of more original technological engagements.

As well as seeking to counteract the rigidity imposed on performance by mechanical technologies, Chunky Move also endeavours to elicit specificities unique to interactive frameworks:

> We began to look at noise and to release it more into the system, to control it broadly but not in the details ... and use that information. What ends up happening ... is that you create this sense of environment that's almost organic, or foreboding, almost living, like a ghost in the machine.
>
> (Obarzanek 2012)

This noise is created by a spurious accuracy that is a by-product of the motion-tracking system. The exact shape of the performer's silhouette varies from one video frame to the next because of interference caused by the dancers' shadows and frequency flicker from the lights. When the display software iterates through them at thirty frames per second, it gives the appearance that the outline vibrates. Weiss cleverly re-harnesses this representational idiosyncrasy to fabricate the 'shimmering, shifting world' that Obarzanek describes. In bringing such unique specificities to the scenographer's palette, the system asserts its technicity, that is, its influence over the creative outcome. The discovery of this noise-based scenographic trope and the success of its adoption to the dramaturgy convinced the collective to investigate other avenues for choreographing indeterminacy via algorithms derived from natural phenomena.

> We started looking into much more complex algorithms that were producing, what we called semi-autonomous particles. And by that, I mean light that has a direct relationship to the body and that uses the information from the body, but that also has various other computations that give it behavioural forms, that give it its own independent sense of the movement – its coming to life, its own death.
>
> (*Gideon Obarzanek's Digital Moves* 2009)

The introduction of these naturally derived algorithms injects an artificial life into the system because they give the visuals their own autonomous organic movement, like an ecosystem to be mutually engaged (Langton 1997; Whitelaw 2004). This is typical of how evolutionary developments in art production are vectorized by the technical milieu. It concerns an aesthetic shift from the mimetic regime towards that of simulation, from artefacts that *look* like natural organisms to those that *work* like them. The more that produced artefacts reproduce a task or movement of an organism the more blurred the distinction becomes between what is natural and what is synthetic (Riskin 2007). The superimposition of dancers onto the visuals fragments the distinction between scenographic simulation and organic interactors, embracing an aesthetics of movement over imitation – interactions between human and non-human entities. The scenographic paradigm reasserts dance as an important territory for experimenting with digital technologies by recuperating aesthetic strategies of predecessors like Nikolais. Digital technologies provide ways of improvising with lighting that were fundamentally impossible for Nikolais during his era. By showing an original deployment of Nikolais' aesthetic in the context of digital technologies, Obarzanek's choreography demonstrates a reengagement with his ideas and a reactivation of his artistic knowledge. Ultimately, *Mortal Engine* shows how improvisational performers and software engineers can fuse their knowledge to reinvent new types of digital artefacts, revealing generative worlds developed using hybrid knowledge.

Sublime Aesthetics of *Mortal Engine*

The responsivity underpinning the choreo-scenographic relations contributes to the positioning of the system as a quasi-organic environment. The visual fusion of the environment and human interactors conjures hybrid, unnameable entities, challenging the audience's perception of what is real or fictional. Obfuscated by inky black shadows that swell and bulge, the human figures become difficult to decipher from each other and the scenographic elements. The conglomerations of dancers appear animalistic and zoomorphic, adding a sense of uncanny horror to the thematics.

In several of the scenes the individual and collective choreo-scenographic compositions focus on challenging perception and 'the limits of anthropomorphic form' (O'Dwyer 2015b: 50), comprising a sort of horror show. Obarzanek colourfully articulates the imagery: 'Crackling light and staining shadows represent the most perfect or sinister of souls. Kinetic energy fluidly metamorphoses from the human figure into light image, into sound and back again' (Obarzanek 2008c). Weiss elicits the interactive and precise affordances of the digital to acquire exquisite control over the lighting design, creating a 'bio-fictional' world 'in which the limits of the human body are an illusion' (Obarzanek 2008c). Various aggregations of impressively flexible bodies with blinding light and deep, inky shadows reveal and conceal sculptural assemblages that manifest and disintegrate throughout the temporal exchanges of the live event. These challenge preconceptions of anthropomorphic possibility (see Figure 4.2). Bereft of a symbolic referent the interpreting audience is cast back into itself and challenged into questioning the limits of knowledge and presuppositions underpinning existence, generally. These compositions that deliver the audience to a place of disturbance and unease are most thinkable through Kant's 'Analytic of the Sublime'.

Kant's *Critique of Judgement* (1790) is unparalleled in the purview of projects to which it has been applied for aesthetic discourse. Notwithstanding its numerous rehearnessings, it has an apparent capacity to rejuvenate itself in every application, continuing to provide fresh, original and topical analyses. Its application to Chunky Move's *Mortal Engine* does not portend to buck this trend. Kant's aim is to show how the human mind operates towards definitively reconciling nature and understanding. He declares that sublime aesthetics operate on the basis of outraging the sensible faculties of intuition and contravening judgemental processes, occasioning a terrifying experience. But he suggests there is a certain feeling of 'delight' that proceeds from this, which he describes as an unintuitively 'negative pleasure' arising from 'admiration and respect' (Kant and Pluhar 1987: 98). For Kant, 'what is sublime, in the proper meaning of the term, cannot be contained in any sensible form' (Kant and Pluhar 1987: 99); only the radical subjectivity of the mind could scaffold pleasure around a clearly disagreeable confrontation and, henceforth, procure satisfaction from it. He surmises the delight as something akin to an ascendancy over nature;[6] therefore, there is a feeling of autonomy from nature, giving rise to further satisfaction. Kant discerns a taxonomic split in sublime experience, based on the imagination's referral of the 'agitation either to the *cognitive power* or to the *power of desire*' (Kant and Pluhar 1987: 101). He categorizes the first type as 'mathematical' and the second as 'dynamical' (Kant and Pluhar 1987: 101). Both types are relevant to this discussion for different reasons.

The dynamical sublime corresponds to an overbearing experience, a dreadful horror that obstructs the will, rendering the subject incapable of action. It operates on the basis that it 'blocks the ability of the imagination to act in accordance with the understanding' (Shaw 2006: 81). Here Kant is describing a moral experience concerning the emotions, as opposed to rational thinking. He associates the apprehension with an anxiety arising from an encounter with unpleasant, overpowering forces analogous to the terrifying forces of nature. He defers locating the sublime in the thing under observation, thus reinforcing his claim that the sublime is 'a subjective condition of the imagination that is experienced as an agitation of the emotional faculties' (O'Dwyer 2016a: 366). Counterintuitively, he contends that the instigating object of reflection 'becomes all the more attractive the more fearful it is, provided we are in a

FIGURE 4.2 *Photo: Andrew Curtis. Performer: Harriet Ritchie (courtesy of Chunky Move).*

safe place' (Kant and Pluhar 1987: 120). The reassurance of a safe distance affords the subject time and space to contemplate the situation and derive satisfaction (or 'delight') from, firstly, an appreciation for the fragility of the human and, secondly, the ability to understand the situation. The second aspect operates by transmitting *'mighty'* attributes away from the object, towards the onlooker's intellect, thereby affirming a transcendental faculty and a capacity for intellectual ascendancy.

The dynamical sublime is particularly relevant to *Mortal Engine* because of the unnameable, uncategorizable zoo-anthropomorphic assemblages formed by the high-contrast light projections and the silhouetted composition of dancers' bodies. The unidentifiable, uncanny configurations arouse fear, anxiety and horror in the mind of the spectator, but these agitations are reconciled through intellectual reasoning, from the safety of the auditorium. However, there is another type of sublime experience present in this performance and, indeed, all performances discussed in this book. What is it about digital technology that conduces an experience of the sublime? This question can be engaged by approaching it through Kant's other, already mentioned, taxonomy: *the mathematical sublime*.

The mathematical sublime is also related to a shortfall in understanding, but in this case it is the inability of the imagination to comprehend something implying the idea of enormity 'beyond all comparison' (Kant and Pluhar 1987: 103). It is an experience of being overwhelmed, arising from an encounter that demands quantitative estimation, but the imagination fails to present a unit 'for the estimation of magnitude [... of] a substrate that is large beyond any standard of sense' (Kant and Pluhar 1987: 112). As a result of the failure, the subject is cast back into itself in the face of the *unknown*; that is, the 'inadequateness' of the imagination is exposed by the idea of absolute magnitude and infinity, as well as 'the infinitely small' (Kant and Pluhar 1987: 106).

For Kant, the mathematical sublime is essentially related to a spatial experience; whereas, for Edmund Burke, theorizing before Kant, the sublime experience is founded on temporality. There was a movement in twentieth-century philosophy to relocate the sublime to an experience of time, evinced in Heidegger's work on *Das Ereignis* (the 'event of appropriation' or 'enowning') (Heidegger 1999), and event theory extending from Jean-Francois Lyotard (1992) to Alain Badiou (2005b). Now, via the digital-cultural analytic of Stiegler, the predominant spatio-temporal conceptualization of mathematically sublime experiences can be rethought along the lines of a fundamental, transcendental speed (Ekman 2007; O'Dwyer 2016a). The phenomenon of speed is an essential consideration when engaging the techno-aesthetic-political question in a hyperindustrial socio-economy propped up by the increasingly ambitious goals of efficiency, data transfer speeds and technological development, that is, the speed of calculation multiplied by 'the speed of technical evolution' (Stiegler

1998: 17). The experience of the sublime in technologically engaged theatre and performance is inseparable from the presence of new technologies and, although akin to the theories of Event or technological rupture (which hinge on the concept of newness), sublime experiences can be further reduced a fundamental constituent of speed.

Thinking about Chunky Move's performances in terms of a technological sublime reveals that the aesthetic experience is fundamentally related to an encounter with new technologies that is conditioned by a mindboggling speed. The machine's ability to capture video, process data, perform calculations and symbolically respond in the blink of an eye exposes the ethical aporia of the continuing evolution of light-speed electronics as both infinitely prosthetic and dehumanizing. The speed of technological processes combined with the speed of technological evolution 'is transmissive of the horrific idea of technology over-taking the human, replacing the human, proletarianising and decommissioning the human' (O'Dwyer 2016a: 372). A sublime experience of technology engenders a set of self-reflexive sociohistorical and ontological questions, relating to the ubiquity of digital soft and hardware and the disorientation of the individual therein. However, as per Kant, the faculties of reason furnish a rationalization of the situation that affords positive aesthetic ascendancy. The positivity is salient in the innovativeness of the work and the artists' ability to *change the rules.* By revealing an innovative cultural re-configuration of technology, the Obarzanek–Weiss collaboration 'shows how art ideas offer a means to travel faster than the message in circuit, that is, faster than light-speed and to think with greater power than any computer executed calculation' (O'Dwyer 2016a: 372). This argument can be traced through all the discussed artworks in this book and it is crucial to the edification of these avant-garde works as positive pharmaka that counteract toxic (incorporated) employments of the technology.

Performing Digital Individuations: Organology

Obarzanek and Weiss's inclination to partner humans with semi-autonomous, quasi-organic systems with degrees of freedom supports the claim that their collaboration involved discovering new possibilities in performance. This methodology 'acknowledges the computer as a contributing agent that can and does bring its own specificities to the artistic development of the work' (O'Dwyer 2015b: 54). The software, constituted by algorithmic rules, influences the dancers' gestures, informing choreographic decisions and the overall mise-en-scène. As in the case of all the performances in this genealogy, Chunky Move's process proposes a change in attitude towards technology that could help formulate new ways of working and thinking about human and non-human collaboration.

Obarzanek affirms the mise-en-scène is a metaphor for the dualistic conflict between 'the real, tangible world of recognizable objects and situations', and the *other* interiorized, intangible yet 'more imaginative, eternal world that is co-existing' (Obarzanek 2012), which we all also inhabit. Although he does not employ the term, these thematics contain the concept of individuation; that is, they express the relations between the material exterior and subjective interior worlds of existence, played out through the intermediary milieu of technology. Interestingly, Obarzanek frames the work in terms of creating a 'synergy' between the digital audio-visual environment and the human performers. This is resonant with Obermaier's inclination to frame his work in terms of a 'symbiosis'. Obarzanek similarly articulates an objective to unify heterogeneous human and mechanical agents under a multifarious assemblage consisting in individual and collective human biological organs, and prosthetic technological organs. The aesthetic dogma underpinning the work is one expounded on the basis that the totality of the live event is determined by numerous contingent human and non-human elements. It is an investigation into what choreographic fictions can arise when humans and computational programmes are allied as performance partners. Therefore, algorithmic agency – with its new potentialities and shortcomings – plays as much of a role in the determination of the piece as human agents.

Stiegler's concept of a *general organology* (which describes the co-individuation of psychic organs, social organizations and technical organs) again provides a useful methodology for explaining how well informed Obarzanek's thematics are because it describes a shift in the understanding of technology from means–ends to organic immanence. Contrary to the perception of technology as the diametric Other of nature, understood in its organological sense, it is undergoing organic processes of evolution every bit as much as biological organs and social organizations. Contemporary operations of individuation involve the transfer and modification of knowledge and information across electronically networked linkages between senders, receivers and servers. These transactions mirror and extend the infra-corporeal messaging that takes place through the interaction of synapses with biological central and peripheral nervous systems, which connect the various psychosomatic organs that constitute awareness, behaviour and physicality. Weiss' scenographic framework supports this quasi-biological analogue. Computer vision technologies extract the dancers' biometric data and the procedural algorithms modify it and reinsert it into the interchangeable human–computer feedback loop that modulates alterations of the dancers' bodies and scenography. As such, the spectacle is constituted by a staging of (organological) individuation, founded on a three-way tension between the individual, the group and the electronic milieu; the mutable scenography evolves in parallel to the becoming of the characters.

The evolutionary metaphor is compounded by Weiss' deployment of mitosis[7] and fractal algorithms for generating the scenography. These (robotic) scenographic agents draw graphics from the centre of the dancer's position, which resemble expanding fungi or rhizomes (see Figure 4.3). When they execute, the outcome of the image they draw is indeterminate. Thus, the scenographic environment is emergent and chaotic in its essence; that is, it captures the highly organizational logic of pure nature, which concerns a multiplicity of contiguous systems affecting one another. The decision to perform the choreography as floor movement establishes a paradigm where the dancers, always answerable to gravity and subjected to a predefined set of possible body movements, can approach the stage (or canvas) from all sides. The canvas has its own internally pre-programmed dynamics, which simulate fractal-based natural phenomena, and the dancers intervene as symbiotic agents, or viruses. The total system provides an abstract metaphor of pure nature at an elemental cellular level that invites reflections on processes of evolution, or decay. One could say that the architecture of the stage itself evolves, or individuates; the mutable and emergent quasi-organic scenography develops, shifts and mutates due to the periodic mutual, commensal or parasitic interventions of a more mobile human species.

FIGURE 4.3 *Photo: Andrew Curtis. Performer: Antony Hamilton (courtesy of Chunky Move).*

Delegation of Responsibilities: Towards AI

To suggest that the computer is an intelligent or autonomous agent would be erroneous. But its software *is* affecting, and *being affected by*, the human dancers. The programme consists of a rule-based system that can and does respond if certain kinaesthetic conditions are met. In this sense, the computer is taught a selection of rudimentary skills for responding to the language of dance, which is always idiomatic and, therefore, exceedingly difficult to teach to a machine. Rather than trying to get the computer to recognize, interpret and force meaning upon specific poses and phrases, the scenographer engineers quasi-organic worlds that are modelled on physics libraries and algorithms. These factor-in the physical characteristics of objects, such as speed, force, mass and size, to simulate the interactions and behaviours of real, tangible objects in the natural world. When the computer sees a dancer moving in a certain direction with a given intensity, it can react because this is the type of data that makes sense to the software. Analogously, the audio-visual responses demand further embodied replies and may even engender new, singular and original gestures in the dancer's somatic repertoire; therefore, the scenography exhibits an agency that is supportive of an emergent choreography.

By indulging the machine with creative privileges Chunky Move is contributing to a vogue of contemporary dance practice that advocates the computer, not as a tool, but as a prothesis of both body and mind, that amplifies developmental processes and methods and affords a deeper understanding of choreo-scenographic practices. Such practices open new epistemological areas for reflection and scholarly discourse because they fundamentally challenge dominant configurations of knowledge. They are derivative decompositions of the epochal technological shock, occasioned by the advent of digital technologies. Cybernetics should be understood as a *Grand* technological innovation because the scale of the disruption it has caused to society, culture, economics and politics is monumental. Grand innovations occur infrequently. This one is analogous to the arrival of mechanical automation, in terms of its ability to reorganize society. Immanent in an epochal rupture is the opportunity to remedy societies' maladies or to exacerbate them.

The Pharmacology of the Second 'Scenographic Turn'

Considering the specificities of digital technologies (outlined in the introduction) their incorporation into scenographic processes brings about different meanings and intentions. It is possible to employ new cutting-edge technologies to do the jobs of old analogue types. This is a logical harnessing because digital technologies are more efficient, user-friendly, and give more control over various media. In theatre, these evolutionary benefits are obvious in the fields of lighting and sound design. However, this positive aspect is not the dominant case in AV design, which has, broadly speaking, fallen foul of a phenomenon that Bolter and Grusin define as *remediation* (Bolter and Grusin 2000). They argue that new visual media achieve their cultural significance by aping, rivalling, refashioning and alluding to earlier media such as film, photography, painting and so on. This tendency – interpreted here as largely toxic to creativity – can be found in the use of computers for executing simple tasks like AV playback and scene queuing. This employment is hardly surprising, given the speed and convenience with which computers can access and replay a variety of sound and vision objects. However, the tendency to ape the formal qualities of analogue performances also 'implies a predisposition to ignore the *fundamentally new* specificities of digital technology: calculation and simulation' (O'Dwyer 2015b: 58). This can lead to a stagnation of performances employing screen-based enhancements and occasions a situation where the devices are employed simply to signal the contemporaneity of the work (J. Feral and Bermingham 1987: 469). Audiences become expectant of them, no matter how inconsequential to the story, and are disappointed by their omission. Obarzanek and Weiss demonstrate a will to elicit the specificities of digital technologies and push them to their limits, cohering the collaboration as a powerful trans-epistemic breakthrough that elevates the project above criticisms of remediation and historical repetition.

The example of remediation disinters a dichotomy concerning the positive and negative aspects of digital technologies and the *way* that they are harnessed for the live stage and beyond. Obarzanek described his experience of working with the motion-tracking techniques as very exciting 'and without the tedium of the dancer having to respond accurately to pre-rendered video' (Collins and Nisbet 2010: 303). This release from rigorous timing and celebration of improvisation were also apparent in Obermaier's progression from *Vivisector* to *Apparition*. However, interactive/computational technologies can also exert a constraint on creative practice because technical know-how is transferred to a machine, occasioning a situation in which the human actor is marginalized and sometimes even eliminated. In the case of live performance there is a risk that, with the advancements of 'modern science, the major discoveries are paid for with an increasing decline of theoretical education' (Horkheimer and Adorno 2002: xiv); as more practitioners engage with responsive computer software, the embodied knowledge of classical or traditional techniques becomes eroded or, at worst, lost. This quandary is especially relevant to dance, which is a mode of artistic expression that does not have a standard form of written notation. As articulations and actions, processes and ideologies become attached to increasingly mediatized norms and values (not just in dance, but in culture generally), knowledge types that cannot easily be 'legitimated' by the statistical, 'denotive' pragmatics of governments and administration risk becoming excluded, or lost (Lyotard 1984: 37). Thus, the survival of oral narrative knowledge and embodied skills become increasingly pertinent to sociocultural wellbeing. This is why technology, as a prosthesis of the mind and the body, should be considered a *Pharmakon*, that is, both a poison and a cure.

Obarzanek and Weiss collaborate to produce a work that is classifiable under the positive taxonomy because they embrace the affordances of digital technologies to genuinely expand the field through PaR. Their methodology and technical setup transform the theatre into a performance research laboratory where phenomenological movement is grammatized, discretized and formalized, and then reinterpreted and reharnessed towards an output whose final configuration is unknown. The encumbrances of the technology on process are detectable in Obarzanek's reflection:

> In some ways *Mortal Engine* didn't progress in an interesting way, choreographically; it was often hijacked (the rehearsal periods) by technical problems. But, on the other hand it brought in a certain simplicity that made the work *work* in a different way. So, I don't regret it.
>
> (Obarzanek 2012)

For a dance collective that are focused on pushing the limits of choreography by performing with objects, it is an unusual scenario to have to simplify somatic practices in a compromise to non-human apparatuses. This illustrates the dichotomy of grammatization: in an artistic situation concerning the discretization of embodied skills and techniques, what are the affordances that retain and extend the idioms that constitute the foundation of artifice and poetry?

Analogous to *Apparition*, *Mortal Engine* is a work that mobilizes new tools (software and algorithmic operations) in order to elicit the particularities of digital technologies, which positions it as genuinely innovative PaR. It contributes to the establishment of a new genre in live performance, based on the digital grammatization of gesture.[8] Operating through a repurposing of motion-tracking technologies, these artistic innovations represent an epistemic progression of aesthetics advocated by choreographers like Merce Cunningham and Alwin Nikolai. However, contrary to analogue multimedia elements, digital apparatuses are employed for more than simple embellishment; the machine is afforded performativity. Henceforth, it is technicity, brought to the stage by the confluence of performers and machine, that constitutes the lion's share of the conceptual tensions in the work. Just as in *Apparition*, it is the unblinking gaze of the motion-tracking system that occupies centre stage in terms of the aesthetic concept.

The synergy between the performers and the machine presents an appropriate metaphor for how processes of psychic and collective individuation are mediated through and affected by technology, and how the technology is itself affected by the human. The work should be read in terms of the organological themes that it abstractly conveys, that is, how subjectivity and identity are formulated, affected and mutated by a relational interplay of the psychic individual, the collective organization and the technical milieu. This represents the basis of how Weiss and Chunky Move contribute to the opening of new circuits of knowledge in the field of performance research, in particular, and in socioculture, politics and economics, generally.

Expanding the Theoretical Lens

All technological advancements can be interpreted as Pharmaka. Every surge in technical evolution occasions a chance for either an enhancement or a hindrance of processes of individuation. On the one hand, biometric technologies afford the documentation, examination and processing of physiological information with increasing efficiency, expanding knowledge of embodied, gestural expression, while on the other, they coerce a situation wherein knowledge is forgotten because certain tasks are either delegated to software or deprecated altogether in favour of new techniques. This 'pharmacological' characteristic can be easily expanded to consider beneficial and stupefacient characteristics of developments in, for example, mobile computing, where intuitive knowledge of a city's organization is renounced in favour of accurate technologically assisted location positioning. There is a modulating relationship between technological advances and knowledge transmission that, depending on the various societal demands, can lead epistemes to either obsolescence or enhancement and prolongation. In terms of scenography, if technology is employed simply for efficiency, fashion or gratuitous embellishment, it may detract from an appreciation of the performer's live presence and the dramaturgy, but *Mortal Engine* represents a positive development because the artists forge new collaborations, expand epistemological boundaries, develop new techniques and evolve new roles.

The logic of the Pharmakon insists that there are ambivalences to these technological developments beyond the locale of stage performance. The technologies of motion-tracking and projection-mapping have enjoyed a certain burgeoning since these early digital avant-garde explorations of the technologies. Projection-mapping, especially, has experienced exponential growth due to its urban architectural applications and potential for garnering public attention through its scalability and spectacular nature. True to Adorno's thesis on the culture industry, these avant-garde technological and cultural inventions 'have been subjected equally to the concept of purpose and thus brought under a single false denominator: the totality of the culture industry' (Horkheimer and Adorno 2002: 108). By acquiring every stylistic and technical innovation available, the culture industry continually reasserts itself as the perfect manifestation of liberalism. In the context of the techno-cultural innovations revealed by Troika Ranch, Obermaier and Chunky Move, there is the alarming suggestion heralding the potential transformation of urban landscapes towards the ends of advertising and persuasion, where every building and wall becomes a potential projection surface, and every citizen becomes a potential vehicle for mobile signs. The next chapter, on one hand, charts the artistic spatio-paradigmatic shift in the deployment of projection technologies, from small, interior, experimental theatre spaces to large, outdoor, public city spaces, and on the other hand, delivers an analysis of how the these technologies operate, impact on citizens and reorganize socio-politics.

5

Architectural Projection-Mapping: OnionLab Beaming on a Grand Scale

Introduction

This chapter examines an early foray into the new expressive genre of architectural projection-mapping. Of special interest to this section of the book is the evolution of the technical milieu. Having gone through an embryonic stage in the protected, interior spaces of experimental theatres, the expressive technique then poured out into public spaces of the urban landscape, lighting up the night skylines of the most modish cities. One company that is among the early movers and shakers of the genre is OnionLab, an audio-visual company based in Barcelona. This chapter examines one of their early outdoor projection-mapping projects exhibited for the fifteenth anniversary of the architectural studio, A-cero (2011). There are earlier architectural projection-mapping projects and this chapter does reference some important ones; however, OnionLab's project was, at the time, unparalleled as an audio-visual spectacle because of its speedy, snappy and fluid graphical sequences and its synchronization of visuals with a custom sound design. In a move that is inconsistent with the rest of the book, the chapter also analyses a film scene from Denis Villeneuve's *Blade Runner 2049* (2017) to open an important discussion about projection-mapping technologies in the context of the culture industry and biopolitics.

A-Cero 15th Anniversary: Description

In June 2011, Spanish AV designers OnionLab exhibited a 3D architectural projection-mapping project the goal of which 'was to explain the language of the architecture studio and its evolution' (Fernandez 2020), using non-narrative, innovative visual effects. Although not exactly the first of its kind,[1] it was among the revolutionary ventures into the new genre and it was an undeniable technical leap in quality, speed, precision, responsiveness and immersiveness. These qualities contribute to the audience's perception of witnessing a genuinely original spectacle. The event was quite groundbreaking and pushed the limits of what was thought to be possible in terms of artificial lighting and scenographing 3D visuals. In this performance, OnionLab pioneered many of the projection design tropes that are now part and parcel of many live projection-mapping shows. These include:

- simultaneous but discrete amination of multiple building surfaces;
- luminous lines that trace, highlight and accentuate the outlines and edges of various facades, planes and door/window openings;
- horizontal or vertical scanlines that rove across the various faces;
- simulated 3D texturing of surfaces with block-work or slabs, which spin, rotate or bulge in various combinations and patterns;
- fragmentation of the structure into stacks of cubes, which are deconstructed and reconstructed using combinations of time-lapse and slow-motion (see Figure 5.1);
- shattering or obliterating the facade;
- converting the structure into a malleable wireframe structure that is twisted, bent and distorted;
- parallel lines repeated across the faces of planes at varying angles, which interfere with perception and the ability to comprehend the totality of the structure (similar to Obermaier's scenography in *Apparition*);
- particle systems and fluid simulations that give the impression the building is melting or warping;
- perspectival tropes and trompe l'oeil, giving the illusion of being able to see into the building, or that the building is turned inside out;
- a shifting directional/global light;
- and synchronized music and sound effects that accentuate the visual movement.

Fernandez (Director) describes how the narrative was divided into four main scenes based on thematic groups present in the architects' vision: rationalism and minimalism; inclined surfaces, an evolution of the complexity of the

FIGURE 5.1 *Photo:* A-Cero 15th Anniversary *(courtesy of OnionLab).*

previous group and 'retrofuturist' shapes; procedural architecture, curves and design evolution; and, lastly, OnionLab's interpretation of the architecture of the future (Fernandez 2020). The final scene involved visuals communicating ideas of 'walls made out of liquids, robots, artificial intelligence, and space and time transportation' (Fernandez 2020) (see Figure 5.2). Rather than giving a detailed description of the scenographic event, the rest of this chapter is dedicated to showing that this future vision of architecture is not all that fictitious; in fact, it is looming ever closer. It gives renewed, alarming pertinence to the idea of 'the society of the spectacle' (Debord 1967) and it has profound implications for spectators, that is, the citizens of the world's hyperindustrialized cities where the technology is now regularly deployed.

The entire performance was only about nine minutes long; however, given the complexity of implementing a multi-projector projection-mapping setup and developing the multi-surface graphics, it was an amazing achievement at that time. There were other similar, innovative and spectacular projects emerging at the time.[2] However, it is not important who exactly was the first art collective to produce this type of work on a grand architectural scale; the important point is that this period hosted the emergence of a new genre of spectacular public light-art exhibitions, in which the sophistication of the work evolved rapidly over a relatively short period. An obvious reason for this is because digital projection technologies improved greatly during this time; the power, luminosity, throw ratio, resolution and portability of projectors became advanced enough for their deployment in outdoor settings, covering large areas.

FIGURE 5.2 *Photo:* A-Cero 15th Anniversary *(courtesy of OnionLab).*

Another reason for the success of the genre was that, although cutting-edge projectors were very expensive, the marketing and advertising opportunities were immediately obvious to commercial sponsors and investors. Therefore, development of the technique became a priority for companies and cash was injected into financing the genre. The artform is now used widely at the openings of festivals and sports events, big pop/rock concerts, luxurious product launches, or for corporate advertisements that envelope entire façades of skyscrapers. It is now quickly becoming ubiquitous in the urban landscapes of the most modish, industrialized and wealthy cities. This transition of techno-cultural knowledge from small, experimental, independent artists to large, wealthy, commercial corporations typifies Adorno and Horkheimer's influential theory of the culture industry, which is widely viewed as an axiomatic condition of contemporary, late-capitalist culture.

Theodor Adorno: Aesthetic Theory and the Culture Industry

Adorno's aesthetics agree with Kant's view that fine art is characterized by formal autonomy and combines this notion with the prominence that Hegel gives to the work's social function (in relation to education, morality, community, politics, social status and, above all, spiritual freedom), as well as Marx's insistence on its embeddedness in the broader societal programme.

Adorno's aesthetic magnum opus, *Aesthetic Theory* (1970), is a body of work which thinks through the significant complications brought to art and culture under the modern, industrialized global exchange of late capitalism.[3] It is a cornerstone of avant-garde theory and remains a key referent for understanding (modern) art in terms of its autonomy (or lack thereof), intellectuality and socio-political function as 'the social antithesis of society' (Adorno 2002: 8). He writes: 'Insofar as a social function can be predicated for artworks, it is their functionlessness' (Adorno 2002: 227); that is, through their state of non-functioning they call into question the capitalist paradigm of streamlined production and means–ends rationale. Per Marx, Adorno focuses primarily on 'the fetishism of commodities' (Marx 2012) as a vector for critiquing the ideologies that capitalism sustains and needs. This constitutes his staunchly leftist discourse that pursues ideas of freedom and equality in society while maintaining that, due to the historical totality formed by the relationship between culture and society, that quest 'is inseparable from the pursuit of enlightenment in culture' (Zuidervaart 2015). On this point Adorno's aesthetic theory owes much to his earlier collaborative efforts with Max Horkheimer under the aegis of the Frankfurt School.

In *The Culture Industry: Enlightenment as Mass Deception* (1944) Horkheimer and Adorno employ a critical aesthetics of dialectical materialism to argue against the emergence of an industrialized system of cultural production, which seizes and monetizes cutting-edge artistic styles and techniques on a massive scale. Their thesis outlines how innovative cultural artefacts, techniques and concepts (avant-garde artworks) quickly become appropriated by an industrial system of production, which commodifies and recirculates them for mass exchange and consumption. They assert that what consumer masses experience in quotidian life is a homogenized cultural gestalt, which gathers into itself all styles and themes, without exception, discrimination or scruples: 'The irreconcilable elements of culture, art, and amusement have been subjected equally to the concept of purpose and thus brought under a single false denominator: the totality of the culture industry' (Horkheimer and Adorno 2002: 108). Through processes of general artefactual homogenization, the social functions of autonomous artistic devices and techniques are stymied and replaced by socio-politically and economically weighted symbols that penetrate deep into the psychic and social subjective fabric of individuals and communities. This cultural phenomenon has a two-fold social repercussion: it causes individuals to 'increasingly experience themselves as exchangeable "things" within a social arena dominated by principles of market exchange' (Sinnerbrink 2009: 3) and it conflates art and marketing, causing 'a condition of universal spectacle and narcissistic consumerism that increasingly precipitates regressive forms of failure to achieve ego independence' (Sinnerbrink 2009: 3). Ultimately, capitalism's abstract, hyper-rational processes of instrumentalization occasion the replacement of autonomous subjectivity with commodified forms of 'pseudo-individuality' (Sinnerbrink 2009: 3), undermining avant-gardist attempts to challenge audiences to critically self-reflect on their increasingly homogenized and impoverished social and intellectual status.

Adorno and Horkheimer's political-cultural critique is very influential but they were writing in a time that was concretely positioned in the epoch of mechanical reproducibility. Technology and socio-economics have undergone substantial evolutionary mutations since the mid-twentieth century and critical discourse has analogously responded. Their dialectical-materialist subject–object, means–ends model of instrumental reason still falls foul of the criticisms levelled at Structuralism by the postmodernists. Notwithstanding the ontological reductionism, their critical reflections on politics and culture laid the foundations for developments in aesthetic scholarly discourse throughout postmodernity and remain pertinent in the (post)digital era. The genealogy from Foucault, through Deleuze, to Stiegler is inherently and fundamentally linked to the Frankfurt School's identification and analysis of 'the politico-libidino-technologico-industrial problem' (Stiegler et al. 2012: 168); indeed, all that they write about and analyse would essentially be impossible if it were not for the foundations laid by the Frankfurt School – specifically Adorno, Horkheimer, Benjamin and Marcuse. This book is particularly interested in Stiegler's contributions because he has enjoyed the privilege of living well into the digital epoch. This permits him the ability to build on the theories of his predecessors while also backing-up speculations with concrete historical-material evidence, giving rise to remarkably lucid aesthetic–political assessments of the new digital-cultural situation.

The greater part of the waking hours of a substantial portion of global populations is now predominantly lived-out in front of screens because they work, play and socialize over digital networks. This techno-sociological development can be read pharmacologically, that is, it is both toxic and beneficial. Staying with Adorno's theory of the culture industry, this chapter mainly discusses the toxic aspects; an argument for a remedy is posited in the following chapter.

From the Culture Industry to the Programme Industry

At the outset of digitally networked society and robotic automation, many theoreticians hoped that these apparatuses would induce a more democratized, equal and freer socio-political paradigm, ending 'an epoch of laborious, consumptive masses' (Stiegler and Rossouw 2011: 54). However, these hopes have failed to materialize. Multinational media corporations increasingly control data flows, monitor activity and surveil users.[4] The utopian ideal of cyberspace as a free territory that could offer intersubjective equality has been eroded by the global dominance of a liberal capitalist paradigm and its advocation of proprietorship, commodification, consumerism and marketing. Reflecting on the contemporary situation, Stiegler writes:

> Not only does the proletariat remain very significant ... it has in fact grown as employees have been largely proletarianised[5] ... As for the middle classes, they have been pauperised ... The growth of leisure ... isn't at all evident, since current forms of leisure do not at all function to free individual time, but indeed to control it in order to hypermassify it: they are the instruments of a new voluntary servitude. Produced and organised by the cultural and program industries, they form what Gilles Deleuze called societies of control.
>
> (Stiegler and Rossouw 2011: 54)

Stiegler aligns himself with the biopolitical legacy from Foucault's 'discipline societies' (1975; 1976) to Deleuze's 'societies of control' (1992). In the latter thesis, Deleuze declares that the distinction between the activities of work and leisure has become confused because the walls of institutions are disintegrating in ways that do not halt their logics but, instead, generalize them in fluid forms across the social field; 'striated' spaces (institutionalized knowledge) in disciplinary societies give way to the modulating, 'smooth' (event–matter) spaces of control societies. Stiegler adds to this by showing how the channels, platforms and interfaces for accessing work are the same as those for accessing leisure. He renames the contemporary manifestation of the culture industry as 'the programming industries' (Stiegler 2008: 3) because, through the creation of a vast repertory of consumable audio-visual programmes or 'industrial temporal objects' (Stiegler 2014: 17–18),[6] media corporations are afforded the power to organize, re-programme and control the lives of the masses, who voluntarily access the programmes as a matter of duty and leisure. The programme industry exerts a profound efficacy over contemporary citizens because it captures individual and collective attentions (the time of consciousness), usurping free time and exploiting this time to modify behaviour, 'especially ... patterns of consumption' (Stiegler and Rossouw 2011: 57) and political persuasion. As an analogue to how oil fuels industrial capitalism, *attention* represents the new 'fuel [of ...] hyper-industrial capitalism' (Stiegler and Rossouw 2011: 54).

The arguments for and against spatio-cultural transformations under globalized multinational capitalism are well-documented: globalized intersubjectivity can erode the separate cultures and traditions of individual 'socio-ethnic programs' (Stiegler and Rossouw 2011: 57) or it can reduce nationalist, xenophobic metanarratives. However, Stiegler points out that very little attention has been given to the homogenization of separate histories. He calls this '*hyper-synchron*ization' (Stiegler 2009a: 50). It is a consequence of bringing the lived experiences of separate global communities into synchronization, whereby consumers' identities and psyches are all governed by the same set of character-constituting experiences; by consuming homogenized global content, individuals' pasts and futures become more alike. Therefore, processes of individuation are increasingly rarefied, and this leads to herd-like behaviour. Stiegler writes:

> The program industries tend on the contrary to oppose synchrony and diachrony in order to bring about a hypersynchronisation constituted by the programs, which makes the singular appropriation of the pre-individual fund impossible. The program schedule … is conceived so that my lived past tends to become the same as that of my neighbours, and that our behaviour becomes herd-like.
>
> (Stiegler and Rossouw 2011: 57)

Global audiences are subjected to a cultural–political paradigm of temporal coalescence that conduces a dilution of historical and cultural independence. This clandestine by-product of globalization emerges as a control mechanism because it short-circuits processes of individuation by devaluing unique histories and disarming citizens of the intellectual tools that could aid the development of a singular identity to critique socio-political totality. Furthermore, the types of knowledge preserved and the means of passing them on to ensuing generations also become homogenized because wisdom and skills that cannot be translated into the 'pragmatics' of rational scientific governance are delegitimated and lost (Lyotard 1984). The type of knowledge that is admitted is discretisable and grammatisable. These knowledge types, which come to constitute the make-up of reality, are increasingly homogenized because the pool of cultural diversity whence they are produced is itself shrinking, perpetuating 'a paradigm of diminishing returns' (O'Dwyer 2020). When content is increasingly produced within the remit of centralized media institutions, the possibility of individual adoption (diachrony) is replaced by a mass gavage of governmentally legitimated symbols, purveyed as knowledge; therefore, there is a foreclosure of richer and more varied processes of individuation.

Symbolic Misery

In terms of creativity, concrete applications of skills and craftsmanship become more scarce because automated machines (like cameras) takeover manual tasks (like drawing) and digital audio-visuals increasingly dominate the basis of symbolic/artefactual exchange in an economy where the masses, instead of contributing, are disenfranchised and marginalized, fuelling it through their undivided attention. This is a denial of the exaltation experienced by amateurs in learning and executing handicraft. *Monological* mediation short-circuits and replaces the *dialogical* transactions of knowledge exchange between teacher and student, in which the student learns through repetition. But the machine produces exact repetitions; it is, *automatic*, repeating without thought. Whereas human repetition is *idiomatic*; it is a *re-membering*, an active piecing-back-together, a participatory rebuilding process that is hermeneutic and fundamentally contingent. Sometimes the product is worse, but often it is better. This 'loss and forgetting of the *experience* of repetition, which is to say, of repetition *as apprenticeship* [... is the condition ...] that Deleuze sought to isolate as difference in *Difference and Repetition*' (Stiegler 2015b: 86). For Stiegler, the loss of participation suffered by the masses under the aegis of industrialized symbolization negates the possibility of *trans*individuation (showing by making). This leads to symbolic misery:

> Aesthetic ambition in this sense has today largely collapsed. And this is because a huge proportion of the population is totally subjected to the aesthetic *conditioning* of marketing, now hegemonic for the vast majority of the world, and is, therefore, estranged from any *experience* of aesthetic investigation.
>
> (Stiegler 2014: 3)

Symbolic misery describes a condition arising from the ongoing tendency, throughout the twentieth century, for the masses to be increasingly excluded from participating in creative cultural processes. There is a persistent propensity for the creative skills and labour of individuals and groups to be replaced by automated machinic processes, which precipitates a dis-individuation (a loss of knowledge). The programme industry perpetuates a situation in which a powerful minority who, as per Marx, owns the means of (symbolic) production controls the lives of the majority, by organizing the symbolic order. Industrially produced temporal objects that are emotionally charged can affect the sensibility of geospatially non-contiguous individuals and groups, facilitating the synchronization of experience, 'and therefore desire, and therefore behaviour, to the point of ... threatening the destruction of desire itself, and therefore politics, if not indeed economics' (Ross 2009). This affirms aesthetics as a pivotal constituent of contemporary politics; indeed, in the opening lines of his aesthetic magnum opus Stiegler states: 'The question of politics is a question of aesthetics and, vice versa' (Stiegler 2014: 1).

The spectacular nature of industrial temporal objects diminishes the possibility of fulfilment through embodied, interpersonal interaction, resulting in increased reliance on digital (non-human) intersubjectivity; that is, industrial temporal objects are highly addictive, to the demise of human interaction. In digitally reticulated society, the apparatuses of power and control operate by conditioning 'the time of consciousness and the unconscious [..., replacing] the sensory experience of social or psychic individuals' with technologically intensified experiences, towards a generalized goal of 'hypermassification' (Stiegler and Rossouw 2011: 58). Said differently, there is increasing enticement for individuals and groups to conduct more and more aspects of work and leisure-related activities through electronic networks and screen-based media, under the pretence that it is better that way. That illusion is always perpetrated through the lies of the marketing and public relations industries, which, as Freud posited, are founded on the exploitation of desire.

Desire

Desire is central to the libidinal economy. The Frankfurt School's apprehension of the political, libidinal, technological and economic question in relation to the culture industry provides a crucial foundation for Stiegler's examination of the continuing exploitation of these subjectivities in the digital age. Many early Frankfurt School theses attempt to think these questions through the relations between drive and desire, and this was certainly innovative and important. However, Stiegler points out that in many cases their examinations are misrepresentations of the relations between these instincts; that is, until Freud engages the topic, but even post-Freud they are still 'surprisingly naïve' (Stiegler et al. 2012: 168).[7] This results in enormous confusion on the difference between drive and desire and their relationship to one another. Stiegler says: 'In Freud's second period ... the drive only becomes libido because it has been bound [to desire], which Derrida calls "stricture", the "bind", and that is libidinal economy' (Stiegler et al. 2012: 177). What is interesting about Stiegler's thesis is that he uses Simondon's theory on the relations between technics and individuation to re-read Freud's instantiation of the problematics of desire. This compels him to assert that the problem is always rooted in technics, that is, in exteriorization. Stiegler maintains that the libidinal economy emerged during the first mechanical turn of sensibility because the emergence of new visualization techniques, (that could order the real) enabled film to pose 'as the libido's means of production' (Stiegler et al. 2012), by penetrating deep into the temporal fabric of consciousness, as per Benjamin and Deleuze. The complex structure that organizes the production of the libido is, itself, a set of relations produced by the *transformation* of drives into libidinal energy, which Freud describes as the idealization of the ego. Invoking Freud is not without its problems given Deleuze and Guattari's denouncement of familialism (1972), but Stiegler's rereading in the context of technical exteriorization is an important reworking that opens new ways for thinking through the exploitation of libido, in the context of commodification and consumption in the digital age.

As Stiegler seeks to interrogate the technical object in terms of desire, Donald Winnicott's practice-led clinical research provides a crucial link between the psychoanalytical and ontological speculations of Freud and Simondon respectively. As a paediatrician and psychoanalyst, Winnicott posits that the original construction of desire is located in what he calls a 'transitional object' (Stiegler 2013: 1). A cuddly toy constitutes an ideal example of this because, for the child, it has the quality of being simultaneously real and false; therefore, it occupies a 'transitional' milieu between the child's imagination and the real (outside) world, manifesting firstly in the mother. In playing with the transitional object the mother and child can 'encounter' each other across its 'transitional space' that is 'infinite' precisely because 'it does not exist' (Stiegler 2013: 1). Stiegler observes that the teddy bear is always firstly a *technical* object, which, read through Gilbert Simondon's relational philosophy, provides the basis for a *transduction*, that is, it 'opens up possibilities of internal resonances in a process of psychic and collective individuation, and that thus (re)constitutes its terms' (Stiegler 2009b: 47). The transduction, in this case, is that care established in the mother–child relation. Transitional objects represent an important early bridge between self and other, which can either help children with genuine projections to exteriority or, in cases of character disorder, facilitate the construction of false, untruthful personalities (Winnicott 1992). Stiegler declares, 'the transitional object is the first pharmakon' (Stiegler 2013: 2) because it reveals a profound care, affirming that 'life is worth living' all the while edified on a fabrication, a lie. In the beginning, the object is perceptible as a sign, but then it becomes a supplement for desire. For Stiegler, this is *the* key aspect of the economy of desire. It is the main question that needs to be addressed and, tragically, the only sectors doing it (very effectively) are marketing and public relations, which represent 'the science of transitional objects' (Stiegler et al. 2012: 179).

The anticipation of a purchase, the ritualistic pairing away of carefully assembled layers of packaging and the tender stroking of sleek, streamlined, electronic objects are the actions that comprise a narcissistic consumerist ceremony known as 'unboxing',[8] a social phenomenon that is only conceivable in a capitalist economy that places desire at the centre of each and every consumer's universe. The only objects that really count in such an economy are objects of desire because everyone is consistently told so by marketing campaigns. As per Freud, the ironic fact is that objects of desire *do not actually exist*; they are 'only idealised as a support for idealised projections' (Stiegler et al. 2012: 182), which are ultimately hallucinations or phantasms, like imagined virtues projected onto the subject of a love interest. Idealized projections are not a bad thing; they are necessary because they edify a profound concern that is central to well-being and human cooperation. Neither the transitional object of desire nor its phantasms are themselves problematic; however, there is an urgent need to address the *abuse* of these phenomena perpetrated by marketing and public relations since they were founded in the 1930s by Edward Bernays.[9]

Desire and the Programme Industry

In terms of the programme industry, many transitional objects that are now produced and consumed are mediatized and intangible; nevertheless, they are technical objects. The system that produces these digitally mediatized objects offers an illusion of choice because it functions on a paradigm of 'on-demand', user-centred programme selection. To some extent, the level of choice is an improvement on its predecessor: analogue television. However, the choice is specious for two reasons. Firstly, the objects are still part of a hegemonic, top-down model of production and diffusion, which means that the set from which they are selected remains consistent, albeit more accessible. Secondly, the system is still an exponent of a homogenizing paradigm, commanding that masses engage with identical objects. As already explained, these factors inhibit processes of individuation because the diversity of the 'pre-individual fund' becomes more diluted and subjects are coerced into interfacing with exteriorized, fragmented and fictitious personalities of (non-human) 'technical individuals [l'individu technique]' (Simondon 2012: 15) over real, embodied personas. This tendency results in the erosion of the cogitative and discerning capacities of individual and collective consciousnesses, invariably curtailing critical thought and, ultimately, pauperizing culture. However, an aspect not yet addressed is the relationship of this tendency to desire: it destroys the mind's 'capacity for *projection* – for *desire* – which can only be *singular* (objective)' (Stiegler 2011a: 4). The idealized projections that were originally located in tangible objects of desire become dissipated and re-located in the temporal, mediated and ephemeral flux of the programme industries and the subject of those idealized projections – a mother, father, child, friend or foe – become analogously fragmented and distributed; that is, the phantasm becomes the subject of the projection, in another paradigm of diminishing returns. Becoming increasingly isolated, an individual responds by:

Either embedding itself in the archi-flux[10] of the programming industries or being trapped in the webs of 'user profiling' – whose goal is to subdivide and tribalize them into subcommunities through devices that can observe the behavior of the programmed consumers.

(Stiegler 2011a: 4)

Either option is equally unfavourable. The former leads to a passive, mindless lethargy; the latter leads to a paradigm of surveillance, anticipation and control, via the exposure, industrialization and examination of personality and behaviour. This dystopian situation of cultural consumerism is, for Stiegler, one arising out of the devastation of aesthetic experience caused by the fragmentation and dissipation of desire, a phenomenon that has become *the* object of the culture industry.

At this point it is useful to return to the artistic technique under inspection: projection-mapping. However, instead of continuing to analyse OnionLab's project – which was chosen on the basis that it was a pioneering feat of sculpting light and represents the kernel of a genre that has far to go – what follows is a discussion of an example that exists only within the imaginary world of a science fiction movie: *Blade Runner 2049* (Villeneuve 2017), which is a scenographic feast. Given the newness of projection-mapping technologies, the analysed scene from this movie contextualizes the speculative discourse and typifies Stiegler's definition of an industrial temporal object produced by a cohort of creative artists that has 'turned its back on those who founder' (Stiegler 2014: 3) in the face of the spectacle.

Blade Runner 2049: 'Everything You Want to Hear/See' and the Horror of Joi

The *Blade Runner* series is based on Phillip K. Dick's 1950s sci-fi novel, *Do Androids Dream of Electric Sheep?* (Dick 1968), which is set in a post-apocalyptic future where 'replicants' (genetically engineered humans) are exploited as slaves. 'Off-world' colonies are established with a view to preserving human genetic integrity because the atmosphere on earth is too poisonous, following the fallout from a global nuclear war. *Blade Runner 2049*, directed by Denis Villeneuve and written by Hampton Fancher and Michael Green, is the sequel to Ridley Scott's original neo-noir classic (1982).

K (the protagonist), a 'replicant' who is employed as a police officer, is charged with the mission of hunting down and 'retiring' (destroying) the offspring of two replicants. As a slave-race, replicants were genetically programmed to be reproductively sterile so the child's existence is perceived as a threat to political stability. The child's birth records were destroyed to conceal her identity and she was disappeared. K's detective work leads to the capture of Deckard (the child's father and main protagonist in the prequel) whose interrogation would inevitably put the 'miracle child' in the hands of Niander Wallace, CEO of the Wallace Corporation. Wallace wants to dissect her so he can discover the secret to creating sexually reproductive replicants, with a view to expanding interstellar colonization. After discovering the identity of his target, K is faced with a dichotomy: atone for his shortcomings by rescuing Deckard and allowing him to meet his daughter, or kill Deckard. Mid-quandary, he stands on an elevated walk-way that overlooks a skyscraper, which is transformed into a giant screen. He is confronted by an enormous, personalized holographic advertisement for a virtual escort programme called 'Joi'.[11] The advert begins as a projection-mapping of a naked woman (visually archetypal of the hyperfeminized type commonly used for advertising) on the façade of the skyscraper. The screen representation transforms into a giant 3D hologram, decouples from the surface of the building, and approaches K. She strikes several (semi-pornographic) seductive poses in front of him and whispers alluring phrases, indicating that she can relieve him of his stress and loneliness. The advert ends with the hologram returning to the surface of the building where she resumes her position as a 2D mapped projection, her fully naked, slender body stretching the full height of the skyscraper, dominating the urban zone. The enormous advert includes the caption, 'Joi: Everything you want to hear/see', flashing in simulated, neon-style text.

Under the technical–aesthetic–political–libidinal theories of the culture/programme industries, this scene foregrounds the problem of putting projection-mapping technologies in the hands of marketing and PR. Although the work undertaken by Obermaier, OnionLab and other early pioneers of the genre is genuinely creative, epistemically exploratory and inventive, there is nothing to stop advertising companies hijacking the techniques and exploiting them towards the ends of mass persuasion. Per Stiegler, industrial appropriation of art ideas in mass media is tied to generating wealth and securing power through the exploitation of desire. Joi's nudity, submissiveness, willingness and general hypersexualized nature constitute the object of male libidinal fantasy. Advertising always targets consumers on this basis and is often within a hair's breadth of using full frontal nudity in mainstream culture. Signifiers that command the attention of consumers are already highly pervasive in urban zones, with marketing companies having access to consumers through computers, phones, tablets and printed signage on billboards, trains, busses, shop frontage and so on. The possibility that every building's façade and potentially even the ground beneath one's feet is lit up with attentional solicitations is a future scenario that is wholly unpalatable, but not unlikely.

The techno-cultural paradigm – begun by Obermaier, expanded by OnionLab and taken towards its limit by Villeneuve – opens and conveys an urban spatial paradigm that threatens privacy and erodes the ability to rest, to switch-off from the circulation of persuasive symbols. This is what Jonathan Crary describes as 'the incapacitation of daydream or of any mode of absent-minded introspection' (2014: 88), which contributes to a disempowerment of the subject. Crary describes how the industry of user-profiling creates digital doubles of citizens that are functionally integrated as virtual consumers in '24/7 markets and a global infrastructure for continuous work and consumption' (2014: 3). In this sense, the avatar overtakes the human. In the digital epoch, proletarianization – the setting-to-work of unskilled, devalued labourers – does not just involve the physical gesticulations of workers' bodies; so too are the mental activities of speaking, listening, thinking and imagining put to work. Because the digital traces created by users' articulations over digital networks are reorganized towards feeding and sustaining the 24/7 global economy constituted on consumer-proxy datasets. The traces that constitute an individual's past are mobilized towards controlling and configuring the future choices of individuals and collectives. The pharmacology of automation in the context of big data and machine learning, which promises both total obsolescence and infinite prosthesis, is a theoretical problem that is taken up and discussed more thoroughly in the next (final) chapter.

The comparison of the A-Cero exhibition with the scene from *Blade Runner 2049* is not without its problems; one is a light performance that takes place in the tangible world in real-time, the other is a science-fiction film that relies heavily on special effects and laborious post-production processes. There is no erroneous intention to conflate the fields of performance and film studies; however, with the rapid evolution of computer-vision and display technologies[12] combined with 'the death of scandal' (O'Dwyer 2016b: 148–54), the horrifying advent of massive, explicit advertisements for depressing applications like Joi is not that far-fetched. With the imminent general deployment of holographic and augmented reality technologies to the mass market, the internal tensions between the artistic avant-garde and the culture industries beg the questions: What are the new technologies that make these symbolic experiences possible? Who develops them? And how are they used?

The Pharmacology of Software as Art Material

The new digital tool that is central to the two projection-mapping projects under scrutiny in this book is computer vision software. It literally confers visual perception capabilities upon machines, and it constitutes a major contributing factor of Obermaier and OnionLab's techno-cultural fusions. The merger of machine vision technologies with culture was a new, original art idea that has begun to take hold as an established cultural practice becoming increasingly employed by advertising. The technology is fundamentally new in the sense that it has only become available to humans since the outset of digital technologies; in the analogue epoch there was no means of automatically analysing video/film frames. Computer vision techniques operate through that instrument taxonomy that is quintessential to the digital epoch: software. That tool, that language, that is used to send electrical pulses through various configurations of circuits, components and microchips that store binary memory in transistor matrices, so that speech, gesture, time and space may be captured, stored, duplicated and analysed. It is software that controls these processes, it is software that obsolesces human labour through systematic automatization and it is software that proletarianizes through the automatic analysis of data.

Software development is a difficult subject to engage; competency demands years of practice and a natural bent towards mathematics and logic. However, many arts practitioners have difficulties with these subjects, which are the essence of computer languages. In this regard, computer-vision is a difficult tool to employ because it is still a very young technology, with relatively few proprietary packages that would make it accessible to artists and designers. Given the importance that the contemporary art world and programming industries attribute to 'newness' and 'originality', how can artists engage with software tools – that is, *really* engage with them, in the sense of *getting under the hood* – thereby reconfiguring them and repurposing them, in unforeseen ways that allow such techno-experiments to be perceived *as art,* and not simply as technical exhibitionism? Stiegler blames 'the art-world' for the catastrophe of symbolic misery because, he maintains, it has abandoned 'the question of politics' for the short-term financial gain of manufacturing stupefying, industrial temporal objects in the service of the culture industry (Stiegler 2014: 1). Considering the immanence of aesthetics to politics, he appeals to the art-world to stand up and accept accountability for its role in combatting the pestilence of symbolic misery. This can be achieved by rediscovering the question of the avant-garde and by engaging, re-harnessing and allocating innovative cultural integrity to cutting-edge technologies that are predominantly used for over-rationalized governmental control procedures or mass cultural commodification. Avant-gardist engagements could awaken audiences to reflect on the totality of the socio-economic situation and the increasingly marginalized position of the individual. However, when the majority of artists are not at all fluent in computer programming languages, and educational institutes (which change direction about as efficiently as the Titanic) are still not equipping new cohorts of art students with the skills *and languages* required for *deeply* engaging with digital media, how can artists be expected to answer Stiegler's call?

Computer Vision: A Digital Resource

Computer vision was originally developed for military and security applications and was initially incredibly expensive because it required sophisticated optical hardware and powerful processors and graphics cards to analyse consecutive video frames. As in the case of all technologies, these financial obstacles have been overcome by mass reproduction and the inevitable cheapening of digital hardware. Now, even basic webcams will suffice for motion-tracking and most modern laptops have adequate processing power to run video analysis algorithms.

Open Computer-Vision (OpenCV) 'is an open-source computer vision and machine learning software library' ('OpenCV.Org | About' n.d.) that interfaces with electronic hardware. It is composed of more than 2,500 optimized algorithms and is written natively in C++. It is distributed freely under the BSD-License (Berkeley Software Distribution License), which allows unlimited redistribution for any purpose as long as its copyright notices and the license's disclaimers are maintained. This makes it easy for its utilization in all types of projects, from cultural, academic and research to commercial ones. In 1999 it was officially launched by Intel Research, whose goals included:

1. Advancing CPU-intensive vision applications by using open and optimized code.
2. Disseminating vision knowledge by providing a common framework.
3. Promoting vision-based applications by providing free, portable, performance-optimised code, without the need for costly or restrictive licenses. (Bradski and Kaehler 2011: 6)

The community released its alpha version at the IEEE Conference on Computer Vision and Pattern Recognition (2000), achieving a milestone in making the intellectual property available to the global community. In the six years following its first release, and under the aegis of a globalized open-source peer-review community, it underwent multiple revisions, refinements and improvements resulting in the first 1.0 release in 2006 (Bradski and Kaehler 2011: 7). In 2008, OpenCV obtained corporate support from two main sources: Willow Garage (a cutting-edge robotics enterprise) and Itseez (which specialized in computer vision algorithms) ('Happy 20th Anniversary to OpenCV Library!' n.d.). Following their patronage, a much-improved 1.1 version was released. These companies provided a core team of programmers who maintained code and oversaw development; however, they had the privilege of receiving feedback from a learned, global community user-base exceeding 47,000 people ('OpenCV.Org | About' n.d.), who contributed, reviewed and trouble-shot complex C++ code, and provided critical feedback, identified bugs and memory leaks, and so on, *for free*. The library of algorithms forming the foundation of any electronic object using computer vision applications is the result of an altruistic global effort, which epitomizes the benefits of a bottom-up system of knowledge-transfer and development. This model is indebted to that positive offshoot of global interconnectivity: *an economy of contribution*. At this stage of its development OpenCV epitomizes the positive qualities of this economy, where a collective of amateurs critique, intervene and contribute 'to the organization of the processing algorithms', co-individuating through the love of work and a care for the community (Stiegler 2010a). Thus, the computer vision library cannot be classified as intellectual *property* because no one individual can claim ownership of it; it is collectively owned and is therefore more akin to a natural resource.

In 2016, 'Intel signed a definitive agreement to acquire Itseez Inc.' (Davis 2016). While it appeared that, by establishing the open-source community, Intel were conducting an act of magnanimity, they in fact emerge as the clear winners in this global effort of free labour because they now control the OpenCV resource and its team of core developers, who have been supported by a global community for free for many years. In this story of apparent collective, global knowledge creation, the problem of proletarianization emerges again because the attentional, creative and problem-solving faculties of masses are seized and put to work under a new, clandestine regime of voluntary servitude. The emergence of a new economic model that promises democratized participation ends in a *hyper-*disenfranchisement because the fragments of information contributed by many altruistic individuals, which at an individual level might seem negligible, are gathered and exploited to the benefit of a privileged corporate few, resulting in a scenario where contributors are neither credited nor remunerated for their input, thereby exacerbating the destruction of the ego – a hidden taxation of the soul.

The OpenCV story, charting the progress from shared creation towards monetization within the contributive economy, is representative of a three-stage resource–wealth redistribution paradigm that Kojin Karatani stresses is common to all socio-economic iterations throughout world history. Karatani defines these as the 'four basic modes of exchange' (Karatani and Wainwright 2012: 38) that move from: (1) 'reciprocity of gift and return' (shared community knowledge), through (2) 'plunder-redistribution' to (3) 'commodity exchange' (Karatani and Wainwright 2012: 38). This cycle then necessitates a fourth and final, recursive mode: the recovery of the reciprocity stage at a higher level. The OpenCV software example is exemplary of Karatani's paradigm that describes the nation-state-capital relationship, which is common across history. Karatani writes: 'These four types [of exchange modes] coexist in all social formations. They differ only on which of the modes is dominant' (Karatani 2014: x). It is also possible to superimpose the OnionLab versus culture industry example, over the resource–wealth redistribution trajectory of OpenCV. The avant-gardist, experimental work occurs at the shared community knowledge stage, where the tool is established as a valid means of creative expression. Following the success of the artists' practical synthesis of computer-vision and projection-mapping, there emerges an abundance of exciting independent projects. This generates a surge in interest by software companies, who race to adopt the intellectual property, repackage it and sell it as a tool that can facilitate fashionable, modish work (plunder-redistribution). Finally, the inevitable torrent of commercial software products and marketing campaigns ensues (commodity exchange).

The Pharmacology of Software as an Art Material

Software programmers want remuneration for their investment in developing complex intellectual property. Why should they not? They invest huge amounts of time and labour in developing the code into graphical user interfaces that aid code-illiterate (creative artists) to engage with technical IP. Paradoxically, these artists are required to do commercial work to pay for the expensive software licences and, therefore, have little or no time, energy or resources to engage political, avant-garde thematics.

The *OpenCV* library is a great resource if you know how to programme using the computer scientific language of C++, but if a user is not trained in programming logic or reading the syntax then they might as well be looking at an alien script. The OpenCV library has been assimilated into many real-time data-processing software packages, and many of the tools are now available to professionals and amateurs alike. Some software packages are free to download and deploy for non-commercial work;[13] others require a proprietary license because they are more refined, user-friendly and technically supported.[14] These types of software packages make the new computer-vision techniques – specific to digital media – available to people untrained in computer programming;[15] however, these tools still only offer a predefined set of options and menus that the artists select from. In fact, most packages only use a small number of the available algorithms in the CV library and this may homogenize the type of work produced, especially in the case of cultural audio-visual projects. For digital media artists to *really* explore the possibilities available they either need a formal education in computer programming or they need to collaborate with computer scientists. The latter makes techno-scientific art experiments very expensive because artists ultimately have to pay computer programmers a wage. This means digital media art experiments are highly dependent on external, third-party funding – like arts councils or private philanthropy – which are inevitably highly competed for and usually underfunded. This precipitates a situation where avant-garde digital media experiments depend on magnanimous contributions by computer scientists, making such outputs rarer. This indicates that computer programmers are potentially better equipped to be the avant-garde of the twenty-first century, begging the question: should Stiegler not redirect his appeal to the computer scientists, who plunge headlong into the service of manipulating information, developing expensive software tools and fabricating the infrastructural base of the programme industry?

Computer scientific professionals are not doing themselves any favours by placing short-term financial gain at the forefront of their work ethos. Considered in the context of the late capitalist penchant towards automating *everything*, to maximize profits and reduce labour costs, computer scientists now frequently work on projects that spell their own redundancy. This ultimately exacerbates the increasing demographic of unemployment in Western technocracies, lessening the contributions of humans to both industrial *and* cultural production in the new hyperindustrial economy.

Summing Up Projection-Mapping and the Programming Industries

In the genealogy from OnionLab to *Blade Runner 2049*, this chapter discusses how the culture industry repurposes avant-garde ideas and exploits desire for commodification, profit, political powerplay and control. The chapter also traces the evolution of the OpenCV resource in the context of wealth redistribution and the contributive economy. The barrage of projection-mapping projects released since OnionLab's pioneering experiment is testimony to the validity of the critical theory. The artist's idea comes full circle. Originally conceived to break away from the mediocrity of continuity, rupture positions of conservatism and provoke art publics to question their socio-political and economic position, the avant-garde artwork instead contributes to the enforcement of the liberal capitalist paradigm that it set out to rupture.

Anyone who resists can survive only by being incorporated. Once registered as diverging from the culture industry, they belong to it as the land reformer does to capitalism. Realistic indignation is the trademark of those with a new idea to sell… The more immeasurable the gulf between chorus and leaders, the more certainly is there a place among the latter for anyone who demonstrates superiority by well-organized dissidence.

(Horkheimer and Adorno 2002: 104)

Through its incessant acquisition of styles and techniques, the culture industry epitomizes the goal of liberalism. Whereas OnionLab's work represents an innovative repurposing of state-of-the-art techniques in a cultural context, Villeneuve's scene represents the horizon of possibility. As the genre develops, more enormous buildings and mobile bodies/vehicles become potential candidates to host advertisements that engulf individual and collective fields of vision. As such, modernized cities are threatened with a commercial paradigm that involves the continuing erosion of privacy and a negation of the down-time that Crary calls 'absent-minded introspection' (2014: 88) and Stiegler describes as a denial of 'intermittence' and 'dream-time' (2016: 65–92). Aside from speculations on the speed of technical evolution, the thematic, subjective and biopolitical development from OnionLab's work to the dystopian scenario depicted in *Blade Runner 2049* is not over-the-top. The industrialization of traces described by Crary and expounded by Stiegler theorizes an imminent future involving pervasive surveillance and powerful algorithmic control procedures that invade the interior of consciousness, determining individual and collective destinies, foreclosing the possibility of qualitative embodied individuation and curtailing freedom.

These are key problems that will be explored in the final chapter by examining *Karen* by Blast Theory, a performance collective from the UK that have been practising immersive and location-based performance for three decades. This last chapter continues tracing the increasing sophistication of the technical milieu by charting the influence of the most up-to-date technologies (big data, deep learning and AI) on scenography. The increase in sophistication is traced here in order to open up a discussion on the potential of these techno-phemonena in performance practice and the socio-political challenges that they open. As such, there is a digression from the spectacular, visual aspects of digital performance (which have dominated much of the subject-matter in this book) to dialogue-driven content.

6

Ubiquitous Computing, Behavioural Profiling, Big Data and Machine Learning: Blast Theory

Introduction

The increasing ubiquity of mobile computing devices – initially phones and tablets, but now also augmented reality (AR) head-mounted displays (HMDs) – is transforming the lives of contemporary citizens because digital media (and their anytime–anywhere accessibility) are steadfastly embedded in the fabric of urban life. These technologies have occasioned new possibilities for active, enthusiastic, mobile and exploratory audiences. Early theoretical speculations on the transformational potential of mobile and ubiquitous technologies (Benford and Giannachi 2011) in the performing arts have become reified in the rich collection of work that comprises the new genre of site-specific, immersive theatre which has blossomed since the turn of the century. Such artworks have created 'new forms of performance and spectating which combine "real" and "virtual" worlds, that respond to participants' locations, or that are finely interwoven with the patterns of their daily lives' (Giannachi and Benford 2008: 60). Therefore, it would be erroneous to conduct a genealogy of digital scenographic innovations without including this important, influential genre. Notwithstanding that digital mobile phone networks ease the logistics of deploying site-specific theatre, this type of performance is not unique to the digital epoch.

Traditionally, this type of theatre can be traced back to ritualistic festivals that seek to transmit culture through oral, performative storytelling. For example, the Ramlila [Rāmlīlā], a dramatic enactment of the Hindu epic Ramayana, has been held annually since the 1830s. Over a period of thirty-one days, the audience follows the actors through the city and congregates at site-specific focal points to watch the drama. In the context of contemporary performance, Richard Schechner expounded his theory of 'Environmental Theatre' (1968; 1973) aimed at defining a new aesthetics of 'interaction and transformation' by reconfiguring theatre space and audience relationships and contradicting theatrical tradition. His dogma was founded on the basis of 'six axioms':

1. 'The theatrical event is a set of related transactions', between multifarious parts (audience, performers, text, sensory stimuli, architecture, equipment, technicians, etc.) that combine to form a coherent whole.
2. 'All the space is used for performance; all the space is used for audience.' The goal of this was to challenge spatial conventions cemented by prosceniums and audience distancing.
3. 'The theatrical event can take place either in a totally transformed space or in "found space".' This is obviously pertinent to site-specific work.
4. 'Focus is flexible and variable', as opposed to the singular and fixed object of attention in traditional theatre.
5. 'All production elements speak in their own language.' This aims to shift prominence from the 'outstanding' actor towards peripheral roles and non-human elements.
6. 'The text need be neither the starting point nor the goal of a production.' This aims to dethrone the rigorous script and encourage an aesthetics of emergence (Schechner 1968: 41–64).

Under these criteria, Schechner was instrumental in shifting the conceptual landscape of theatre and how practitioners thought about producing work, especially in relation to site specificity and audience participation, under his second and third axioms.

Another important innovator in the genre was Agusto Boal, who developed audience-engagement strategies since the 1960s under his broader revolutionary praxis coined *Theatre of the Oppressed* (Boal 1979). One strategy, *Forum Theatre*, constituted his concept of 'simultaneous dramaturgy', whereby, faced with a crisis, the protagonist consulted the audience to suggest a course of actions for the actor to perform to overcome the problem. Although suggestions are interpreted by the actors under poetic licence, the methodology was framed as an endorsement of a contributive form of learning. Another strategy, *Invisible Theatre*, consisted of surprise or spontaneous performances in random urban locations, similar to the contemporary Flash Mob genre. The goal of his aesthetics was to motivate education, political engagement and social justice by challenging people to question how society draws the lines between various states of reality, catalysed by indeterminate erections and obliterations of the fourth wall in his performances (Boal 1979).

Since those early explorations, the site-specific genre has burgeoned into a rich performance research area with a wealth of scholarly work, including, but not limited to, site-specific art (Kaye 2008) and autobiographical reflections on performance practice (Pearson 2010), and historiographical compilations that chart the field from the seventeenth century, through modernism, to contemporary examples that depend on digital technologies (Birch and Tompkins 2012; Birch 2012). This variety of approaches to the field expresses a 'fascination with how different types of spatial arrangements affect our understanding of and relationships with performance' (Birch 2012: 1). The genre has undeniably been invigorated by the explosion of mobile digital technologies, which have been zealously engaged by Blast Theory whose work in immersive, site-specific theatre is internationally acclaimed and features in many books and top performance art research journals.[1]

The bulk of work that engages mobile technologies for performance consists of narratives that explore embodied encounters arising from the new mobility of audiences under the aegis of mixed reality technologies (Benford and Giannachi 2011). They operate by moving (participatory) audiences around urban zones and engaging them in situated action using live actors or real-time mediated interactions. This type of work represents an important contribution to the immersive theatre genre; however, the predominance of this method begs the question: what potential alternative applications of mobile technologies in performance remain unexplored? In an attempt to open new areas of discourse, this chapter examines an unusual and pioneering addition to the mixed reality performance genre because it involves participants accessing pre-recorded video footage over mobile devices (at random times and locations). This itself is not an innovation, but the way the videos are linked is. The narrative is assembled so as to simulate a series of videoconferencing sessions and the user interacts with a piece of software (or robot) posing as a human, via instant messaging and multiple-choice questions. The artwork in question is called *Karen* (2015) by Blast Theory[2] and, in terms of its thematics and audience-engagement paradigm, it is more resonant with the overarching techno-philosophical, biopolitical argument of this book than the audience-mover models already widely discussed.

Karen

Karen is an experimental, participatory, software-driven drama application (aka 'app-drama') created for engaging audiences over mobile phones and tablets. Blast Theory has been effecting technology-enabled site-specific performances since 1991 – the entire time-line of this genealogy. In terms of originality and innovation, it puts them on a par with other early adapters covered in this book: Troika Ranch and Klaus Obermaier. Blast Theory was 'augmenting' reality using crude mobile phones and hacked wireless gadgets long before the AR idea ever came near the radars of giant tech-sector companies, who are now investing billions in the technology.[3]

This book has primarily focused on digital scenographies that appeal to the visual regime. However, Blast Theory's work has been selected for the final chapter of this book because of their deep engagement with specifically digital themes, that is, the types of stories they tell, how they tell them and how they design the stories around the new specificities of mobile and ubiquitous computing technologies. Although they are best known for location-specific theatre, immersive storytelling and audience participation methods, the app-drama was chosen because it draws on the specificities of tracking, surveillance and user-profiling technologies. Therefore, it continues the discussion introduced in the last chapter, while demanding a deeper engagement with the critical theory concerning biopolitics, privacy, big data and machine learning. These are the techno-subjectivities of the moment. It would be erroneous to write a book on digital scenography and omit these imperative factors concerning, perhaps, the most important subjective mutations of the contemporary era.

Description

Emerging from the new conditions of access, that is, the new ways audiences can access content and artists can access audiences, *Karen* is an original and innovative contribution to the 'app-drama' genre located at the intersection of live performance, pre-recorded video, social networking and gaming. The app-drama consists in a series of discrete video sessions, in which the character directly addresses the user. These are woven into a narrative that hybridizes storytelling, theatre, film and gaming by combining the videos with text-based questions demanding interactive input (see Figure 6.1). According to the data provided by participants, *Karen* modifies and personalizes her conversations to the point that it starts to become

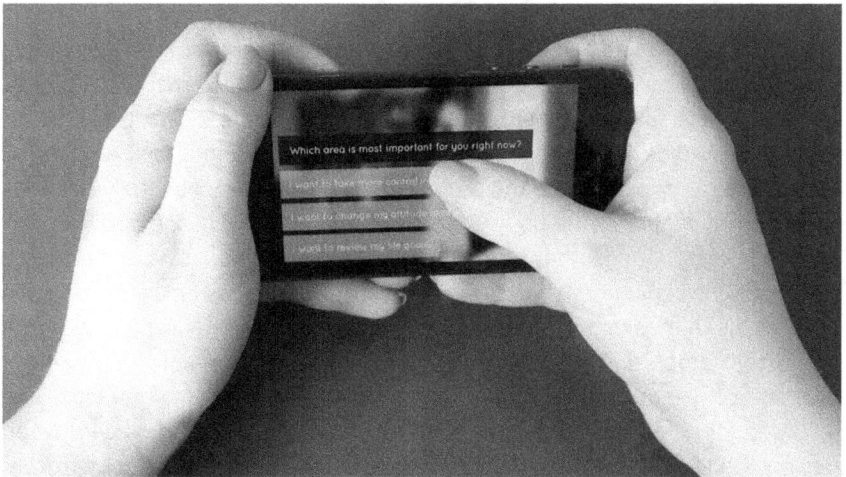

FIGURE 6.1 *Photo: Multiple-choice interface for* Karen *(courtesy of Blast Theory).*

a little disturbing regarding how much she knows about you. Behavioural metrics carried out on the inputted data do not 'affect the plot of the story; they affect *how* Karen talks to you' (Adams 2019). This storytelling strategy sets up an uncanny mode of audience participation because it is difficult to separate the human interactions from the machinic ones. As such, the audience undergo a narrative experience that is not unlike the human–computer dynamic depicted in Spike Jonze's *Her* (2014), although *Karen* is more intimate due to the first-person conversational paradigm.

Mise-en-scène

The app is eloquently and innovatively assembled, in the way it engages users. Karen (Claire Cage) speaks directly to the camera and addresses the user in the first person but the user cannot reply orally. After Karen poses a question, the user is prompted to reply, via the mobile touchscreen interface, using a menu of options that they must choose from.

As with all interactive video narratives, the juxtaposition of scenes is a complicated affair and, unlike traditional film, there is no universal language for handling this. Blast Theory added the complication of trying to simulate dialogue within the scene. They developed some clever techniques around moments of pause and deferral, which traditionally would have been represented by 'cuts', within a filmic scene. For example, when Karen asks a question, the video image blurs (although it is still clear that Karen is waiting in the background), and loops back and forth, giving the impression that she is rocking or nodding, while waiting patiently for your answer. The videos are shot in a way that they are booked-ended with the same generic pose of Karen's face filling the frame. This facilitates the juxtaposition of various videograms because, when combined with the blurring and unblurring tropes, the minor variance in the protagonist's positioning caused by the edits is barely noticeable to the user. Based on the user's input, the app instantly and seamlessly loads the videogram that corresponds to the selection, assembling a sequence of videos supporting the impression that a sensible dialogue is happening. These devices combine to establish a real-time montage method that provides a slick solution to the interactive storytelling problem of sustaining a naturalistic dialogue between an interactor and recorded footage. Karen also sometimes turns away from the camera when responding to some of the inputted answers, so you cannot see her lips move. This allows the app to load different audio-bites (appropriate to each answer) without having to film separate sequences for every answer. Although such conversational interactions do not strictly have a bearing on the overall story, they certainly give the impression that a more naturalistic conversation is happening in real time.

Considering the difficulty of creating believable real-time dialogue in interactive video, it is tenable that, in *Karen*, Blast Theory starts to establish a grammar for the dialogical problem that has baffled experimental interactive filmmakers since the beginning of the genre. Aside from the establishment of a technique for staging interactive dialogue with a computer, there is also the question of how to integrate the user's (audience's) private data and structure a narrative on the basis of behavioural profiling.

At the beginning, one is required to type basic profile information, like name, email address and so on. At one point you are also asked to enter the name of your 'significant other' (see Figure 6.2). This is an alarmingly personal detail that implicates a loved one beyond the bounds of the fiction, but it is a detail that becomes harmlessly pertinent to the narrative towards the end. On starting up the app, one must also grant permissions to allow the app to access the mobile device's location-based data. Blast Theory backs this up with a promise that doing so will enhance and help personalize the experience. If one is willing to give away their data to the 'internet giants', which make no bones about disclosing the fact that the personal data they harvest contributes to big data sets used for machine-learning under the rubric of enhanced consumer experiences, then why would one not give one's data to a small arts collective who contrarily promise to do nothing with it outside of the immediate app-drama? One should not lose sleep over giving location data to Blast Theory for the sake of art; however, sleep deprivation might kick in when Karen starts contacting you at night!

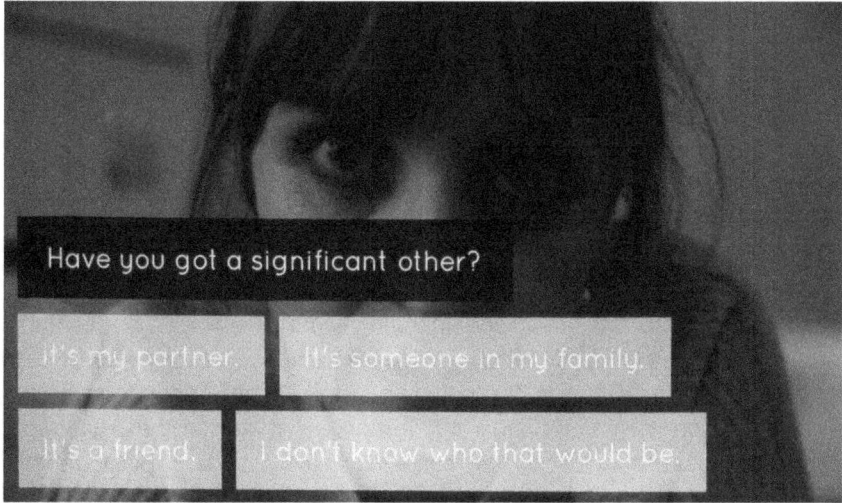

FIGURE 6.2 *Screenshot:* Karen. *Performer: Claire Cage (courtesy of Blast Theory).*

Dramaturgy

According to the makers, the work was conceived in order 'to create a personal and intimate experience for smartphones in which you interact directly with the lead character' (Adams 2015). The dramaturgy (or game-aturgy) is formulated on the basis that users are invited into an online life-coaching programme to be guided by the protagonist and mentor, Karen, but quickly get sucked into her chaotic world that confuses 'boundaries between her personal and professional lives' (Adams 2015).

From the outset, alarm bells start sounding because Karen presents as a flustered but charming free-lancer who greets the user on her doorstep, donned in a track-suit with hands full, immediately disintegrating expectations of professionalism. In the next video, as she begins her personality assessment, she assumes a more professional tone and dresses more appropriately to someone offering professional life-coaching services. However, in ensuing videos, the user is treated to increasingly informal encounters, from awkwardly interrupting her munching her breakfast or applying makeup, through a voyeuristic surveillance of her getting drunk with her roommate, to wallowing in her pyjamas and pining over her lost love. She increasingly crosses the line, contacting the user from her bedroom late at night, taking offence if you do not keep up regular contact, or 'cheekily pushing her friendliness into new areas' (Adams 2015). She becomes overly forthcoming with details about her personal life and, in return, expects reciprocation from the user, demanding frequent attention and wanting to know increasingly intimate details. 'You are aware that she is slightly intrusive, but if ... she's a slightly seductive figure, ...

a little bit chaotic and slightly comic, there's a greater tendency for you to give her a free pass' (Adams 2019), that is, to trust her, stay engaged in the app and answer truthfully. Adams explains: 'The driver was: in what ways could we collect data about each audience member in such a way that is both very rich, in terms of the experience we give them, and invites them to reflect on how [data were] collected and manipulated?' (Adams 2019).

In developing the narrative, Blast Theory worked with Dr Kelly Page (a Chicago-based researcher) whose work investigates 'web-profiling, data-harvesting and psychometric testing' (Adams 2019), which has led her to foster both a deep fascination and apprehension of the new socio-economic paradigm of dataveillance, which 'is the systematic use of personal data systems in the investigation or monitoring of the actions or communications of one or more persons' (Clarke 1988: 499). As noted, in the digital age, harvested data is the fuel of the marketing and PR sectors. Blast Theory's goal was to challenge 'how honest and open' (Adams 2015) people are, and how readily users surrender personal, private, vital details to friendly digital applications purporting to be personal companions. Frequently referred to as *intelligent personal agents* (IPAs), these are a new breed of software applications that simulate interpersonal interaction and are designed to appeal to users through emotive, psychological techniques. IPAs actively learn about users through information garnered from their digital footprints and carefully crafted questionnaires based on an established psychological-scholarly legacy of behavioural profiling. 'The app uses a combination of mood repair tests and psychometric evaluation systems, like the five-factor model, which companies routinely use to construct our consumer identities' (Khan 2015).[4] Through these techniques, *Karen* gathers information about a given user, based on phone usage and responses to her questions. 'Pretty much anytime Karen asks you a question we are drawing an inference from that question, about you. And so a profile is being built up in the background' (Adams 2019). Then, in the intermittences between video calls, she runs diagnostics on the data, learns from them, and modifies her own tone, dialogue and behaviour according to the type of interactor. As such, *Karen* is a provocative and 'deliberately unsettling experience' that challenges users into questioning 'the way we bare ourselves to a digital device' (Rose 2015).

Durational Time, Intermittence and Subversion of the Author–Audience Relation

The story-game is durational; it is designed to be experienced over a period of one-and-a-half to two weeks, but can last longer if one allows the 'appointments' slide. The video sessions, each lasting only a couple of minutes, take place on a daily, intermittent basis and increase in frequency as the story advances. The 'fictional interactions are interspersed with other quotidian activities of real life, blurring the lines between fiction and reality' (Mee 2016: 169). Their periodic, brief, punctuated and hyper-attentional nature makes them indistinguishable from other audio-visual and textual symbols that solicit our attention and comprise the fabric of daily digital cultural life. By surreptitiously becoming yet another attention-grabbing temporal object, Karen places demands on audiences to be at an appropriate place at the right time to take a session.

> Thus Karen offers ... a new location in which theatre can occur (on your smartphone) and a new time-frame for theatre (both in the sense that 'the play' takes two weeks to complete, and in that it is always and everywhere available via a phone app – and for an indefinite run).
>
> (Mee 2016: 169)

The videos 'ubiquitously install themselves in our daily life' (Stiegler 2011a: 146), redefining what Stiegler would call, our 'calendarity' and 'cardinality' (Stiegler 2011a: 146). Common across all socio-ethnic groups, these terms describe 'primordial' conditions of temporal and spatial organization (respectively). Historically constituted by night and day and geographical instincts, they have been deeply disturbed by the ability of the programming industries to solicit our attention anywhere on a 24/7 basis, thanks to that exosomatic prosthesis of mind and body: the smart phone. Analogous to the urban projection-mapping models discussed in the last chapter, this causes a deprivation of intermittence. Blast Theory taps into these conditions by mimicking the spatio-temperal operations of the programming industries, cajoling the audience into reflecting on the 'whole idea of *how* data is collected. And the idea of how *you* are the product' (Adams 2019).

The plot in *Karen* is peripheral to the rule-based setup, where the audience enter into a contract of participating in numerous sessions with Karen established as a life coach. It quickly becomes apparent that this convention turns the audience–author relation on its head. We are not watching Karen; she is watching us. The audience is the subject of the performer's inquisitive gaze; she, or *it*, 'is learning from us and feeding back to us' (Adams 2019). As Mee writes:

> The app itself, as it gathers data about me, is the audience – or spy ... *Karen* switches up traditional theatrical roles and relationships: I am not 'just' a 'passive spectator' I am cast in the play – as the lead character. My participation is both medium and message.
>
> (Mee 2016: 171)

Karen is not a protagonist who we watch empathetically; rather, she is the agent for an introspective investigation of the self and the new reality of sociocultural engagement over mobile devices. Adams says: 'we were fascinated to explore … what is it about us that makes us drawn to machines that reflect ourselves back at ourselves. Clearly there is a compulsion here which goes beyond purely a utilitarian model of technology' (Adams 2019). This statement clearly resonates with Stiegler's cogitations on the libidinal force at the heart of transitional objects and the economy of desire that they erect (discussed in the last chapter).

As opposed to technologically intensified site-specific performances that are experienced collectively, *Karen* is a performance game that is experienced in isolation. This negates the 'feedback loop of emotional contagion not just between performer and audience member, but also among audience members themselves' (Mee 2016: 168), which hinges on the paradigm of a collective experience of empathy. Therefore, Blast Theory subverts the experiential flow between the public and private realms that constitute the author–audience dynamic. *Karen* operates on the basis that participants' private experiences are externalized and publicized via process of data collection, which is contradictory to the traditional audience format of internalizing and interpreting an actor's public gesture. Adams says: 'A lot of the works we make in Blast Theory sit on the boundary between the very private and the very public' (Adams cited in Mee 2016: 168). Mee continues to analyse the significance of the inversion of privacy but deploys her argument on the basis of a dualism between the 'public' and the 'private', holding that the lesson of *Karen* is concerned with highlighting 'how and when we constantly shift between public and private in the course of our daily lives' (Mee 2016: 168). This is absolutely correct, but the discourse on the increasingly confused margins separating the private and public spheres is a thoroughly debated topic since Kant, through Foucault, to Deleuze. Aside from making the well-known claim that digital media further confuse those margins, Mee falls short of analysing, firstly, how digital surveillance and profiling technologies exacerbate the problem by causing a fundamental mutation in the cognitive sphere and, secondly, how they operate (especially by intercepting messages and interpreting them for us) and what the consequences are for the audience–public. In the next section it is shown how Blast Theory's employment of dataveillance and behavioural profiling frameworks exposes a fundamental cognitive mutation that has huge consequences for the intersubjective conditions of the contemporary sociocultural and political economy because the interior (private) realm is laid bare, discretized, reconstituted as digital traces in the exterior (public) realm and plundered by a technical agency, towards the goals of liberalism.

Algorithmic Governmentality and 24/7 Capitalism

When the user becomes embroiled in Karen's complicated love life, her flatmate Dave coxes you into being complicit in searching through her private affairs.[5] This is staged as a voyeuristic act of inverse surveillance because he brings the videophone into her bedroom and positions it so that you can watch him rifling through her personal possessions. Ironically, he retrieves *your* client file, gloats mischievously, then promptly hangs up. Karen then traces the data trail, exposes your breach of trust and confronts you about it, leaving you feeling utterly guilty and hypocritical. As such, one is impelled to reflect on the issue of trust through a sort of self-examination that follows a relationship crisis. The question of trust thus surfaces as a dominant theme in the app-drama; 'if you break her trust, she will absolutely interact with you in a very different way, than if you maintain confidentiality' (Adams 2019).

The fact that Karen is able to surveil our actions, make a character judgement and modify her own behaviour based on the results is deeply significant because it is representative of the horizon of activity taking place in the economy of profiling, tracking and big data – what Stiegler describes as 'the industry of traces' (Stiegler 2016: 22). The hyperindustrial global economy is founded on the condition that everything and everyone create traces (a digital footprint) – through interfaces, sensors and various electronic devices – that are recorded, stored, prepared and re-routed to big data sets, so that calculations can be performed on them by high-performance computers. These techniques represent 'the most advanced stage of a process of grammatisation' (Stiegler 2016: 19), in which previously intimate and private details – like individual behaviour and social relations – are laid bare and subjected to calculability.

The owners of the traces – who are not the people who made them – use the data to fabricate digital doubles of individuals, with a view to exploiting them for profit and political persuasion. As shown in the last chapter through the analysis of projection-mapping and Joi, these data-doppelgangers are commodified and plugged into the unceasing electronic transactions of the 24/7 economies of hyperindustrial capitalism and algorithmic governance, where they are subjected to automated calculations that control consumer behaviour and influence decision-making. The owners of *the means of calculation* (the means of control) exploit the traces in a way that occasions a new, clandestine form of proletarianization, where the consumer's mind and spirit are put to work simply by being connected to the network. Furthermore, these hegemonic controllers of traces have the power to intervene in – intensify or curtail – the processes of individuation that determine the becoming (or non-becoming) of individuals and collectives.

The existence of an interpretative faculty is crucial for any possibility of individuation because interpretation is central to the process of individuals consolidating singular present experiences with their unique fund of past experiences (diachronization). The effect that industrial temporal objects have on this process – by denying individuals the possibility of singular experiences and filling them instead with generic, mediocre and mass-produced ones – has been explicated. However, still more deleterious is the consequence that processes of individuation are short-circuited by a *denial of the opportunity to interpret* because hermeneutic processes are automatized; that is, human subjects are overtaken by their digital double, who interprets in their place. To bypass interpretative processes is to systematically impede the fundamentals of thinking and this constitutes the control strategy of 'algorithmic governmentality' (Rouvroy and Berns 2013). *Karen* stages this problem superbly because the act of interpretation, previously within the purview of the spectator, is surrendered to the machine; the machine interprets the spectator's private data and enacts a performance on the garnered knowledge. There is a proletarianization of the spectator because they are reduced to a function of the app-drama, which is fuelled by the human (audience) data. The proletarianization occurs on two levels: firstly, the programme cannot progress without the psychosomatic clicking/swiping (work) of the human; secondly, the noetic exteriorizations (the traces of the mind) of the spectator are harvested by the app and *put to work* in the service of generating the narrative. There is, henceforth, a putting to work of the cognitive aspects of the human psyche, as well as the physical aspects, that parallels techniques used in the contemporary hyperindustrial economy.

Automation is now so ubiquitous and penetrates so deeply into the fabric of cognitive processes that it dominates the formulation of thought itself, not by way of a subconscious hypnosis or brainwashing, but through *pure speed*, by outpacing and overtaking the human mind and its ability to conjure thoughts from its own depths. In the digital era, *protentions* become automatized in equal measure to the expanding pervasiveness of *tertiary retentions* which formulate experience and therefore identity.[6] The reticulated logic of algorithmic governmentality operates by segregating networked individuals, flooding their consciousnesses with prefabricated experiences and outstripping the mind's ability to anticipate, or theorize (Anderson 2008). The protentions that are formulated are, henceforth, homogenized, mundane and lacking critical potency. Thus, the prevalence and embeddedness of automated processes in quotidian intersubjectivity reveal the technological milieu as having a profound political and economic efficacy. Through ubiquitous nested processes of automation, reticulated digital networks occasion a situation that gives rise to another surreptitious mass exclusion (in addition to the existing exclusion from symbolic production). The perpetual, unceasing metrics that are performed on the statistical simulation of the self comprise a deeply rooted 'technological performativity' that opens an overpowering and esoteric new regime of truth (Rouvroy and Berns 2013: 164). Stiegler explains:

> This regime of truth is founded on the permanent capture of data, on the computational operations performed on this data, and on the digital doubles that are formed as a result. These digital doubles interact in real time with those whom they double, and with the new data these doubles generate and extract by going faster than those they double – hence producing an immediate retroactive effect on the operating sequences of populations.
>
> (Stiegler 2016: 103)

The embodied individual is overtaken by its digital doppelganger, which can act-out in the automated economies in a superhuman capacity, tirelessly, without sleep or intermittence. The owners of the means of calculation carry out metrics on the digital double, profiling it, quantifying it, averaging it and categorizing it with a view to corralling it into sets that simplify singularities into shared qualities for the sake of statisticalization. These automatized operations manifest as a short-circuiting of individuation because the exchange of knowledge takes place between proxies that substitute the individual and collective, homogenizing consciousnesses. Considering that the culture industries of the twentieth century created a situation in which the consumer (the receiver of messages) was proletarianized under the economy of attention, now we are 'reaching a stage where it is possible to purely and simply destroy the proletariat, that is, to replace the proletariat by machines' (Stiegler 2015a). The ability for the proletarianized consumer to select a consumable and choose to take action is short-circuited by the automated algorithm that selects and acts in their place.[7] This precipitates a situation which is even more deleterious than that of analogue media because consumers, led to believe that they have infinite choice, unbounded freedom and are acting on spontaneous impulses, are actually making choices within an automatically generated set – gathered and served up by automated robots – that offers all the illusions of freedom without any of the existential payoffs.

Blast Theory astutely stages this paradox of proletarianization. In the app-drama, the efficacy of computation determines and progresses the narrative structure, analogous to the *computer-as-performance-partner* paradigm explored by Troika Ranch, Obermaier and Chunky Move; however, Blast Theory structures the framework in a way that engages the audience under the contrivance that they are interacting with a human agent. *Karen* is ultimately a performance concerning the performativity of a non-human, robotic software application, dressed up as a human life-coach; a human is assigned the role of being the face of a participatory performance that is anything but human.

Under the pressure exerted by the technical milieu, the actor also suffers a proletarianization, which is a metastasis of the type instantiated by the film camera in cinema. As previously mentioned, the interpersonal relation experienced through the performer–audience feedback loop is short-circuited by the audience's solipsistic interaction with the automaton. The hyper-rationalistic conclusion of this is, just like the audience, the performer is overtaken by the machine and reduced to a function of the algorithm. *Karen* opens the thought of a situation in which the performer and the audience are obsolesced because the performing algorithms (robots) perform for the digital doppelganger – human presence is a footnote to the performance. By connoting a proletarianization of the minds and bodies of both the audience and actor, the application satirizes the hyperindustrial economy, challenging the audience to reflect on the totality of the contemporary sociocultural, political and economic situation, and its trajectory towards generalized and total automatization.

Socio-politically, the paradigm aims 'to reduce decision-making time [and] to eliminate the useless time of reflection and contemplation' (Crary 2014: 40). These activities are 'useless' to the logic of capitalism because, given that attention and connectivity fuel the economy, independent thought is not calculable (monetizable) and it has the potential to disrupt wealth distribution. It is in the interests of the incumbents (the owners of the means of calculation) to minimize contemplation by interacting with, and reprogramming, the digital double, to install a prevailing global despondency and a *disbelief* 'that it is possible to change human behaviour' (Stiegler 2018: 35). The interaction between hypercapitalist algorithms and digital doubles occasions a situation where we all live 'under the weight of a common protection that is massively negative on a worldwide scale' (Stiegler 2018). For Stiegler, capitalism represents nihilism on a grand scale, which achieves the epitome of its manifestation in the global emergency of the Anthropocene.[8] In the current epoch of digitalized automation, the industrial production of tertiary retentions amounts to the fabrication of impotent protentions that foreclose the will to act in accordance with the prediction of a catastrophic future. Stiegler writes:

> The combination of the network effect, the self-production of traces, user profiling and real-time supercomputing indeed generates an industrial short-circuit and a systemic elimination of those protentions that are incalculable, subjecting all will to a form of levelling.
>
> (Stiegler 2018: 37)

Stiegler's analysis of the current stage of the Anthropocene concludes that capitalism has generated a general negative protention that collectively railroads the world economies towards a scenario of self-harm; that is, hypercapitalism promotes a totalizing 'protention of nihil, of nothing' (Stiegler 2018: 37) and, therefore, can be understood as the fulfilment of nihilism par excellence. Stiegler's philosophical programme attempts to unpack what positive aspects and approaches can be elicited from the current techno-economic situation; what values, attributes and knowledge paradigms can be mobilized in the opposite direction to the nihilistic global despondency, without denying the serious legitimacy of the situation?

A New Critical Vocabulary for the New Economy

In an attempt to think innovatively on the impasse of aesthetics, socio-politics and economics, Stiegler employs *systems theory* to discuss these problems. He describes the symbolic misery produced under the economic mode of twentieth-century capitalism as an *entropic* process (Stiegler 2015a).[9] By the law of entropy, capitalism is a chaotic system produced by singularly organized parts that usurp resources, dissipating energy towards the stabilization of the collective through socio-economic processes that are fundamentally regressive. Hyperindustrial capitalism is entropic in character because: (1) the receiver of a communication is *only* a receiver, not at all a producer, participant or dialogist; (2) it squanders time and energy by co-opting the attention of consumers; and (3) it inhibits differentiation by statisticalizing and homogenizing personae, reducing cultural diversity and curtailing the potential for processes of individuation, ultimately cauterizing knowledge and exacerbating the potential for the destruction of thought – thinking itself runs the risk of annihilation (Stiegler 2015a). Therefore, the unitary challenge in contemporaneity is to address the catastrophe of the Anthropocene by *reversing* the entropic flux, that is, by generating *negative entropy*.[10] Economic policies must be rethought in the context of a responsible organology that places care and concern at the heart of its programme. There is an urgent need for humanity to be re-injected into the hyper-capitalist system, which has been set to autopilot.

The Goal of Art in the Hyperindustrial Economy

Stiegler maintains that the individualistic creative force of the artist maintains the ability to rupture – or *bifurcate*[11] – the entropic tendency of the programming industries. He constructs a pseudo-scientific metaphor based on *bifurcation theory* to describe a type of avant-garde, technical poiēsis that is provocative and inventive and has an inherent ability to disrupt, shock and perhaps even reverse the destructive entropy of the programming industries. He writes: 'Becoming ... requires inventiveness – it requires *"inventivity"*' (Stiegler 2018: 43). This 'inventivity' constitutes the bifurcations that can completely reverse the topology of a system of *non-becoming*, of no future. For Stiegler, artistic creativity can turn the entropic economy into a *negentropic* one, catalysing the transition from the Anthropocene to the Neganthropocene – from the Entropocene to the Negentropocene (Stiegler 2018). The key enquiry for contemporary art is, what questions can be asked of the *current* technologies – which organize the cerebral impulses that constitute perception, memory and anticipation – that could help positively rebuild individual and collective identities in the digital epoch? Art must continue along the political agenda of the avant-garde and engaging technology is key to this. Although he is not afraid to employ the term (despite its historical baggage), Stiegler tries to conceive a new vocabulary for art to proceed along political lines. He suggests that the creative endeavours of the new world economy need to be *negentropic* in character:

> I believe that we haven't articulated really, really strongly the artistic questions, the aesthetic questions, that are always questions of singularity. And singularity is always the *bifurcation*, in the sense of systems theory, of *negentropic* systems theory. A bifurcation is that which is producing a negentropic stage, a *new* negentropic stage of a system. The goal of arts, not only art, but particularly of arts, in society, is to produce such negentropy.
>
> (Stiegler 2015a)

Stiegler is clear on his opinion that art, as a singular (unique and exceptional) process and outcome, embodies a small and smooth external force which, when input into the hyperindustrial system (which is suffused with processes of automation, standardization and symbolic duplication), can cause a bifurcation that could dramatically change the topology of the socio-economic landscape. Art can rupture, change and even reverse the pernicious entropy of the programming industry, which is, in its current stage of automatic proletarianization, the epitome of nihilism: capitalism. Capitalism always tends towards entropy, towards dissipation. Avant-garde praxis embodies the bifurcation necessary to drive the global economy towards a negentropic model, so these bifurcations need to be inputted regularly and frequently. The singularity of art stands in opposition to the programming industry's hyperautomatized production of symbols because, firstly, the care and attention that constitute artistic praxis condition an irreproducibility that flies in the face of automated symbolic production and, secondly, the conditions of its engagement and associated milieu subvert and evade the programming industry's production–distribution paradigm of statisticalized, profile-based viewership. This provides *a way around* that disindividuating short-circuit that leads to the proletarianization of the consumer and then to the destruction of the proletariat. *A bifurcation is an avant-garde gesture.* A contemporary bifurcation is a technologically engaged work of art that undermines the dominant symbolic and socio-economic regimes. But how? What are the strategies?

Bifurcation Points in the Hyperindustrial Economy

In the context of increasing regimes of speed – that operate now, in digital automata, at the speed of light – it is thinking that possesses the 'infinite speed of the power to rupture, to effect breaks, that is, to cause bifurcations by disautomatizing repetitive regularities and by changing the rules' (Stiegler 2018: 41). Changing the rules that formulate the basis of socio-economics and politics levels an abstract critique at their totality, compelling audiences to reflect on the oppressive nature of automated retentions and protentions, thereby reinvigorating the singularity of psychic and collective thought, and the diversity of individuation, generally. Stiegler declares that *to change the rules* is to go faster than the bewildering light-speed processes by which digital automata operate. Changing the rules concerns a technologically engaged noesis that can counteract the system of *total automatization* that is responsible for the seizure, co-option and simulation of memories, perception, ambitions and, therefore, care. This challenge is brought into unprecedented urgency by the rollout of digital technologies that impel not only a hyper-acceleration of socio-economic and productive processes but also a situation of total *grammatization*, that is, a *hypermodernity* in which 'we are experiencing the industrialisation of all things' (Stiegler 2014: 47), including the spirit. Thus, the essential question is, how can we proceed with *care* and *responsibility* in relation to our socio-economic condition of dataveillance, big data, user-profiling and machine-learning, when these tools are being exploited by public relations for radicalizing politics, especially by right wing neoliberalists?[12] The prolongation of neoliberalist policies is placing a huge strain on the environment and, in the context of the Anthropocene, threatens the future of the species as a whole. Thus, for Stiegler, grammatization is the core socio-technological phenomenon that needs to be addressed. Given the ecstasy experienced by calculation – in its coming to rule not just productive processes but, indeed, all aspects of life and knowledge – how can artists continue to communicate the idioms that give art its unique and mysterious power, while also engaging the latest technological developments in a way that is negentropic, that is, humane, holistic and progressively moral? Artists need to produce poetry which, on one hand, engages the dominant subjectivities of hypermodernity, concerning the impact of technology and reticulated systems on the bodies and minds of publics and administrations, and on the other hand, repurposes, re-invents and gives new meaning to the rapidly evolving tools and technologies, by employing them in innovative and surprising ways.

As in the case of all instrumental advancements, the computer changes the relations between knowledge, intersubjectivity and methods of expression and, therefore, alters the entire modality of epistemology. However, the computer does so in a monumental fashion, by positioning calculation at the root of all expression. It is at the level of automated calculation and the befuddling speed of electronic networks that the contemporary status of being-in-the-world needs to be critiqued. The deployment of a critical art practice that interrogates the essence of calculation (and the impact it has on the technical, cultural, political and economic landscapes) could help re-route public attention towards the significance of its omnipresence and the ontological and epistemological agency it has in modernized societies. This is precisely why Blast Theory's engagement with digital media's most cutting-edge specificities, in *Karen*, is so significant.

Eliciting the New Specificities

In *Karen*, amongst many of their other works, Blast Theory employs computational specificities that are only possible now in the digital age, establishing themselves as quintessentially digital performance artists. Their praxis is not simply a case of employing computers to assist expression; they tackle the essence of digital culture by engaging computation itself – the algorithm. As both material and process, numbers are the essence of digital culture. By quantifying their audience and performing calculations on the data, Blast Theory identifies this dual characteristic of numbers and highlights its new cultural importance. They demonstrate inventiveness by mobilizing profiling and tracking techniques in a direction that was previously unthought, that is, towards an epistemic territory that is neither dramatic art nor science, but somewhere between. In this sense, the work defies classification and this quality maintains the power to rupture – that is to bifurcate.

By engaging digital technologies at their fundamental essence, Blast Theory draws out the specificities of contemporary computational culture, which are the multi-layered processes of automation (enacted on the server side) that perform metrics on users' biological, behavioural and geospatial data on a permanent, non-stop basis. Blast Theory's dramaturgical reorganization of these techniques towards a cultural innovation is an example of inventive storytelling. *They change the rules.* In this work we witness an innate ability to reconfigure the regulatory matrix, that is, to travel faster than the speed that fibre-optics pulse messages into the retentional reserve of the human cognitive faculty. Their amalgamation of automated user-metrics with drama compels a reinterpretation of surveillance technologies as having a semi-autonomous creative force, with an efficacy that is far more advanced and powerful than the cognitive technologies of previous eras. Blast Theory not only demonstrates the negentropic quality of its praxis, but also shows how inventive and unusual employments of technical know-how can open up new epistemological pathways.

The artists direct an activism at both the institute of art and the broader topology of the socio-political economy because their work calls for a revaluation of both the work and the audience. This innovative uptake of cutting-edge computational techniques and materials that were previously unavailable to artists, combined with a socio-political provocativeness, testifies to the avant-gardist nature of their work. Furthermore, their work subverts calculation and rational scientific method because the technical knowledge is deployed towards an end that has no goal other than the advancement of an artificial narrative. Tracking technologies and behavioural profiling algorithms, originally conceived for automatically identifying, segregating, persuading, manipulating and commodifying individuals (all specifically hyperindustrial objectives), are repurposed towards artifice and fiction: idioms. Thus, contemporary socioculture is exposed and subverted; its meaning is undermined because what is essentially a hyperrational framework, for cajoling individuals into becoming 'dividuals' (Deleuze and Guattari 2004: 376), is mobilized for the output of a comic, emotive and self-reflexive app-drama – an artefactual exercise that holds very little *value* under the capitalist barometer of value.

Karen is original, novel and inventive. It demonstrates the creative potential of new variations on established scientific methods and systematic processes that constitute contemporary quotidian existence. By re-harnessing and repurposing the new tools and technologies, Blast Theory reconceives the manner in which they are mobilized and the ends which they serve, offering new possibilities for the role of automatons in narrative disclosure and revealing the curative aspects of automatization. Importantly, it is not just the tracking technologies and behavioural modelling techniques that are repurposed and subverted in this artwork; more significantly, the artists' satirical reinvention implicitly highlights the pernicious potential of the convergence of computer science and psychology when deployed under the remit of a neoliberalist agenda. Since the 1920s, marketing and public relations have been refining methods of targeting and persuading demographics with ever greater effectiveness; now, by inputting harvested data to deep learning computational models, they have been furnished with a method for discretizing, examining and isolating individuals with unprecedented accuracy, ultimately, achieving the goals of neoliberalism.[13]

The ends of scientific research are very different to those of artistic research. The sciences must always qualify their findings within the ambit of a specific field of study; the arts attempt to dissolve boundaries and blur distinctions. The sciences set very specific and attainable goals, with an envisaged output for a specific use; the arts do not set goals beyond the totality of the work itself, nor does it generally have a specific end in mind, beyond the ambit of the sensible. The sciences work to prove a hypothesis, erect 'value tables' and make them fact, to construct reality; the arts hypothesize through work to question values, to disprove the facts which are perceived as an edifice for reality, a fiction whose rules change depending on the dominant socio-political ideology. The sciences are restricted by industrial parameters, monetizable goals and ethics committees; the arts and humanities are too, but they can move faster. Therein lies the power of art: by undermining use value, or quantifiable worth, it is set free to conduct forays into unknown territory beyond the carefully mapped catchment areas of science and to wander unrestricted in uncultivated domains; it is up to the sciences to catch up, to stabilize the terrain. This is exactly what Blast Theory is doing; by appropriating computer scientific and psychological knowledge – such as data harvesting and behavioural profiling – and directing the methods down pathways that science simply could not conceive, they are sojourning in the open space of pure creation. In mobilizing scientific processes towards original, innovative creativity in interactive digital storytelling, Blast Theory is injecting a bifurcation into the utilitarian topology of the techno-scientific economy, contributing to its reconstitution as a negentropic system. They achieve this by repurposing *both* the psychological knowledge and the automatized efficacy of machine learning and *hot-wiring them*. That is, they reconfigure the circuits of knowledge, rerouting rational, quantitative techno-scientific processes towards generating irrational, qualitative artifice.

Conclusion: Towards a Nascent Grammar of Digital Scenography

At the outset of this book it was stated that the goal is to produce a nascent grammar of digital scenography, which is epistemically and pedagogically useful for practitioners in articulating aesthetic endeavours and for scholars in reflecting on work and engaging related critical discourse. Over the six chapters, I have traced a particular genealogy of experimental scenographic works at the nexus of the performing arts and technology to assemble a narrative that corroborates the need for and usefulness of such a grammar. The case studies of Troika Ranch, Stelarc, Klaus Obermaier, Chunky Move, OnionLab (and *Blade Runner 2049*) and Blast Theory were selected because the genealogical trajectory through their avant-garde innovations – negentropic bifurcations – affirms the emergence of new modes of expression, and these demand a new characteristic grammar that will help map this rapidly evolving field. This nascent grammar should not be simplistically interpreted as exhaustive or exclusive; that is, it is not a list of qualities that works must satisfy to gain admittance to the genre, nor is it definitive. The field of digital scenography is evolving rapidly because so is technology; therefore, as the field matures and expands so too will the grammar have to be refined and extended in future scholarly discourse. Also, by attempting to articulate a grammar it is not intended to close down the field by naming it, but to help nurture a methodology and vocabulary that creatives and scholars can identify with and employ for decoding digital scenography. With this in mind, I suggest that this nascent digital scenographic grammar is defined along the following lines: political agency, singularity, (in)determinism, innovative repurposing, digital specificity, noetic reactivation and increasing technological performativity.

Political Agency

Digital scenography tends to be inherently political because, by employing the (now digital) material artefacts and techniques that constitute contemporary reality, it challenges audiences to examine the industrial temporal objects and mediated transactions that comprise contemporary existence. As shown in the introduction, activism levelled at the institution of art and at the broader socio-political regime is an unavoidably avant-gardist characteristic that has generally become a defining quality of contemporary art. Through its experimentalism, technologically engaged art is manifestly linked to the avant-garde; therefore, it is inherently political because, by implementing various material superstructural elements of capitalism, it impels a critique of the abstract, exploitative base. The digital scenographies engineered for the intermedial performances that comprise this genealogy mimic and parody the computational processes (like biometrics, tracking, dataveillance and so on) enacted under the ambit of the digitalized socio-economy.

Capitalism functions by placing a (numerical, monetizable, calculable) value on everything. Anything that cannot be 'valued' under its quantitative criteria is deemed invaluable, labelled an exception, denied 'legitimacy' and perceived as a threat to the statistical and denotative pragmatics of late capitalism (Lyotard 1984). This huge emphasis on *calculability* is undergirded by the positioning of exchange value at the heart of socio-economics and by mobilizing it as a barometer or unitary scale; thus, capitalism places a numerical value on all things. This is how capitalism warps 'the essential question touching on the life of human societies' (Stiegler 2018: 60). By insisting that everything (including art which fundamentally challenges functionality) be shoehorned into a denotative, over-rationalized and numerical model, capitalism strips everything of those values that bear no relation to economics and functionality; the very meaning of value itself becomes distorted. Temporal avant-garde gestures tend to elude the massive interpenetration of capitalism and art because capitalism struggles to superimpose its hyper-rationalistic yardstick over transitory, furtive intersubjective experiences that cannot be bottled and resold; that is, avant-garde outputs 'are those so-called unproductive expenditures' (Stiegler 2018: 60) that create bifurcations within the entropic topology of the capitalist means–ends paradigm. Furthermore, since the early aesthetic cogitations of Kant, it is widely agreed that aesthetic judgement operates through a system of morals; the reflexive judgement at the heart of aesthetic reflection is essentially a moral judgement. Art flies in the face of capitalism because it demands a moral judgement of the subject; capitalism responds by attempting to redefine aesthetic judgement on the basis of a numerical value.

CONCLUSION

For Stiegler, the singular and event-based nature of *avant-garde* art manifests in its ability to destabilize and subvert the capitalist conception of *value*. This can affect change in the socio-economic system that is taking increasing liberties with privacy, tracking, dataveillance and so on, to the demise of individuality, in particular, and the principle of individuation, generally. In the spirit of Nietzsche, Stiegler calls for a 'transvaluation'[1] of the 'economic values and moral devalorizations' (Stiegler 2018: 38), which are the derivative decompositions of that epitome of nihilism – unrestrained capitalism. Stiegler says:

> The goal of arts, not only art, but particularly of arts, in society, is to produce such negentropy ... that is, the production of non-calculable value. This is what Nietzsche calls 'the value of value' ... because it is in the arts that the experience of 'the value of value' as non-calculable is obvious for everybody.
>
> (Stiegler 2015a)

When Nietzsche speaks of value, he is referring to morality (Nietzsche, Clark and Swensen 1998: 33), but morals are non-calculable and are, therefore, counter-intuitive to the logic of capitalism. In this regard, immanent in Stiegler's reference to Nietzsche is the desire to reposition the question of morality back at the locus of a sociocultural and economic discourse that is currently dominated by discretization, statisticalization and calculation. These qualities serve only to short-circuit morality, ethics and *care* because they eliminate singularities in favour of dehumanized, homogenized sets. Art holds the means to reinvigorate, or 'transvaluate', morality (Nietzsche and Ludovici 2013: sec. IV 'The Will to Power in Art').

All the artists examined in this genealogy engage various specificities of digital technology to produce politically charged work, using practice-based methodologies founded on thematics that are abrasive towards dominant, homogeneous culture; that is, they are negentropic in character. Their practical reifications of intensive theoretical and technical critique each constitute an aesthetic rupture that fundamentally moves art-going publics to question, firstly, the fallaciousness at the centre of the artwork's receding towards autonomous artifice and, secondly, the fictions and narratives that contrive dominant, socio-political ideologies, and reality in general. Aside from the works themselves, the interviews with each of the artists testify to a predominance of the will to agitate incumbent tastes, aesthetic dogmas and political-cultural ideologies, validating the persistence of socio-political abrasiveness in contemporary digital scenographic expression. It is the domain of (critical and political) avant-garde art to produce the bifurcational ruptures that could interfere or transform the entropic flux of hyperindustrial capitalism.

The bifurcations of which Stiegler speaks are a pseudo-scientific metaphor for the socio-political provocations originally carried out by the artistic avant-garde and which are now the task of contemporary digital artists. It is through techno-political art that a transvaluation of value is possible *'because it is in the arts that the experience of "the value of value" as non-calculable is obvious for everybody'* (Stiegler 2015a). It is for these reasons that a nascent grammar of digital scenography, and of all digital art, should firstly be expounded along the lines of a political agency.

Singularity

It was established that every technological development is pharmacological – simultaneously toxic and remedial. In terms of socio-economics and systems theory, this can be understood as the ability for technical developments to either cause an 'acceleration of entropy' (Stiegler 2018: 41) through the dissipation of energy, the control of protentions and the industrial standardization of psychic and collective individuations or an 'accentuation of negentropy' (Stiegler 2018: 41) through new, singular, acts of ingenuity, which are processes of 'artefactual ontogenesis' (Stiegler 2018: 43). This is why the question of the valuation of value, the transvaluation of *moral* values, is so pertinent, because the fundamentals of the dominant political, socio-economic ideology and its rationale for making, doing, expressing, communicating, listening and interpreting are in need of an urgent revaluation of morals. Given that human phylogenesis is tending towards stasis and equilibrium (see Chapter 2), it is the artistic ontogenetic surges that hold the potential to create bifurcations necessary to interrupt hypercapitalist topologies. Stiegler's mobilization of systems theory gives affirmation to his insistence on the responsibility of the arts to take up its political (*avant-garde*) duty and create the much-needed ruptures (*bifurcations*) within this system, by producing unique, new, singular and, therefore, therapeutic work that counter-acts that toxic, homogenizing type mass-produced under the ambit of the programming industries.

Each example of digital scenography analysed in this book is singular, in the sense that it is unique and monumental. In the cases of Troika Ranch's and Stelarc's productions they are once-off performances – at least, very difficult to repeat. In the case of the others, they are repeatable, but subsequent iterations vary considerably because the automatons behave indeterminately based on singular interactions. Hyperindustrial production does not compute the 'singular', only replication, duplication and standardization. Thinking about this in terms of socio-politics, the singularity of these works flies in the face of hyperindustrial society because its reliance on the database model demands that everything and everyone be identified, categorized, tabularized and placed in standing reserve for easy access and processing. Troika Ranch, Stelarc, Obermaier, Chunky Move, OnionLab and Blast Theory all apply hyper-rational, techno-scientific knowledge in fundamentally irrational and singular ways, producing gestures of *incalculable value*. Scientific knowledge is usually employed for conducting very fine-grained empirical experiments concerning the appraisal of how given elements relate and react under very specific, controlled conditions. However, under the remit of artistic experimentalism the knowledge is employed for producing events of fascination – pure artifice. Experimentalism is crucial to both knowledge domains; however, the open-ended and indeterminate outcome of artistic praxis subverts the rigorous, tightly controlled laboratory conditions of the sciences that insist on the reproducibility of the subject. This agitates against the dominant perception that 'the digital' automatically means reproducibility, thereby levelling an abstract political statement at hypercapitalist socio-economics, and this represents the locus of the rationale for emphasizing the importance of singularity in any grammar of digital scenography.

(In)determinism

The digital scenographies examined in this genealogy are mobilized in the opposite direction to that of symbols produced for mass culture because the collision of the human and automaton at the heart of the system is unpredictable; the processes are uncertain and experimental, and the outcomes are unforeseen and expressionistic.

The indeterminate processes and artefacts are the result of mischievous introductions of artistic performance practices into highly rationalized, computational frameworks. They playfully undermine the technically scaffolded promise of societal progress through rationalization and structure because the works give primacy to spontaneity and improvisation over adherence to a fixed script. The expressionistic subject–object relations of non-narrative performance have a rich heritage in the historical avant-garde, which is concerned with drawing attention to the 'invisible propaganda, which ... establishes and perpetuates itself as ... common-sense' (Foulkes 1983) through the culture industry's production of fantastically distracting and emotive popular cinema. Avant-garde improvisation operates along a methodology of advancing the notion of infinite possibility, abstractly drawing the audience's attention to the rigorous determinism and constraint scheduled into their lives via the technocratic programming industries. This determinism constrains end users, whose increasingly suppressed impulse and restricted freedom precipitate a disenchanted public.

The digital scenographers in this genealogy take their impetus from the praxis of the historical avant-garde and they seek to operate in an analogously agitative manner. However, in these digital works, agitation is introduced by the performer–material relations that can be metaphorically interpreted as a sort of viral infection injected into the (algorithmic and mathematical) rule-based systems that also scaffold broader technocratic control procedures. Pertinently, this is in keeping with Norbert Wiener's thesis on cybernetics, asserting that organic lifeforms, 'which locally swim upstream against the current of increasing entropy' (Wiener 1989: 32), represent necessary injections of indeterminacy that help transform simple closed mechanical systems into 'life-imitating machines … that [can] exemplify locally anti-entropic processes' normally only visible in the 'physical, chemical, and spiritual processes of life' (Wiener 1989). Capitalism's entropic drive towards control and regulation (always for profit) is evinced by the pressure exerted on governments by wealthy, influential internet service providers to introduce a two-tiered internet that would end net neutrality (Pil Choi and Kim 2010; McCabe 2019) – a move that is counter to the positive potential of cybernetics explained by Weiner.

Digital scenography is essentially founded on a paradigm of interfacing humans with cybernetic systems; the life-affirming potential of which Wiener speaks manifests through the mise-en-scène of computers and performers. Humans are the indeterminate element in cybernetic systems that can drive the overall topology towards negentropy. Expanding this modality to algorithmic governance (total automation) insists that humans must stay involved and digital scenography represents the domain where unrestricted experimentalism can help define future potentialities and standards. This explains why digital scenography, as the leading domain investigating *the intersection of human performativity with technical performativity*, must maintain indeterminism at the heart of its praxis.

Innovative Repurposing

Technological engagements are of course the means of achieving avant-garde goals; however, simply employing technology to stage old ideas was neither enough for a project to make the cut for inclusion in this book nor is it enough to build a grammar on. Each of the projects discussed here involved the repurposing of a cutting-edge technology – biometric sensing, plastic surgery and genetic engineering, computer vision, motion-tracking, projection-mapping, mobile GPS tracking, data harvesting or user profiling – towards the development of a bespoke, new application. The artists adopted a common strategy of reconfiguring current technological innovations and automatized processes with a view to subversion, producing hardware and/

or software applications that amounted to indeterminate, irrational artifice, yet energized monumental art Events. As such, the works operate by a subliminal parody of hyper-rationalized automatism because the artists are feeding the machines idiomatic, non-calculable data that results in performance events that are singular, indeterminate, unrateable yet cutting-edge. These qualities scaffold a strategy based on mimetically adapting to the capitalist consumer paradigm that is inherently tied to newness and innovation, which underpin the spectacle. By doing so, the artworks abstractly expose the importance that capitalist ideology places on innovation and automation. Hence, on the one hand, they establish their eloquence by subscribing to the capitalist celebration of the new and, on the other hand, they exhibit an intolerance for artworks and audiences that are traditional, inoffensive, unintellectual and non-political – that is, works that are devoid of noetic thought. It is the task of digital scenographers to innovatively re-harness technology and champion new potentialities in performative human–computer spectacles.

Digital Specificity

Just as digital specificity was an important qualifying criterion for the genealogy, so too now is its place in the nascent grammar as essential. Each project engages specificities of digital technologies and/or thematic aspects of digital culture in a unique way, whether that be: the biometric sensing of Troika Ranch, the medical and surgical interventions of Stelarc, the motion-tracking and projection-mapping of Obermaier and their epistemic furtherance by Chunky Move, the large-scale urban projection-mappings of OnionLab, or the biopolitical dataveillance and behavioural profiling of Blast Theory.

All processes of expression – whether aesthetic, noetic, technical, political or otherwise – are constituted by the exteriorized trace, which is, in the digital epoch, a highly complex, fluid, interactive, fragmented, networked, modularized, discretized, automated, participatory and multifarious object. It is the task and test of the digital scenographer to create artefacts that elicit these specificities and mobilize them in a direction that gathers: a nuanced interplay of form and content, a poetic indeterminacy, a unique and singular identity and an inspirational quality. The best technologically engaged artworks are always those that invite us to ask: 'What is the thought that the [digital] is thinking or inviting us to think? What happens inside the virtual … unto itself? Where does art collide with technology?' (O'Dwyer et al. 2020: 211). Thirty years on, the ontology of the digital 'is still incredibly interesting, and philosophically problematic, as to what it is and how we exist within these virtual domains' (O'Dwyer et al. 2020: 208).

The design-led performances selected for this volume all, in some way, elicit digital specificities, thereby drawing attention to the internal workings of the thing itself and begging questions concerning mechanisms that undergird the socio-political and economic bases. By doing so, they abstractly probe deeper and deeper into the ontology of the digital, that is, into questions of being and existence concerning the contemporary hypermodern human subject. There is nothing to stop contemporary practitioners firing a digital projection onto the stage and calling it digital performance, but for the work to be noticed, and commended, it needs to interrogate the essence of 'the digital' by drawing out its specificities. Art that draws attention to its own internal mechanisms – and, by complicity, to the analogous external, efficacious mechanisms of the socio-technical milieu – is noetic.

Noetic Reactivation

Stiegler writes: 'It is ... imperative to completely rethink the noetic fact, and to do so in every field of knowledge, whether of living, doing or conceptualizing' (Stiegler 2018: 38). When art ceases to be noetic – and this is very much the case for mainstream symbolic production under the programme industry – it is indicative of a society that has lost the will to think independently; art should inspire thought. This point also reiterates the importance that Stiegler allocates to the role of artists as critical political commentators in the new hyperindustrial economy. Just as the aesthetic question is a political question, the noetic question is a technical question because 'the noetic soul is a technical form of life' (Stiegler 2018: 40). Given that the avant-garde is a techno-political domain, it is logical that it should be the front-line of aesthetic-noetic endeavours. This convergence of noetic experience with aesthetic experience infers that it is through avant-garde artistic praxis that noetic experience can achieve its highest state. Therefore, digital scenography – as an arbitrator of performance practice and technical expertise – represents a domain of high potential for taking up the mantle of the avant-garde and levelling topical political critique at the hypercapitalist economy.

Each artist in the genealogy identifies with the need for a recursive reworking of the techno-aesthetic-political question – that is, the avant-garde question – and therefore *shows* the invaluable value of historical referencing in the formation of noetic praxis, in the manner that an apprentice would watch a master. This is the apprenticeship that Deleuze sought to elucidate as difference, that is, learning through careful repetition. As described in Chapter 4, this noetic reactivation, which concerns seeing 'a work by showing *what it makes us do*', is what Stiegler describes as 'a circuit of *transindividuation* (of the formation of an epoch)' (Stiegler 2010b: 17). It is in art's ability to create circuits of transindividuation – which are inherently linked to the technical milieu – that possible sites for reinvigorating noetic thought can be identified. The inventiveness at the heart of the avant-garde inspires new generations of art-makers who *show* their reinterpretations and critical reengagements with extant themes through the new, idiosyncratic tools and techniques that disinter consistent idiomatic motifs through innovative styles, particular to the given techno-historic moment. Thus, Stiegler's technological aesthetics provides a useful grammar for explaining the technological–historical–sociopolitical internal tensions of the various digital performances; conversely, the genealogical narrative gives concrete expression to his crucial philosophical concept of transindividuation.

The genealogy that begins with Troika Ranch and ends with Blast Theory shows that, despite the recursive socio-political and economic tendency towards entropic processes of automatization (that homogenize, proletarianize and stupefy), there is no limit to human ingenuity and the noetic thought that outstrips the speed of computational automation. The artists show that, by deploying infinite thought in singular and original ways, they can create bifurcations in the entropic, nihilistic economy that characterizes 24/7 capitalism and algorithmic governmentality, *showing* the way towards inaugurating new conceptions of the future.

It is a duty of the digital scenographer to reactivate noetic thought by keeping a keen eye on the past, taking up the unresolved questions and understanding the importance of engaging the difficult, incomplete and challenging long circuits of transindividuation that are numerous and lie scattered among the symbolic debris of the history of traces. The great failures are always the result of a forgetting of *human values* in the face of an acceleration towards an increasingly rationalized ecology. Paradoxically, this over-rationalization also precipitates a tendency towards reductive binarisms in which technology is mistakenly perceived as an *other* entity, obfuscating its phenotypical origin at the source of hominization.

Increasing Technological Performativity

Each unit of the grammar described above can, with certain caution, be folded into an updated aesthetics of the avant-garde and contemporary (digital) art generally. However, there is an important story that should be read between the lines of the overall genealogy that is neither apparent nor articulated in other earlier digital art/performance books: the progressive emergence of a technological performativity.

The definition of technological performativity – the ability for technology and artefacts to exert a psychosomatic agency or influence over the human that has real-life impact – is explained in Chapter 2, and the concept arises repetitively throughout the book. From beginning to end of the genealogy, there is an increasing sophistication of the digital scenographies and a continual deepening and entanglement of technologies in working processes, delineating their growing importance. The first chapter discusses artists who use bend sensors and MIDI messages to quantify biomechanical movement, which influences and expands the dramaturgical and scenographic possibilities in the performances. In Chapter 2, although more concerned with advances in medical science than digital technologies per se, Stelarc's inherently cyborg-themed project is used for explicating theories of individuation and cybernetics, and the reconception of the body as a fluid entity. In Chapters 3 and 4, while the techno-performative paradigm remains constant, the reliability of the data and the sophistication of the methods increase in parallel with the evolution of computer vision techniques, affording more scenographic and dramaturgical possibilities. In Chapter 5, the evolution of projection technologies and the 'immense accumulation of spectacles' they afford are given renewed efficacy to intervene in the subject's architectural and vital experience of urban space in a similar way to that apprehended by Guy Debord in *The Society of the Spectacle* (1967). Finally, in the last chapter, the performance invades personal mobile devices (which have already been consolidated as exosomatic organs) and interfaces directly with the spectator, perpetrating a situation in which the audience are led to believe they are interacting with a performer but are, in fact, interacting with a piece of software that subjects them to an intense act of surveillance and data profiling.

The genealogy of digital scenographies shows the increasing levels of technological agency in the performing arts which parallel general developments in the technical milieu, exemplified by the programming industries and their production of (temporal) symbolic products that are becoming more enmeshed in the nature of being. Each branch of the genealogy supports the argument that (digital) technology, catalysed by increasing levels of autonomy and agency, is gathering an ever more profound ontological efficacy. This axiom also raises the pharmacology of this situation: automatization (underpinned by a transcendental speed) simultaneously withholds the promise of infinite psychosomatic prosthesis and the danger of an endemic lethargy and indifference, leading to a loss of nature and humanity (O'Dwyer 2016a: 374). This demands a reiteration of the urgent need for a transvaluation of values, wherein the task of responsibly reorganizing epistemology along the lines of an evolved technological intersubjectivity must be engaged, thereby opening new ways for a shared participation in the creation of new realities.

The digital scenographies selected for this genealogy are by no means the only examples that reveal the techno-performative potentialities that constitute this component of the grammar; there are other historical lineages that could support this thesis. Demarcated as a series of aesthetic ruptures, the works have primarily been selected for their pioneering, experimental and influential qualities that combine to establish the new, emerging genre of digital scenographic practice, which not only is answerable to the evolving technical milieu but also is, in fact, a pivotal research area creatively leading the uptake and mobilization of the technologies and innovatively investigating the cutting-edge of human-computer interaction. The onus is on the digital scenographer to collaborate with directors, dramaturgs, computer scientists and so on, to embrace the increasing efficacy of the technological milieu and to allow the technology to influence the outcome of the work – that is, to allow the work to emerge organically, or *organologically*.

A Final Word

This genealogy attests to a specific line of development in which the successive innovative fusions of digital technologies with performance design bring forth increasingly autonomous, naturalistic and quasi-organic scenographic frameworks that consecutively question and deepen the relations between humans and technology. The predominant theme that is repetitively recuperated with each digital scenographic reworking is the mutating role of the human artist–performer vis-à-vis the evolving performativity of the machine; that is, the agency and operative functioning of technology is inseparably and indeterminately entangled with the becoming of individual and collective identities. This affirms the ontological force of the technological milieu and its immanent potential for engineering positive futures. 'The machine has become more than a mere adjunct to life. It is really a part of human life – perhaps the very soul' (Francis Picabia cited in Tomkins 2014: 100). Digital technology is neither the cure nor the exacerbator of hyperindustrial hyper-rationalization; humans are. Because *we are digital*.

Notes

Introduction

1. The *Event* is a central theme of discussion in several chapters. According to Alain Badiou an Event is something that ruptures pre-existing codes and rules of 'the situation' (existence), causing a psychological and collective upheaval, ultimately reorganizing ways of being (making, doing, intersubjectivity etc.) (Badiou 2005a).
2. The term 'cybernetics' is largely attributed to Norbert Wiener, who coined the phrase to describe the study of self-regulating mechanisms in his book *Cybernetics, or Control and Communication in the Animal and the Machine* (1948). The discipline, more broadly speaking, emerged through collective investigations and dialogues, the main proponents of which were Wiener, William Ross Ashby, Alan Turing, Warren Sturgis McCulloch, Arturo Rosenblueth and William Grey Walter.
3. The specificities of digital technology can here broadly be defined along criteria that set digital technology apart from its analogue predecessor: discretization, interactivity, responsivity, control, networking, telepresence and so on.
4. Perhaps the most valuable contribution that Salter's book offers is in the last two chapters, where he demonstrates acute practical and theoretical knowledge, deftly interweaving the two strands into a nuanced critique of kinetic machines, robotic devices and responsive environments.
5. The book is a novel collaborative effort by the International Federation of Theatre Research's (IFTR's) *Intermediality in Theatre and Performance* working group.
6. See, for example, Matthew Causey's analysis of the Wooster Group in *Theatre and Performance in Digital Culture* (2006).
7. A crucial factor in the success of internet technology was a decision by CERN not to patent it and keep it open-source and royalty free, forever. Berners Lee maintains: 'Had the technology been proprietary, and in my total control, it would probably not have taken off. You can't propose that something be a universal space and at the same time keep control of it' ('History of the Web' n.d.).
8. *Casual creative* is a term used in computer science to refer to practitioners in the creative-cultural sector who use digital media tools, but do not engage in their development.

Chapter 1

1. The extended vocal technique involves the inclusion and mixing of alternative non-sung sounds, like spoken word, rapping, falsetto, glottal sounds, yodelling, ululation, screaming, growling, inhaling helium, as well as non-vocal sounds like clapping, stamping, shuffling feet or artificial electrical/electronic enhancement.
2. In 1975 Bella Lewitzky produced an 'interactive' performance, entitled V.C.O. (Voltage Control Oscillator), using analogue radio transmitters strapped to the limbs of several dancers. The opening episodes were composed of soloists emphasizing 'one part of the body ... including the ankle, elbow, knee, wrist and shoulder ... after which other dancers performed variations in which the basic phrases broadened into movements for the entire body' (J. Anderson 1979). And in 1969, Lee Harrison's 'Scanimate' project, a predecessor of MoCap technology, was featured on the ill-fated TV show *Turn-On* (Smith 2017).
3. Mark Coniglio (Music & MidiDancer), Dawn Stoppiello (Choreography), Ilaan Egeland (Choreography), Peter Seidler (Set Design), Sten Rudstrom (Text), Cathy Galeota (Video), Betsy Herst (Lighting), Meredith Alex (Costumes).
4. Coniglio identifies *Interactor* as 'the father of *Isadora*', his current proprietary digital performance design software: https://troikatronix.com/
5. http://www.ecafe.com/museum/history/ksoverview2.html
6. Troika Ranch was officially incorporated with the Federal Government as a non-profit corporation in 1994.
7. Both Coniglio and Stoppiello maintain that Galloway and Rabinowitz are under-recognized for their pioneering contribution to the field of digital performance. They were the first people to explore remote connections on the basis that simultaneous events can happen in distant places, and that separated audiences and performers can have a relationship and a shared, yet different, experience of a singular event (Stoppiello 2018; Coniglio 2019).
8. This does not include the latency involved in transmitting the image across the telephone network, decoding it and re-visualizing it on the remote video display.
9. The Open Theatre was collectively founded by Megan Terry, Sam Shepard, Peter Feldman and Joseph Chaikin in 1963.
10. The Living Theatre, founded in 1947 by Judith Malina and Julian Beck, was one of the first experimental theatre groups in the United States.
11. This concept would include the film object.
12. In *Phaedrus*, Plato declares that the inscriptive technique of writing is a pharmakon – a poison and a cure – because (1) although the written word aids memory it hinders pure recollection and thought, and (2) it short-circuits real, interlocutory presence, advances rhetorical contamination and affords (mis)interpretations, or untruth. Jacques Derrida uses Plato's passage as the basis for critiquing the predominance of logocentrism in Western culture and advocating the benefits of written word (Derrida 1981:

67–119). Stiegler, Derrida's tutee, supports the argument and applies it to modern technologies of inscription, for example, tape recorders, cameras, computers and so on.

13. Stiegler establishes a definite accordance with Adorno and Horkheimer's thesis on the culture industry. This shared position is explored in detail in Chapters 5 and 6.

14. A nanosecond is a unit of time equal to one billionth of a second (10^{-9} or 1/1,000,000,000 s). This is the standard unit of measurement for clocking hardware such as processors and graphics cards.

15. Benjamin discusses 'the very crisis in which we see the theatre' as a result of the emergence of film technology (Benjamin 1999: 223).

16. Following the profound increase in the use of screens, projections and media technologies on the live stage, even the validity of the presence of the live (embodied) actor is challenged (Causey 2006: 13–29). The polemics of the technological determination of theatrical ontologies is also born out comprehensively in the Peggy Phelan versus Philip Auslander debate that took place in the late 1990s. The former claiming that 'Performance's only life is in the present' (Phelan 1993: 146) and the latter arguing that mediation is what creates performance in the first place (Auslander 2008).

17. Although it is erroneous to try to define postmodernism as a period, I am here referring to post-1969 (post Parisian student revolutions) through to the beginning of digital epoch (c. 1990).

18. An especially noteworthy performance that Coniglio worked on was a collaboration between David Rosenbloom (Dean of the Music School, in CalArts) and acclaimed minimalist composer, Terry Reilly, which consisted in a transcontinental improvisatory musical duet, between ECI, in L.A., and the CIRM, Centre National de Création Musicale, in Nice (1993) (Joy 2010: 53). Coniglio's role was to create a piece of software, called *Midiphone*, which sent and received MIDI notes over a 56k modem. The piece involved the installation of two Disklavier pianos at each venue. The performance functioned such that the musicians played on one piano at each location, the other was unmanned. They sent the played notes to the opposing remote locations, over the *Midiphone*, which were received and played back by the unmanned pianos, like a player piano. The telepresent improvisational aspect, afforded by the digital technology, was profoundly significant; the ability for the musicians to improvise together over a huge geospatial divide was ground-breaking. The work had a profound impression on Coniglio: 'Maybe that was the moment when I started to understand why Kit and Sheri were right, about the need for improvisation' (Coniglio 2019).

19. Becoming is a term that is mostly associated with Deleuze because he is noted for his thorough work on the theory and its various subcategories, exhaustively explored throughout his corpus. In fact, the crystallization of his theories is indebted to Simondon, whose theses and concepts are either detected implicitly or cited explicitly. They had a close friendship and the concepts for which they are now renowned were teased out over a series of dialogues; indeed, Deleuze is the person most responsible for bringing Simondon's work to the public's attention.

20 IDAT '99 was hosted at Arizona State University and organized by John Mitchell. It was an important event because it was the first conference of its type, which allowed the global community to finally come together and meet face-to-face. There were many important pioneering figures in attendance such as Johannes Birringer, Palindrome and Frieder Weiss, to name a few.

Chapter 2

1 Other artists of critical acclaim working on bio-themed projects during the period included Orlan, Kathy High, Paul Vanouse and the Critical Art Ensemble amongst others.

2 The term is an abbreviation of 'cybernetic organism', and was 'coined by Manfred Clynes and Nathan Kline in 1960' (Ihde 2003: 615).

3 The term *exosomatic* refers to phenomena occurring outside the body. It was originally coined by Alfred J. Lotka, in *Elements of Mathematical Biology* (1924), and then later taken up by Robert E. Innis, in *Technics and the Bias of Perception* (1984), to describe prosthesis of the senses through 'organ projection'; for example, in the way that telescopes extend vision and sonar augments hearing.

4 Telematics describe the integration of humans, computers and telecommunications. Roy Ascott is best known for popularizing the concept, which he refined and developed over several decades in both his theory and arts practice. The theory gained strong currency in the mid-1990s during the cybercultural boom. He defines telematics as 'computer-mediated communications networking between geographically dispersed individuals and institutions ... and between the human mind and artificial systems of intelligence and perception' (Ascott 2003: 232).

5 He also noted that the stem cell procedure was not legal in the United States and was, therefore, executed in Europe.

6 Recent dialogues with the artist reveal a more moderate position, and a more careful use of language for framing the projects.

7 'The amplified body performances began in 1971, the 3 body probes into the stomach, lungs and colon from 1973, and the *Third Hand* project started in 1976' (Stelarc 2020).

8 Leroi-Gourhan borrows this term from the field of biology and Stiegler continues with this language. It describes the process of expression through language and gesture. It is based on establishing the human psyche as an analogue to its environment. The 'exterior milieu is understood as "everything materially surrounding the human"' (Leroi-Gourhan cited in Stiegler 1998: 57); the interior milieu is understood as 'that which constitutes its intellectual capital ... an extremely complex pool of mental traditions' (Stiegler 1998).

9   The term *retention* is drawn from Husserl's thesis on the three-tiered structure of consciousness: primary retention (present perception), secondary retention (recollection) and protention (anticipation). Stiegler adds to this stack by proposing the term *tertiary retention*, which refers to exosomatized memory, beginning with writing and undergirding all cognitive technologies.

10 *Additional Notes on the Consequences of the Notion of Individuation*, appended to his main doctoral thesis, written between 1954 and 1958.

11 The concept of cybernetics evolving from 'the study of observed systems' towards 'the study of observing systems' was developed by Heinz Von Forester over a series of papers published between 1960 and 1974, whereupon he finally concretized it as the 'cybernetics of cybernetics' (von Foerster 1974), later coined second-order cybernetics.

12 A genotype is the genetic constitution of an individual organism. A phenotype is the set of observable characteristics of an individual resulting from the interaction of its genotype with the environment.

13 Phylogenesis is the evolutionary development and diversification of a species or group of organisms, or of a particular feature of an organism.

14 Ontogenesis refers to the development of an individual organism, in terms of anatomical or behavioural features, from the earliest stage to maturity.

15 Nietzsche's notes testify to his view that the creative genius embodies a transitory, ephemeral moment of exceptional, individual, ontogenetic *physis* and, as such, he dismisses the possibility of phylogenetic development as a lost cause.

16 The photographs of the *Ear on Arm* surgery and his portrait with the ear (taken by Nina Sellars) have been exhibited as singular artworks, entitled *Oblique: Images from Stelarc's Extra Ear Surgery.*

17 The bio-art genre does continue to thrive in the aftermath of Stelarc and Orlan but it has experienced a decline in the number of artists actually putting themselves on the operating table as a performative gesture.

18 Eduardo Miranda (University of Plymouth) is researching methods of 'culturing Physarum polycephalum-based memristive components' from myxomycete (slime mould) for building circuits in biological computing (Braund and Miranda 2017).

19 The culture industry is comprehensively explained in Chapter 5.

Chapter 3

1   A complete list of Obermaier's projects is available at www.exile.at.

2   Robert Brownjohn was a student of László Moholy-Nagy at the New Bauhaus (Chicago) where he participated in moving image experiments. Brownjohn is famous for projecting graphics and typography onto female

bodies in the title sequences of James bond movies, like *Goldfinger* and *From Russia with Love*.

3   Merce Cunningham and Alwin Nikolais both 'sought to challenge established choreographic paradigms ... by introducing multimedia elements and random phenomena as determinants of the composition' (O'Dwyer 2015a: 35).

4   The infamous Korean case of a three-month-old baby dying from malnutrition because its parents devoted too much attention to playing a computer game (Tran 2010) shocked the planet, and the publication of research findings confirming the detrimental effects of sitting for prolonged periods (Sjögren et al. 2014), at computers in work and then at home for leisure, stimulated widespread public debate about the hazardous effects of screen addiction.

5   This statement was made in the project synopsis of *D.A.V.E.* but it is a useful provocation that helps articulate the research of the entire trilogy.

6   While the subject of neuro/cognitive-capitalism is pertinent to *Apparition*, it is explored in greater detail in Chapters 5 and 6, in the context of artists directly engaging urbanism, big data and hypercaptialism. However, the avant-garde nature of Obermaier's performance deserves commendation because this work was first exhibited in 2004, before there was widespread public anxiety about data harvesting and its abuse by the marketing and PR sectors.

Chapter 4

1   *Mortal Engine* also included collaborations from Ben Frost (Music) and Robin Fox (Laser light effects); however, for this discussion I am focusing on the digital scenographic projections.

2   The project description and director's notes for *Mortal Engine* were published on Chunky Move's website in 2008. At the time of writing they had removed the webpage but informed me that they are building a new archive section for the website which will host the *Mortal Engine* information. However, there is currently no fixed URL.

3   A professor at Osaka University and group leader of ATR Intelligent Robotics and Communication Laboratories, Ishiguro's work is concerned with human nature and feeling, how 'presence [can] be captured, revived, and transmitted' (Stocker and Schöpf 2010: 218).

4   Geminoids are a type of robot, 'originally planned to be test-beds for studying the individual nature of human beings' (Stocker and Schöpf 2010: 218).

5   William Ross Ashby outlines the fundamental importance of degrees of freedom, and their constraint thereof, to cybernetics (Ashby 1957: 61, 129–31).

6   For Kant, aesthetic experience is 'always confined to the conditions that [art] must meet to be in harmony with nature' (Kant and Pluhar 1987: 98).

7 Mitosis is a process of cell duplication, or reproduction, during which one cell divides into two genetically identical daughter cells. Computer simulations of this process use an algorithmic logic called reaction diffusion, derived from the field of linear algebra.

8 There were several similar research projects in progress at the turn of the twenty-first century. Some of particular note were Scott deLahunta and the Forsyth Company's *Synchronous Objects* project (2009) in collaboration with Ohio State University (an important work that was amongst the primary movers in developing processes for annotating choreography), and the *Motion Bank Project* (2010) initiated by the Forsyth Company, in Frankfurt am Main.

Chapter 5

1 At the turn of the twenty-first century there were various attempts to enhance the immersiveness of site specific events and exhibitions using digital projection design. One notable early example was George Coates' *Blind Messengers* (1998), a multimedia opera staged in the courtyard of the (then) new Golden State Museum (Sacramento, California) against the backdrop of the Constitution Wall. The wall was illuminated using prerendered animations and live video compositing techniques.

2 Nadja Masura gives a useful historiography of projection design projects (including examples from practitioners like George Coates, the Gertrude Stein Repertory Theatre, Troika Ranch, David Saltz, Mark Reaney, The Builder's Association and ArtGrid) produced in the UK and United States between 1990 and 2020.

3 *Aesthetic Theory* was not edited by Adorno himself, but by Gretel Adorno (his widow) and Rolf Tiedemann (his friend). It was assembled from Adorno's working drafts and unfinished manuscripts composed between 1961 and 1969.

4 The Wikileaks controversy, which really blew up in 2010/11, brought with it a debate not just about online security and the lack of privacy for individual citizens, but also about the repercussions that leaked 'confidential' documents could have for national security and the personal safety of government officials.

5 Stiegler uses the term *proletarianization* in the Marxist sense of putting people to work at unskilled tasks in the service of machinery. It describes a loss of knowledge caused by subservience to technical operations, where the human becomes a 'conscious linkage' connecting the 'numerous mechanical and intellectual organs' of the machine, which replaces human 'skill and strength' (Marx 1993: 614–15).

6 *Temporal objects* are a phenomenological concept developed by Edmund Husserl to describe artefacts perceived over time, like a musical melody (Husserl 2012). *Industrial temporal objects* refer to recordings of these events (using electro-mechanical technologies) which can be duplicated, distributed and played back ad infinitum.

7   Stiegler's criticism stems from a more general (post-Derridean) criticism of philosophy's overly reductionist binarisms, for example he critiques Marcuse for opposing the Reality Principle to the Pleasure Principle, something which Freud did not do (Stiegler et al. 2012: 168).

8   Unboxing is a popular neologism that describes the 'ceremonial' activity of unpackaging a newly purchased device – usually an electronic consumable. Many consumers record themselves doing it and then post the video on social networks.

9   Edward Bernays was the nephew of Sigmund Freud. In the 1930s he took Freud's theories on drive and desire and used them as the basis for founding the economy that, today, we call public relations and marketing (*The Century of the Self* 2002).

10 Archi-flux refers to global television network broadcasts that subject masses to a synchronized time of consciousness, founded on the economy of capturing attention (Stiegler 2011a: 121–5).

11 Coined on social media as 'Hello Handsome', this scene is quite close to the end of the film, taking place at approximately the two-and-a-quarter hour mark. Disappointingly, the copyright holders declined to allow me to use an image in the book.

12 Display technologies based on light-field technologies, like *The Looking Glass*, and sophisticated augmented reality HMDs, like the *Hololens* and *Magic Leap* are already widely deployed in the offices and labs of computer vision research groups and leading content providers. While the cost of rollout to the mass market is still quite prohibitive, financial and technological forecasters predict that a general uptake by consumers is achievable within a five- to ten-year period.

13 *Processing* and *Pure Data (PD)* are free digital media software tools commonly used by artists, students and amateurs.

14 Some proprietary software packages include: MAX/MASP, TouchDesigner and QLab.

15 Although these software packages overcome the problem of end users having to read/write code, they still require a high level of mathematical competency and logical reasoning.

Chapter 6

1   Based in the Mixed Reality Lab (Brighton), Blast Theory has, itself, published numerous academic papers, written both independently and in collaboration with various scientific and humanities research groups. For a complete list, see https://www.blasttheory.co.uk/bt/documents/Blast_Theory_Bibliography.pdf.

2   The main proponents of Blast Theory are Nick Tandavanitj, Ju Row Farrand and Matt Adams.

NOTES

3   Blast Theory's background is very well documented in numerous journals and they have an excellent website: www.blasttheory.co.uk/

4   The *five-factor model* describes 'a group of major facets of the human personality. These traits are agreeableness, conscientiousness, extroversion, neuroticism, and openness to experience. Identified by psychologists in the late twentieth century, these facets have been incorporated into a test that can measure and assess a subject's personality. Although the Big Five concept and testing procedures have some shortcomings, they are popular among psychologists and interested individuals alike. Personality assessments may prove useful in broader psychological studies and serve as predictors of behavior in certain areas of life' (Dziak 2019).

5   Even if you resist, Dave is extremely persistent and ushers you into the room, even against your will; it is a measure of 'how much you can resist before he wins' (Adams 2019). This arouses an extreme sense of powerlessness, unlike any I have experienced in any other performance – like a paralysis, awake but unwilling. I wanted to turn off the video, but curiosity and a sense of needing to complete the programme got the better of me.

6   *Protention* is a term that is central to Stiegler's philosophy. Husserl's concept of retention was already explained in Chapter 2 (note 9). In opposition to retention (memory), protention can be defined as anticipation – the ability to predict the future. In terms of embodied knowledge, it constitutes our innate ability to predict the trajectory of a moving object, like a ball; in terms of mindful knowledge, it constitutes the ability to predict the forthcoming notes in a musical composition. For Husserl, protention is modulated by the constant interplay of primary and secondary retention (perception and experience); however, Stiegler argues that since the mechanical turn of sensibility, these are increasingly organized by tertiary retentions (inscribed memories).

7   Netflix is a good example of this paradigm. Based on information harvested through processes of *hyperprofiling*, where vital data is gathered, scraped, swapped and sold on electronic networks, the Netflix algorithm formulates a set of suggested movies for a user/viewer to watch.

8   The *Anthropocene* is a new term referring to a new geological epoch occasioned by industrial human activities and their impact on the earth's ecosystems. It was coined in the 1980s by biologist Eugene F. Stoermer in relation to human impact on the species of fresh waterways in North America. The term was popularized through a collaborative article by Stoermer and atmospheric chemist Paul Crutzen, who insisted that the effects of greenhouse gases released into the atmosphere due to human activity at the lithospheric level are so significant that we must now acknowledge a new geological epoch (Crutzen and Stoermer 2000). 'The Working Group on the Anthropocene' is currently awaiting full, formal ratification of the term by the *International Commission on Stratigraphy*. (Subramanian 2019; 'Working Group on the "Anthropocene"' n.d.)

9   *Entropy* is a term that originates from the scientific field of thermodynamics. It refers to the quantity of energy in a system that is unavailable for

conversion into mechanical work. It can be understood as the amount of randomness, disorder or unpredictability in a system. It is a phenomenon that is present in all systems and has been mobilized by economists for explaining the tendency of marketplaces to descend into chaos.

10 *Negative entropy*, or *Negentropy*, is the opposite of entropy. It describes the idea of chaos moving towards order. In his popular science book, *What Is Life?* (1944), Erwin Schrödinger theorizes that living systems and organisms are 'negentropic' because they take in exterior matter (like food, water, oxygen, etc.) and organize them towards generating cellular growth and energy, for mobility and functionality.

11 A *bifurcation* literally refers to a split of something into two parts; however, in the context of systems theory, it concerns the study of changes in the qualitative structure of a dynamical system, first introduced by mathematician Henri Poincaré (Coates 1998). A bifurcation occurs when a small, smooth change is applied to variable parameter values of the system, triggering an instantaneous, rapid qualitative variation in the topology of the overall system. Birfucation theory has more recently been applied to the field of biology (which is negentropic systems theory), where dramatic changes in the total system (like cyclical transitions in cell division) are understood as paramount to the development, functionality and survival of organisms.

12 The political efficacy of these techniques has been validated in the targeted persuasion campaigns that are known to have influenced the outcomes of the 2016 US presidential election and the 2016 UK referendum on Brexit. Cambridge Analytica is known to have played a substantial role in the campaigns by using profiling, data-mining and dataveillance techniques (Cadwalladr 2017; Hern 2018).

13 A propaganda machine that can propel a president, who espouses neo-fascist rhetoric, into power in a country that purports to be modern and enlightened, and cause a major European state to break away from the Common Market, under a nationalist agenda that threatens the stability of peace, only seventy-five years after the end of the greatest humanitarian catastrophe in modern history, in a bid to make Britain 'the greatest country on earth' (Staunton 2019).

Conclusion

1 The *transvaluation*, or *revaluation, of value* is a concept that Stiegler borrows from the *moral philosophy* of Friedrich Nietzsche, which presents a scathing critique of the predominant and normative moral system of the Western world. Nietzsche's aim is to free ('higher') human beings from their entrapment within a prevailing and fundamentally deleterious false consciousness that is undergirded by a flawed moral value system and is, therefore, inhibitive to the flourishing of high and good characteristics; that is, he philosophizes towards a conception of human perfection,

unencumbered by institutionally imposed moral values. Although Nietzsche is best known for targeting monotheism – exemplified by his attacks on Christianity – as a primary source of moral oppression, he does not confine his pejorative criticisms to this one example; philosophical, social and historical examples are also specifically identified. Nietzsche calls for a *revaluation/transvaluation* of 'values tables' (Nietzsche 2013: sec. 1007) prescribed by these institutes, but curiously, his is not a philosophy founded on human equality. He draws a crucial distinction between the *master morality*, which he conceives so that 'higher,' superior humans can elevate themselves and society through intellectual creativity, and the *slave morality* of the irredeemable masses. Despite this class disparity, there are no grounds for assigning a politics to his philosophy because he does not express systematic views about the nature of society and state. Stiegler on the other hand is expressly political in his views and repeatedly calls for a new politics and a politically engaged art. As such, his mobilization of the concept of transvaluation is one directed at the political economy.

Bibliography

Adams, Matt. 'Karen'. Portfolio. Blast Theory, 2015. https://www.blasttheory.co.uk/projects/karen/.
Adams, Matt. Interview with Matt Adams (Blast Theory). Interview by Néill O'Dwyer. YouTube HD Video, 9 August 2019. https://www.youtube.com/watch?v=k_JCrpkpLrk.
Adorno, Theodor W. *Aesthetic Theory*. London: Routledge & Kegan Paul, 1970.
Allegue, Ludivine, Simon Jones, Baz Kershaw and Angela Piccini, eds. *Practice-as-Research: In Performance and Screen*. New York: Palgrave Macmillan, 2009.
Amsler, Mark E. *Etymology and Grammatical Discourse in Late Antiquity and the Early Middle Ages*. Amsterdam; Philadelphia: J. Benjamins Pub. Co., 1989.
Anderson, Chris. 'The End of Theory: The Data Deluge Makes the Scientific Method Obsolete'. *Wired*, 23 June 2008. https://www.wired.com/2008/06/pb-theory/.
Anderson, Jack. 'Dance: Bella Lewitzky Offers Three Premieres'. *The New York Times*, 4 November 1979, sec. Archives. https://www.nytimes.com/1979/11/04/archives/dance-bella-lewitzky-offers-three-premieres.html.
Anthropology. 'Diffusionism and Acculturation', 24 April 2017. https://anthropology.ua.edu/theory/diffusionism-and-acculturation/.
Appia, Adolphe and Richard C. Beacham. *Adolphe Appia: Texts on Theatre*. London; New York: Routledge, 1993.
Aronson, Arnold. *Looking into the Abyss: Essays on Scenography*. Ann Arbor: University of Michigan Press, 2005.
Ashby, William Ross. *An Introduction to Cybernetics*. London: Chapman & Hall Ltd., 1957.
Ascott, Roy. *Telematic Embrace: Visionary Theories of Art, Technology, and Consciousness*. Berkeley: University of California Press, 2003.
Auslander, Philip. 'Reviewed Works: The Theory-Death of the Avant-Garde by Paul Mann; The Object of Performance: The American Avant-Garde Since 1970 by Henry M. Sayre; Performing Drama/Dramatizing Performance: Alternative Theatre and the Dramatic Text by Michael Vanden Heuvel; Theatre, Theory, Postmodernism by Johannes Birringer'. *TDR (1988-)* 37, no. 3 (1993): 196. https://doi.org/10.2307/1146318.
Auslander, Philip. *Liveness: Performance in a Mediatized Culture*. 2nd edition. London; New York: Routledge, 2008.
Austin, J. L. *How to Do Things with Words: Second Edition*. Edited by J. O. Urmson and Marina Sbisà. 2nd edition. Cambridge, MA: Harvard University Press, 1975.
Badiou, Alain. *Being and Event*. London: Continuum, 2005a.
Badiou, Alain. *Handbook of Inaesthetics*. Stanford, CA: Stanford University Press, 2005b.

Baraibar, Aitor. 'Stelarc's Post-evolutionary Performance Art: Exposing Collisions between the Body and Technology'. *Women & Performance: A Journal of Feminist Theory* 11, no. 1 (January 1999): 157–68. https://doi.org/10.1080/07407709908571320.

Bardin, Andrea. *Epistemology and Political Philosophy in Gilbert Simondon: Individuation, Technics, Social Systems*. Netherlands: Springer, 2015.

Bardin, Andrea and Pablo Rodriguez. 'A Vindication of Simondon's Political Anthropology'. *Australasian Philosophical Review* 2, no. 1 (2 January 2018): 54–61. https://doi.org/10.1080/24740500.2018.1514967.

Baudrillard, Jean. *Simulacra and Simulation*. Ann Arbor: University of Michigan Press, 1994.

Baugh, Christopher. *Theatre, Performance and Technology: The Development and Transformation of Scenography*. London: Macmillan Education UK, 2014.

Baugh, Christopher. '"Devices of Wonder": Globalizing Technologies in the Process of Scenography'. In *Scenography Expanded: An Introduction to Contemporary Performance Design*, edited by Joslin McKinney and Scott Palmer, 23–38. London; New York, NY: Bloomsbury Methuen Drama, 2017. https://doi.org/10.5040/9781474244428?locatt=label:secondary_dramaOnline.

Bay-Cheng, Sarah, Chiel Kattenbelt, Andy Lavender and Robin Nelson, eds. *Mapping Intermediality in Performance*. Amsterdam: Amsterdam University Press, 2011.

Benford, Steve and Gabriella Giannachi. *Performing Mixed Reality*. Cambridge, MA: MIT Press, 2011.

Benjamin, Walter. *Illuminations*. Edited by Hannah Arendt. London: Pimlico, 1999.

Berry, D. and M. Dieter, eds. *Postdigital Aesthetics: Art, Computation And Design*. Houndmills, Basingstoke, Hampshire; New York, NY: Palgrave Macmillan, 2015.

Birch, Anna. 'Editorial'. *Contemporary Theatre Review* 22, no. 2 (1 May 2012): 199–202. https://doi.org/10.1080/10486801.2012.669209.

Birch, Anna and Joanne Tompkins. *Performing Site-Specific Theatre: Politics, Place, Practice*. New York; Gordonsville: Palgrave Macmillan, 2012.

Biro, Matthew. *The Dada Cyborg: Visions of the New Human in Weimar Berlin*. Minneapolis: University of Minnesota Press, 2009.

Birringer, Johannes. 'Postmodern Performance and Technology'. *Performing Arts Journal* 9, no. 2/3 (1985): 221–33.

Birringer, Johannes. *Media & Performance: Along the Border*. 1st edition. Baltimore: Johns Hopkins University Press, 1998.

Blumenthal, Ralph. 'Joseph Chaikin 67; Actor and Innovative Director'. *The New York Times*, 24 June 2003, sec. N.Y./Region. https://www.nytimes.com/2003/06/24/nyregion/joseph-chaikin-67-actor-and-innovative-director.html.

Boal, Augusto. *Theatre of the Oppressed*. London: Pluto, 1979.

Bolter, Jay David and Richard Grusin. *Remediation: Understanding New Media*. 1st edition. Cambridge, MA: MIT Press, 2000.

Bradski, Gary R. and Adrian Kaehler. *Learning OpenCV: Computer Vision with the OpenCV Library*. 1st edition. [Nachdr.]. Software That Sees. Beijing: O'Reilly, 2011.

Braund, Edward and Eduardo Reck Miranda. 'On Building Practical Biocomputers for Real-World Applications: Receptacles for Culturing Slime Mould Memristors and Component Standardisation'. *Journal of Bionic*

Engineering 14, no. 1 (1 March 2017): 151–62. https://doi.org/10.1016/S1672-6529(16)60386-4.

Brautigan, Richard. *All Watched over by Machines of Loving Grace*. San Francisco: Communication Company, 1967.

Brejzek, Thea, ed. *Expanding Scenography: On the Authoring of Space*. Prague: Arts and Theatre Institute, 2011.

Bullivant, Lucy. *Responsive Environments: Architecture, Art and Design*. New York: Harry N. Abrams, 2006.

Bürger, Peter. *Theory of the Avant-Garde*. Minneapolis: Manchester University Press, 1984.

Cadwalladr, Carole. 'The Great British Brexit Robbery: How Our Democracy Was Hijacked'. *The Guardian*, 7 May 2017, sec. Technology. https://www.theguardian.com/technology/2017/may/07/the-great-british-brexit-robbery-hijacked-democracy.

Canguilhem, Georges. *La connaissance de la vie*. Paris: Vrin, 1992.

Causey, Matthew. 'The Screen Test of the Double: The Uncanny Performer in the Space of Technology'. *Theatre Journal* 51, no. 4 (1 December 1999): 383–94. https://doi.org/10.1353/tj.1999.0083.

Causey, Matthew. *Theatre and Performance in Digital Culture: From Simulation to Embeddedness*. London: Routledge, 2006.

Causey, Matthew. 'Postdigital Performance'. *Theatre Journal* 68, no. 3 (20 October 2016): 427–41. https://doi.org/10.1353/tj.2016.0074.

Caygill, Howard. 'Stelarc and the Chimera: Kant's Critique of Prosthetic Judgment'. *Art Journal* 56, no. 1 (March 1997): 46–51. https://doi.org/10.1080/00043249.1997.10791800.

Clarke, Roger. 'Information Technology and Dataveillance'. *Commun. ACM* 31, no. 5 (May 1988): 498–512. https://doi.org/10.1145/42411.42413.

Coates, George. 'Blind Messengers'. George Coates Performance Works, 1998. http://georgecoates.org/BlindMessenger/index.html.

Collins, Jane and Andrew Nisbet, eds. *Theatre and Performance Design: A Reader in Scenography*. London; New York: Routledge, 2010.

Collins, Jane and Arnold Aronson. 'Editors' Introduction'. *Theatre and Performance Design* 1, no. 1–2 (3 April 2015): 1–6. https://doi.org/10.1080/23322551.2015.1028172.

Coniglio, Mark. Interview with Mark Coniglio. Video teleconference, 6 January 2019. YouTube (Private). https://www.youtube.com/watch?v=TuJ244EVfho&t=2686s.

Crary, Jonathan. *24/7: Late Capitalism and the Ends of Sleep*. London: Verso, 2014.

Crutzen, Paul and Eugene F. Stoermer. 'Have We Entered the "Anthropocene"?' Text. International Geosphere-Biosphere Programme, 2000. http://www.igbp.net/news/opinion/opinion/haveweenteredtheanthropocene.5.d8b4c3c12bf3be638a8000578.html.

Davies, Rick. 'Palmtree Instruments Airdrums (MT Dec 1986)'. *Music Technology* (December 1986): 26. http://www.muzines.co.uk/articles/palmtree-instruments-airdrums/198

Davis, Doug. 'Intel Acquires Computer Vision for IOT, Automotive'. Corporate. Intel Newsroom, 26 May, 2016. https://newsroom.intel.com/editorials/intel-acquires-computer-vision-for-iot-automotive/.

Debord, Guy. *La société du spectacle*. Paris: Buchet/Chastel, 1967.

de Lahunta, Scott. 'Klaus Obermaier: Apparition – Background', 2005. http://www.exile.at/apparition/background.html.
de Lahunta, Scott. 'Blurring the Boundaries – Interactions between Choreography, Dance and New Media Technologies'. In *Interface Cultures: Artistic Aspects of Interaction*, edited by Christa Sommerer, Laurent Mignonneau and Dorothée King, 225–36. Bielefeld: Transcript, 2008.
Deleuze, Gilles. 'Postscript on the Societies of Control'. *October* 59 (1992): 3–7.
Deleuze, Gilles. *Cinema II*. London; New York: A&C Black (Continuum), 2005.
Deleuze, Gilles and Félix Guattari. *Capitalisme et schizophrénie. 1. Anti-Oedipe*. Paris: Éd. de Minuit, 1972.
Deleuze, Gilles and Félix Guattari. *Mille plateaux*. Paris: Éditions de minuit, 1980.
Deleuze, Gilles and Félix Guattari. *A Thousand Plateaus: Capitalism and Schizophrenia*. Minneapolis: University of Minnesota Press, 1987.
Deleuze, Gilles and Félix Guattari. *A Thousand Plateaus: Capitalism and Schizophrenia*. London; New York: Continuum, 2004.
Derrida, Jacques. *Dissemination*. Translated by Barbara Johnson. Chicago: University of Chicago Press, 1981.
Desmond, Colm, Jeanette Doyle, Elizabeth Matthews, Cathy O'Carroll, Néill O'Dwyer, Michael O'Hara and Connell Vaughan. 'In Response to Bernard Stiegler: A Pharmacological Avant-Garde'. *In/Print* The History of the Present, no. 3 (2015): 73–92. https://doi.org/10.21427/D7G992.
Di Benedetto, Stephen. 'Embodying Scenography'. *Performance Research* 18, no. 3 (June 2013): 190. https://doi.org/10.1080/13528165.2013.818333.
Dick, Philip K. *Do Androids Dream of Electric Sheep?* Doubleday: Garden City, NY, 1968.
Dixon, Steve and Barry Smith. *Digital Performance: A History of New Media in Theater, Dance, Performance Art, and Installation*. Cambridge, MA: MIT Press, 2007.
Draper, John V., David B. Kaber and John M. Usher 'Telepresence'. *Human Factors* 40, no. 3 (1 September 1998): 354–75. https://doi.org/10.1518/001872098779591386.
Dziak, Mark. 'Big Five Personality Traits'. *Salem Press Encyclopedia*, 2020. http://search.ebscohost.com/login.aspx?direct=true&db=ers&AN=121772787 (accessed 11 January 2021).
Ekman, Ulrik. 'Of Transductive Speed – Stiegler'. *Parallax* 13, no. 4 (October 2007): 46–63. https://doi.org/10.1080/13534640701682792.
Emshwiller, Ed. *Hungers*. Los Angeles: Los Angeles Festival, 1987.
Farley, Kathryn. 'Digital Performance: A History of New Media in Theatre, Dance, Performance Art, and Installation (Review)'. *Theatre Journal* 59, no. 4 (2007): 690–1. https://doi.org/10.1353/tj.2008.0003.
Feral, Josette and Ron Bermingham. 'Alienation Theory in Multi-Media Performance'. *Theatre Journal* 39, no. 4 (December 1987): 461–72. https://doi.org/10.2307/3208248.
Fernandez, Aleix. *A-Cero XV Aniversario. 3D Mapping*. YouTube 720p, 2011. https://www.youtube.com/watch?v=un4L6iCS7rU.
Fernandez, Aleix. 'Dialogue with Aliex Fernandez', 18 June 2020.
Fisher, Mark. *Capitalist Realism: Is There No Alternative?* 1st edition. Winchester: O Books, 2009.
Fitzpatrick, Noel, Néill O'Dwyer and Mick O'Hara. *Aesthetics, Digital Studies and Bernard Stiegler*. New York: Bloomsbury Academic, forthcoming.

Foerster, Heinz von. 'Notes pour un epistemologie des objets vivants'. In *L'Unite de l'homme*, edited by Edgar Morin and Massimo Piattelli-Palmarini, 401–17. Paris: Editions du Seuil, 1974.
Foucault, Michel. *Surveiller et punir: naissance de la prison*. Paris: Gallimard, 1975.
Foucault, Michel. *Histoire de la sexualité*. Paris: Gallimard, 1976.
Foulkes, A. Peter. *Literature and Propaganda*. London; New York: Methuen, 1983.
Freytag, Gustav. *Die Technik des Dramas*. Leipzig: Hirzel, 1863.
Giannachi, Gabriella. *Virtual Theatres: An Introduction*. 1st edition. London; New York: Routledge, 2004.
Giannachi, Gabriella and Steve Benford. 'Temporal Expansion in Blast Theory's Day of the Figurines'. *PAJ: A Journal of Performance and Art* 30, no. 3 (September 2008): 60–9. https://doi.org/10.1162/pajj.2008.30.3.60.
Gibson, William. *Neuromancer*. London: Gollancz, 1984.
Gideon Obarzanek's Digital Moves. Vimeo 720p. PopTech, 2009. https://vimeo.com/7711107.
Greenspan, Alan. 'Greenspan Testimony on Sources of Financial Crisis'. *WSJ* (blog), 23 October 2008. https://blogs.wsj.com/economics/2008/10/23/greenspan-testimony-on-sources-of-financial-crisis/.
Griziotti, Giorgio. *Neurocapitalism: Technological Mediation and Vanishing Lines*. London: Minor Compositions, 2019.
Guattari, Félix. *Chaosmosis: An Ethico-Aesthetic Paradigm*. Bloomington: Indiana University Press, 1995.
'Happy 20th anniversary to OpenCV library!' https://opencv.org/anniversary/20/. (accessed 26 August 2020).
Haraway, Donna. *Simians, Cyborgs, and Women: The Reinvention of Nature*. 1st edition. New York: Routledge, 1991a.
Haraway, Donna. 'A Cyborg Manifesto: Science, Technology, and Socialist-Feminism in the Late Twentieth Century'. In *Simians, Cyborgs and Women: The Reinvention of Nature*. London: Routledge, 1991b. Original Publication 'Manifesto for Cyborgs: Science, Technology, and Socialist Feminism in the 1980s'. *Socialist Review*, no. 80 (1985): 65–108.
Hayles, N.K. *How We Became Posthuman : Virtual Bodies in Cybernetics, Literature, and Informatics*. Chicago, IL: University of Chicago Press, 1999.
Heidegger, Martin. *The Question Concerning Technology, and Other Essays*. 1st edition. New York: Harper & Row, 1977.
Heidegger, Martin. *Contributions to Philosophy (From Enowning)*. Translated by P. Emad and K. Maly. Bloomington: Indiana University Press, 1999.
Hern, Alex. 'Cambridge Analytica: How Did It Turn Clicks into Votes?' *The Guardian*, 6 May 2018, sec. News. https://www.theguardian.com/news/2018/may/06/cambridge-analytica-how-turn-clicks-into-votes-christopher-wylie.
Hoel, Aud Sissel and Iris van der Tuin. 'The Ontological Force of Technicity: Reading Cassirer and Simondon Diffractively'. *Philosophy & Technology* 26, no. 2 (June 2013): 187–202. https://doi.org/10.1007/s13347-012-0092-5.
Horkheimer, Max and Theodor W. Adorno. *Dialectic of Enlightenment: Philosophical Fragments*. Stanford, CA: Stanford University Press, 2002.
Howells, Christina and Gerald Moore, eds. *Stiegler and Technics*. Edinburgh: Edinburgh University Press Ltd, 2013.
Hui, Yuk. *On the Existence of Digital Objects*. 1st edition. Minneapolis: University of Minnesota Press, 2016.

Husserl, Edmund. *On the Phenomenology of the Consciousness of Internal Time (1893–1917)*. Netherlands: Springer, 2012.
'IEEE Conference on Computer Vision and Pattern Recognition (CVPR 2000)'. Hilton Head, SC, USA: IEEE Computer Society, 2000. https://ieeexplore.ieee.org/xpl/conhome/6894/proceeding.
Ihde, Don. 'Beyond the Skin-Bag'. *Nature* 424, no. 6949 (2003): 615.
Irigaray, Luce. *Speculum of the Other Woman*. Ithaca, NY: Cornell University Press, 1985a.
Irigaray, Luce. *This Sex Which Is Not One*. Translated by Catherine Porter and Carolyn Burke. Ithaca, NY: Cornell University Press, 1985b.
Jameson, Fredric. *Postmodernism, or, the Cultural Logic of Late Capitalism*. Durham, NC: Duke University Press, 1992.
Jones, Amelia. *Body Art/Performing the Subject*. Minneapolis: University of Minnesota Press, 1998.
Jonze, Spike. *Her*. Annapurna Pictures, Stage 6 Films, 2014.
Joy, Jérôme. 'Introduction à une Histoire de la Télémusique'. Université Laval Québec, 2010. https://ecitydoc.com/download/la-musique-etendue_pdf.
Kant, Immanuel. *Critique of the Power of Judgment*. New York: Cambridge University Press, 2000.
Kant, Immanuel and Werner S. Pluhar. *Critique of Judgment*. Indianapolis, IN: Hackett Pub. Co, 1987.
Karatani, Kōjin and Joel Wainwright. '"Critique Is Impossible without Moves": An Interview of Kojin Karatani by Joel Wainwright'. *Dialogues in Human Geography* 2, no. 1 (March 2012): 30–52. https://doi.org/10.1177/2043820612436923.
Karatani, Kōjin. *The Structure of World History: From Modes of Production to Modes of Exchange*. Translated by Michael K. Bourdaghs. Durham; London: Duke University Press, 2014.
Kaye, Nick. *Site-Specific Art: Performance, Place and Documentation*. London: Routledge, 2008.
'Kelman Group – Scott Kelman Biography'. http://www.kelmangroup.com/scottBiog.php (accessed 24 June 2020).
Khan, Nora N. 'Managing Boundaries with Your Intelligent Personal Agent'. *Rhizome*, Winter 2015. http://rhizome.org/editorial/2015/apr/07/boundary-management/.
Landow, George P. *Hypertext: The Convergence of Contemporary Critical Theory and Technology*. Baltimore: Johns Hopkins University Press, 1992.
Langton, Christopher G. *Artificial Life: An Overview*. Cambridge, MA: MIT Press, 1997.
Lavender, Andy. 'Mise en Scène, Hypermediacy and the Sensorium'. In *Intermediality in Theatre and Performance*, edited by Freda Chapple and Chiel Kattenbelt, 55–66. Amsterdam, Netherlands: Rodopi, 2006.
Lehmann, Hans-Thies. *Postdramatic Theatre*. 1st edition. London; New York: Routledge, 2006.
Leroi-Gourhan, André. *Le geste et la parole*. Paris: A. Michel, 1964.
Leroi-Gourhan, André. *Gesture and Speech*. Translated by Anna Bostock Berger. Cambridge, MA: MIT Press, 1993.
Lotker, Sodja and Richard Gough. 'On Scenography: Editorial'. *Performance Research* 18, no. 3 (1 June 2013): 3–6. https://doi.org/10.1080/13528165.2013.818306.

Lyotard, Jean-François. *The Postmodern Condition: A Report on Knowledge.* Manchester: University Press, 1984.
Lyotard, Jean-François. *The Inhuman: Reflections on Time.* 1st edition. Stanford, CA: Stanford University Press, 1992.
Mann, Paul. *The Theory-Death of the Avant-Garde.* Bloomington, IN: Indiana University Press, 1991.
Manovich, Lev. *The Language of New Media.* 1st edition. Cambridge, MA: MIT Press, 2001.
Marx, Karl. *Grundrisse: Foundations of the Critique of Political Economy.* Translated by Martin Nicolaus. Reprint edition. Penguin Classics, 1993.
Marx, Karl, Serge L. Levitsky, and Inc Recorded Books. 'Part One: Commodities and Money, SECTION 4: The Fetishism of Commodities and the Secret Thereof'. In *Das Kapital: A Critique of Political Economy.* Washington, DC: Regnery Publishing, 2012. http://rbdigital.oneclickdigital.com.
McCabe, David. 'Court Upholds Net Neutrality Repeal, with Some Caveats'. *The New York Times,* 1 October 2019, sec. Technology. https://www.nytimes.com/2019/10/01/technology/net-neutrality-repeal-broadband.html
Mckinney, Joslin. *The Cambridge Introduction to Scenography.* Cambridge; New York: Cambridge University Press, 2009.
McKinney, Joslin. 'Scenography, Spectacle and the Body of the Spectator'. *Performance Research* 18, no. 3 (June 2013): 63–74. https://doi.org/10.1080/13528165.2013.818316.
McKinney, Joslin and Scott Palmer. *Scenography Expanded.* London; New York: Bloomsbury Methuen Drama, 2017.
'MEDPOR | Stryker'. Accessed 3 April 2019. https://www.stryker.com/us/en/craniomaxillofacial/systems/medpor.html.
Mee, Erin B. 'The Audience Is the Message: Blast Theory's App-Drama Karen'. *TDR/The Drama Review* 60, no. 3 (2016): 165–71.
Moore, Gregory. *Nietzsche, Biology and Metaphor.* Cambridge; New York: Cambridge University Press, 2002.
Moulier Boutang, Yann. *Cognitive Capitalism.* Cambridge, UK; Malden, MA: Polity Press, 2011.
'Net Neutrality: A Two-Tier Internet Would Be Bad for Europe'. *The Irish Times.* 6 March 2015. https://www.irishtimes.com/opinion/net-neutrality-a-two-tier-internet-would-be-bad-for-europe-1.2128078.
Nichols, Bill. 'The Work of Culture in the Age of Cybernetic Systems'. *Screen* 29, no. 1 (1988): 22–46.
Nietzsche, Friedrich, Maudemarie Clark and Alan J. Swensen. *On the Genealogy of Morality.* Indianapolis: Hackett Pub. Co., 1998.
Nietzsche, Friedrich Wilhelm and Anthony M Ludovici. *The Will to Power: An Attempted Transvaluation of All Values.* Vol. II, United States: Obscure Press: Made available through Hoopla digital, 2013.
Obarzanek, Gideon. *Chunky Move: Mortal Engine.* Contemporary Dance Performance. Art Films, 2008a. https://www.artfilms.com.au/item/chunky-move-mortal-engine.
Obarzanek, Gideon. *Mortal Engine by Chunky Move.* HD (Trailer). Melbroune, Australia, 2008b. https://www.youtube.com/watch?v=sbjOMualLVs.
Obarzanek, Gideon. 'Mortal Engine: A Dance-Video-Music-Laser Performance'. *Portfolio.* Chunky Move, 2008c. http://chunkymove.com/.

Obarzanek, Gideon. Interview with Gideon Obarzanek at the Southbank Centre, London. Interview by Néill O'Dwyer. Audio, 7 November 2012.
Obermaier, Klaus. 2019. 'Dialogue with Klaus Obermaier', 13 September.
Obermaier, Klaus and Chris Haring. 'Artist's Statement: D.a.v.e. – Digital Amplified Video Engine'. Portfolio. Exile.At. 1999. http://www.exile.at/dave/project.html.
O'Dwyer, Néill. 'The Cultural Critique of Bernard Stiegler: Reflecting on the Computational Performances of Klaus Obermaier'. In *The Performing Subject in the Space of Technology: Through the Virtual Towards the Real*, edited by Matthew Causey, Emma Meehan and Néill O'Dwyer, 34–52. Palgrave Studies in Performance and Technology. London: Palgrave Macmillan, 2015a.
O'Dwyer, Néill. 'The Scenographic Turn: The Pharmacology of the Digitisation of Scenography'. *Theatre and Performance Design* 1, no. 1–2 (3 April 2015b): 48–63. https://doi.org/10.1080/23322551.2015.1023667.
O'Dwyer, Néill. 'Death and Ecstasy: Reflections on a Technological Sublime'. *Proceedings of the European Society of Aesthetics* 8 (2016a): 354–76.
O'Dwyer, Néill. 'From Avant-Garde to Negentropy: An Aesthetic Deployment of Bernard Stiegler's Genealogy of the Sensible'. Thesis, Trinity College, 2016b. http://www.tara.tcd.ie/handle/2262/83151.
O'Dwyer, Néill. 'Organology, Grammatisation and Exosomatic Memory in Samuel Beckett's Krapp's Last Tape'. In *Aesthetics, Digital Studies and Bernard Stiegler*, edited by Noel Fitzpatrick, Néill O'Dwyer and Mick O'Hara. London; New York: Bloomsbury Academic, forthcoming.
O'Dwyer, Néill and Nicholas Johnson. 'Exploring Volumetric Video and Narrative through Samuel Beckett's Play'. *International Journal of Performance Arts and Digital Media* 15, no. 1 (2 January 2019): 53–69. https://doi.org/10.1080/14794713.2019.1567243.
O'Dwyer, Néill, Nicholas Johnson, Enda Bates, Rafael Pagés, Jan Ondřej, Konstantinos Amplianitis, David Monaghan and Aljoša Smolic. 'Samuel Beckett in Virtual Reality: Exploring Narrative Using Free Viewpoint Video'. *Leonardo* (26 December 2018): 1–10. https://doi.org/10.1162/leon_a_01721.
O'Dwyer, Néill, Gareth W. Young, Nicholas Johnson, Emin Zerman and Aljosa Smolic. 'Mixed Reality and Volumetric Video in Cultural Heritage: Expert Opinions on Augmented and Virtual Reality'. In *Culture and Computing*, 195–214. Springer, Cham, 2020. https://doi.org/10.1007/978-3-030-50267-6_16.
'OpenCV.Org | About'. https://opencv.org/about/. (accessed 26 August 2020).
Oudsten, Frank den. *Space.Time.Narrative: The Exhibition as Post-Spectacular Stage*. 1st edition. Burlington: Routledge, 2012.
Palmer, Scott. 'A "Choréographie" of Light and Space: Adolphe Appia and the First Scenographic Turn'. *Theatre and Performance Design* 1, no. 1–2 (3 April 2015): 31–47. https://doi.org/10.1080/23322551.2015.1024975.
Parker-Starbuck, J. *Cyborg Theatre: Corporeal/Technological Intersections in Multimedia Performance*. Houndmills, Basingstoke, Hampshire; New York: Palgrave Macmillan, 2011.
Pearson, Mike. *Site-Specific Performance*. Houndmills, Basingstoke, Hampshire; New York: Palgrave, 2010.
Phelan, Peggy. *Unmarked: The Politics of Performance*. 1st edition. London; New York: Routledge, 1993.
Piccini, Angela and Baz Kershaw. 'Practice as Research in Performance: From Epistemology to Evaluation'. *Digital Creativity* 15, no. 2 (1 April 2004): 86–92. https://doi.org/10.1080/14626260408520170.

Pil Choi, Jay and Byung-Cheol Kim. 'Net Neutrality and Investment Incentives'. *The RAND Journal of Economics* 41, no. 3 (4 August 2010): 446–71. https://doi.org/10.1111/j.1756-2171.2010.00107.x.

Plato, and Reginald Hackforth. *Plato's Phaedrus*. Reprinted. Cambridge: Cambridge University Press, 1993.

Poggioli, Renato. *The Theory of the Avant-Garde*. Cambridge, MA: Belknap Press of Harvard University Press, 1968.

Poincaré, Henri. 'Sur l'équilibre d'une Masse Fluide Animée d'un Mouvement de Rotation'. *Acta Mathematica* 7, no. 1 (1885): 259–380.

Pritchett, James. *The Development of Chance Techniques in the Music of John Cage, 1950–1956*. Michigan: UMI Dissertation Services, 1988.

Rifkin, Jeremy. *Third Industrial Revolution*. Basingstoke: Griffin, 2013.

Riskin, Jessica. *Genesis Redux: Essays in the History and Philosophy of Artificial Life*. Chicago: University of Chicago Press, 2007.

Rose, Frank. 'Karen, an App That Knows You All Too Well'. *The New York Times*, 2 April 2015, sec. Arts. https://www.nytimes.com/2015/04/05/arts/karen-an-app-that-knows-you-all-too-well.html.

Ross, Daniel. 'Politics and Aesthetics, or, Transformations of Aristotle in Bernard Stiegler'. *Transformations Journal* no. 17 (2009). http://www.transformationsjournal.org/2009-issue-no-17-bernard-stiegler-and-the-question-of-technics/.

Rouse, Rebecca. 'Partners: Human and Nonhuman Performers and Interactive Narrative in Postdigital Theater'. In *Interactive Storytelling*, edited by Rebecca Rouse, Hartmut Koenitz and Mads Haahr, 369–82. ICIDS 2018. Lecture Notes in Computer Science, Vol. 11318. Springer, Cham. http://doi-org-443.webvpn.fjmu.edu.cn/10.1007/978-3-030-04028-4_44

Rouvroy, Antoinette and Thomas Berns. 'Algorithmic Governmentality and Prospects of Emancipation: Disparateness as a Precondition for Individuation through Relationships?'. *Réseaux* 177, no. 1 (2013): 163. https://doi.org/10.3917/res.177.0163.

Russell, Charles. *The Avant-Garde Today: An International Anthology*. Champaign, IL: University of Illinois Press, 1981.

Salter, Chris. *Entangled: Technology and the Transformation of Performance*. Cambridge, MA; London: MIT Press, 2010.

Saltz, David Z. 'Media, Technology, and Performance'. *Theatre Journal* 65, no. 3 (9 October 2013): 421–32. https://doi.org/10.1353/tj.2013.0086.

Schechner, Richard. '6 Axioms for Environmental Theatre'. *The Drama Review: TDR* 12, no. 3 (1968): 41. https://doi.org/10.2307/1144353.

Schechner, Richard. *Environmental Theatre*. 1st edition. New York: Hawthorn, 1973.

Scheer, Edward and Rosemary Klich. *Multimedia Performance*. Houndmills, Basingstoke, Hampshire; New York: Palgrave Macmillan, 2011.

Scott, David. *Gilbert Simondon's Psychic and Collective Individuation*. 1st edition. Edinburgh: Edinburgh University Press, 2014.

Scott, Ridley. *Blade Runner*. The Ladd Company, Shaw Brothers, Warner Bros., 1982.

Shaw, Philip. *The Sublime*. London; New York: Routledge, 2006.

Simondon, Gilbert. *L'individuation psychique et collective: à la lumière des notions de forme, information, potentiel et métastabilité*. Paris: Aubier, 1989.

Simondon, Gilbert. *L'individuation psychique et collective*. Paris: Flammarion, 2007.

Simondon, Gilbert. 'On the Mode of Existence of Technical Objects'. Translated by Ninian Mellamphy, Dan Mellamphy and Nandita Biswas Mellamphy. *Deleuze Studies* 5, no. 3 (1 November 2011): 407–24. https://doi.org/10.3366/dls.2011.0029.

Simondon, Gilbert. *Du mode d'existence des objets techniques*. Paris: Editions Aubier, 2012.

Simondon, Gilbert. *On the Mode of Existence of Technical Objects*. Translated by Cecile Malaspina and John Rogove. Minneapolis, MN: University Of Minnesota Press, 2017a.

Simondon, Gilbert. *L'individuation à La Lumière Des Notions de Forme et d'information [Individtuation in Light of the Notions of Form and Information]*. Grenoble: Editions Jérôme Millon, 2017b.

Sinnerbrink, Robert. 'Culture Industry Redux: Stiegler and Derrida on Technics and Cultural Politcs'. *Transformations: Journal of Media and Culture* 17 (2009). http://www.transformationsjournal.org/journal/issue_17/article_05.shtml.

Sjögren, Per, Rachel Fisher, Lena Kallings, Ulrika Svenson, Göran Roos and Hellénius Mai-Lis. 'Stand Up for Health – Avoiding Sedentary Behaviour Might Lengthen Your Telomeres: Secondary Outcomes from a Physical Activity RCT in Older People'. *Br J Sports Med* 48, no. 19 (1 October 2014): 1407–9. https://doi.org/10.1136/bjsports-2013-093342.

Smith, Ernie. 'This Is What 1970s Motion Capture Tech Looked Like'. *Vice* (blog), 20 March 2017. https://www.vice.com/en_us/article/wnkbzz/this-is-what-1970s-motion-capture-tech-looked-like.

Smith, Marquard, ed. *Stelarc: The Monograph*. 1st MIT Press paperback edition. Cambridge, Massachusetts; London, England: The MIT Press, 2007.

Staunton, Denis. 'The Third-Rate, the Lightweight and the School Mate – Boris Johnson's Cabinet'. *The Irish Times*, 25 July 2019, sec. News: UK. https://www.irishtimes.com/news/world/uk/the-third-rate-the-lightweight-and-the-school-mate-boris-johnson-s-cabinet-1.3967673.

Stelarc. 'STELARC | THIRD HAND'. Portfolio. Stelarc.org, 1980. http://stelarc.org/?catID=20265.

Stelarc. 'Prosthetics, Robotics and Remote Existence: Postevolutionary Strategies'. *Leonardo* 24, no. 5 (1991): 591. https://doi.org/10.2307/1575667.

Stelarc. 'STELARC | EXTRA EAR'. Portfolio. Stelarc.org, 1996. http://stelarc.org/?catID=20229.

Stelarc. 'STELARC | EAR ON ARM'. Portfolio. Stelarc.org, 2008. http://stelarc.org/?catID=20242.

Stelarc. 'Dialogue with Stelarc', 24 May 2020.

Stern, Nathaniel. *Interactive Art and Embodiment: The Implicit Body as Performance*. 1st edition. Canterbury: Gylphi Limited, 2013.

Stiegler, Bernard. *Technics and Time, 1: The Fault of Epimetheus*. Translated by Richard Beardsworth and George Collins. Stanford, CA: Stanford University Press, 1998.

Stiegler, Bernard. *Technics and Time, 2: Disorientation*. Translated by Stephen Barker. Stanford, CA: Stanford University Press, 2008.

Stiegler, Bernard. *Acting Out*. Stanford, CA: Stanford University Press, 2009a.

Stiegler, Bernard. 'The Theater of Individuation: Phase-Shift and Resolution in Simondon and Heidegger'. *Parrhesia* 7 (2009b): 46–57.

Stiegler, Bernard. 'Amateur'. Ars Industrialis, 2010a. http://arsindustrialis.org/amateur-english-version.

Stiegler, Bernard. 'The Age of De-Proletarianization: Art and Teaching Art in Post-Consumerist Culture'. In *ArtFutures: Current Issues in Higher Arts Education*, edited by Kieran Corcoran, Carla Delfos and Floris Solleveld, 10–19. Amsterdam: ELIA, 2010b.

Stiegler, Bernard. *Taking Care of Youth and the Generations*. Stanford, CA: Stanford University Press, 2010c.

Stiegler, Bernard. *Technics and Time, 3: Cinematic Time and the Questions of Malaise*. Translated by Stephen Barker. Stanford, CA: Stanford University Press, 2011a.

Stiegler, Bernard. 'The Proletarianization of Sensibility'. Edited by Calvin Bedient and David Lau and translated by Arne De Boever. *Lana Turner: A Journal of Poetry and Opinion*, no. 4 (2011b): 124–40.

Stiegler, Bernard. *What Makes Life Worth Living: On Pharmacology*. 1st edition. Cambridge: Polity Press, 2013.

Stiegler, Bernard. *Symbolic Misery Volume 1: The Hyperindustrial Epoch*. 1st edition. Oxford: Polity Press, 2014.

Stiegler, Bernard. *Bernard Stiegler – From the Anthropocene to the Neganthropocene [Néguanthropocène] – YouTube*. YouTube HD. Vol. 1. 1 vols. Digital Studies. Dublin, Ireland: Dublin Institute of Technology (DIT), 2015a. https://www.youtube.com/watch?v=CuIStdHApaw.

Stiegler, Bernard. *Symbolic Misery Volume 2: The Katastrophē of the Sensible*. 1st edition. Malden, MA: Polity Press, 2015b.

Stiegler, Bernard. *Automatic Society: Volume 1: The Future of Work*. Volume 1st edition. Cambridge, UK; Malden, MA: Polity Press, 2016.

Stiegler, Bernard. 'The Proletarianization of Sensibility'. *Boundary 2* 44, no. 1 (2017): 5–18. https://doi.org/10.1215/01903659-3725833.

Stiegler, Bernard. *The Neganthropocene*. Translated by Daniel Ross. London: Open Humanities Press, 2018.

Stiegler, Bernard. 'Biopower, Psychopower and the Logic of the Scapegoat: Political and Industrial Criticism of Technology'. *Ars Industrialis*. http://www.arsindustrialis.org/node/2924. (accessed 6 January 2021).

Stiegler, Bernard and Johann Rossouw. 'Suffocated Desire, or How the Cultural Industry Destroys the Individual: Contribution to a Theory of Mass Consumption'. *Parrhesia: A Journal of Critical Philosophy* 13 (2011): 52–61.

Stiegler, Bernard, Ben Roberts, Jeremy Gilbert and Mark Hayward. 'Bernard Stiegler: "A Rational Theory of Miracles: On Pharmacology and Transindividuation"'. *New Formations* 77, no. 1 (1 December 2012): 164–84. https://doi.org/10.3898/NEWF.77.10.2012.

Stocker, Gerfried and Christine Schöpf, eds. *Ars Electronica 2009 ARTBOOK*. Exhibition Catelogues. Germany: Hatje Cantz, 2010. http://www.artbook.com/9783775724982.html.

Stoppiello, Dawn. Interview with Dawn Stoppiello (Troika Ranch). Interview by Néill O'Dwyer. Video teleconference, 20 December 2018. YouTube (Private). https://www.youtube.com/watch?v=qR2g6eq0Ar0&t=2327s.

Stoppiello, Dawn and Mark Coniglio. 'FleshMotor'. In *Women, Art, and Technology*, edited by Judy Malloy, 441–51, Cambridge, MA: MIT Press, 2003.

Stoppiello, Dawn and Mark Coniglio. 'In Plane (1994) | Troika Ranch'. Portfolio. Troika Ranch. http://troikaranch.org/portfolio-item/in-plane/. (accessed 6 March 2019).

Stott, Tim. *Play and Participation in Contemporary Arts Practices*. New York, NY; London: Routledge, 2015.

Subcommission on Quaternary Stratigraphy. 'Working Group on the "Anthropocene"'. http://quaternary.stratigraphy.org/working-groups/anthropocene/. (accessed 30 August 2020).

Subramanian, Meera. 'Anthropocene Now: Influential Panel Votes to Recognize Earth's New Epoch'. *Nature* (21 May 2019). https://doi.org/10.1038/d41586-019-01641-5.

Suchan, Brigitte. 'Vivisector Reviews: Technology Drives Out Dance'. Portfolio. www.exile.at, 9 January 2002. http://www.exile.at/vivisector/reviews.html.

Ranch, Troika. 'The Need (1989) | Troika Ranch', 1989. https://troikaranch.org/portfolio-item/the-need/.

Ranch, Troika. 'Tactile Diaries (1990) | Troika Ranch', 1990. https://troikaranch.org/portfolio-item/tactile-diaries/.

Ranch, Troika. 'In Plane (1994) | Troika Ranch', 1994. https://troikaranch.org/portfolio-item/in-plane/.

The Century of the Self. Documentary. British Broadcasting Corporation (BBC), RDF Media, 2002.

Thompson, Seth. 'Seth Thompson: Troika Ranch on Interactive Performance Design'. Art Education Blog. https://seththompson.info, 2002. https://seththompson.info/essays/video-interviews/troika-ranch-on-interactive-performance-design/.

Tomkins, Calvin. *Duchamp: A Biography*. Revised edition. New York: The Museum of Modern Art, 2014.

Tran, Mark. 'Girl Starved to Death while Parents Raised Virtual Child in Online Game'. *The Guardian*, 5 March 2010, sec. World news. http://www.theguardian.com/world/2010/mar/05/korean-girl-starved-online-game.

Vaccari, Andrés and Belinda Barnet. 'Issue No. 17 2009 – Bernard Stiegler and the Question of Technics', 2009. http://researchbank.swinburne.edu.au/vital/access/services/Download/swin:13936/SOURCE2.

Villeneuve, Denis. *Blade Runner 2049*. Alcon Entertainment, Columbia Pictures, Sony, 2017.

Virilio, Paul. *Open Sky*. London: Verso, 1997.

Weiss, Frieder. Frieder Weiss Interview. Interview by Néill O'Dwyer. Google+ Hangouts on Air, 9 February 2015. https://www.youtube.com/watch?v=dKhDyq7wRGA.

Weiss, Frieder. 'Dialogue with Frieder Weiss', 23 September 2019.

Whitelaw, Mitchell. *Metacreation: Art and Artificial Life*. Cambridge, MA: MIT Press, 2004.

Wiener, Norbert. *Cybernetics or Control and Communication in the Animal and the Machine*. Cambridge, MA: MIT Press, 1965.

Wiener, Norbert. *The Human Use of Human Beings: Cybernetics and Society*. London: Free Association Books, 1989.

Winnicott, Donald Woods. *The Child, the Family, and the Outside World*. Da Capo, Reading, MA: Perseus Pub., 1992.

Winthrop, Robert H. *Dictionary of Concepts in Cultural Anthropology*. New York: Greenwood, 1991.

World Wide Web Foundation. 'History of the Web'. https://webfoundation.org/about/vision/history-of-the-web/. (accessed 9 February 2018).

Zuidervaart, Lambert. 'Theodor W. Adorno'. In *The Stanford Encyclopedia of Philosophy*, edited by Edward N. Zalta, Metaphysics Research Lab: Stanford University, Winter 2015. https://plato.stanford.edu/archives/win2015/entries/adorno/.

Index

A-cero 127, 129, 130, 141
activism 5, 8, 9, 103, 167, 170
Adams, Matt 156, 158
Adorno, Theodor 5, 73, 126, 130–2, 182 n.13, 186 n.3
Aesthetic Theory (Adorno) 130–2, 186 n.3
agency 20, 35, 42, 44, 45, 66, 73, 74, 80, 92, 103, 106, 166, 179
  algorithmic 120
  computer 42, 80
  political 170–2
  psychosomatic 178
  technological 51, 77, 94, 158, 178
AirDrums (Davies) 27
algorithmic governmentality 159–63, 174, 177
Allegue, Ludivine 23
Analytic of the Sublime (Kant) 116
Anthropocene 162–5, 188 n.8
Apparition (Obermaier) 79, 84, 93–9, 100, 102, 107–9, 113, 123–5, 128, 185 n.6
  sociopolitical metaphors of 99–101
Appia, Adolphe 1, 14, 107, 108
archi-flux 139, 187 n.10
Aristotle 47, 65
artefactual ontogenesis 72, 172
artificial intelligence (AI) 122
Ascott, Roy 183 n.4, 183 n.5
Ashby, William Ross 185 n.5
audience-engagement 150–1
audio-visualization 1, 4, 14, 15, 19, 20–2, 24, 26, 31, 33, 36–8, 41, 43, 49, 52, 54, 65, 80, 93, 94, 106, 107, 110, 111, 114, 120, 122, 127, 133, 135, 146, 157
Auroux, Sylvain 108
Auslander, Philip 6, 182 n.16
Austin, J. L. 60

author–audience relation 156–8
automation 19, 40, 108, 111–13, 122, 132, 141, 142, 160, 162, 164, 165, 167, 174, 175, 177, 178
avant-garde theory 4–9, 13, 14, 17, 18, 21, 22, 25–7, 35–6, 42–4, 73, 75, 79, 95, 101, 106, 114, 119, 125, 126, 131, 141, 142, 145, 146, 164, 165, 169–74, 176, 177, 185 n.6

Badiou, Alain 118, 180 n.1
Barbara, Joan La 27
Baugh, Christopher 10
Bay-Cheng, Sarah 15
Bella Lewitzky 26, 181 n.2
Benjamin, Walter 36–40, 132, 136, 182 n.15
Berkeley Software Distribution License (BSD-License) 143
Bernays, Edward 138, 187 n.9
Berners Lee, Tim 4, 18, 180 n.7
bifurcation 164–6, 168–72, 177, 189 n.11
bio art 53, 54, 67, 73, 184 n.17
biological organisms 55, 60, 67, 68, 75, 102, 120
biometric sensing 19, 34, 88, 99, 101, 106, 109, 110, 120, 125, 170, 174, 175
bio-techniques 54–5
Blade Runner 2049 (Villeneuve) 127, 139–41, 146, 147, 169
Blast Theory 4, 9, 12, 16, 21, 147, 149–53, 169, 173, 175, 177, 187 n.1, 188 n.3
  algorithmic governmentality 159–61
  audience 156–8
  capitalism 159–63
  dramaturgy 155–6

hyperindustrial system 163–6
Karen (*see Karen* (Blast Theory))
mise-en-scène 153–5
bleep-bloop method 29
Blind Messengers (Coates) 186 n.1
Boal, Agusto 150
Body Art (Jones) 75–6
body scenography 81–2
body–technology–society relationship 72–5
Bolter, Jay David 123
Bringer, Johannes 14
Bürger, Peter 5

Cage, John 43, 44
calculability 159, 170
California Institute of the Arts (CalArts) 9, 26–7, 35
Canguilhem, George 66, 67, 73
capitalism 39, 52, 100–1, 131, 133, 147, 159–64, 170, 171, 174, 177, 185 n.6
casual creative 23, 180 n.8
Causey, Matthew 15
Centre for Experiments in Art, Information and Technology (CEAIT) 46, 48, 51
Chaikin, Joseph 35
choreo-dramaturgy 94, 95, 98, 108
Chunky Move 4, 9, 16, 21, 22, 51, 103, 105–8, 161, 169, 173, 175
  and computer 122
  general organology 119–21
  grammatization 108–10
  Mortal Engine 116–19
  Pharmakon 124–6
  specificities of digital technology 111–15, 122–5
Coates, George 186 n.1
computer 14, 95, 98, 101, 102, 109–10, 122, 123, 140, 166, 185 n.4
  agency 42, 80
  Apple Mac 28
  assisted 40
  human–computer 16, 42, 79, 94, 114, 120, 153, 175, 179
  languages 142, 145
  programmer 27, 146
  scientists 146

simulations 186 n.7
vision 19, 79, 80, 93, 98, 105, 109, 120, 141–5, 174, 178, 187 n.12
Coniglio, Mark 25–30, 33–5, 42, 43, 45, 46, 48–51, 181 n.4, 181 n.7, 182 n.18
Crary, Jonathan 141, 147
Critique of Judgement (Kant) 116–17
culture industry 7, 22, 40, 73, 79, 126, 127, 130, 133, 136, 139, 141, 142, 145–7, 161, 173, 182 n.13
Culture Industry, The: Enlightenment as Mass Deception (Horkheimer and Adorno) 131–2
Cunningham, Merce 80, 106, 124, 185 n.3
cutting-edge technology 2, 21, 23, 29, 110, 122–3, 130, 131, 142, 143, 174, 175, 179
cyberculture 52–7, 84, 102
cybernetic organism 183 n.2
cybernetic technology 3, 4, 11, 15, 16, 41, 43, 52, 55, 66, 74, 83, 111–13, 122, 133, 174, 178, 180 n.2, 184 n.11
cyborg 11, 15, 33, 52, 53, 55–7, 71, 74, 76, 80, 84, 85, 91, 178
Cyborg Manifesto (Haraway) 55
Cyborg Theatre (Parker-Starbuck) 15–16

Das Ereignis (Heidegger) 118
data processing 20, 88, 110, 145
D.A.V.E. (Obermaier) 79–84, 86, 88, 89, 91–3, 185 n.5
  technical determinacy 84–5
Debord, Guy 178
degrees of freedom 113, 119, 185 n.5
DeLahunta, Scott 79, 84–5, 94–6, 186 n.8
Deleuze, Gilles 8, 47, 132, 133, 135–7, 158, 176, 182 n.19
democratization 15, 17, 30, 31, 36–9, 52, 132, 144
Derrida, Jacques 136, 181 n.12
design-led performance 2, 17, 19, 20, 176
desire 136–8
  and programme industry 138–9

dialectical materialism 8, 131
Di Benedetto, Stephen 53–4
Dick, Philip K. 139
digital
   and cybernetic technologies 83–4
   doppelganger 50, 159, 161–2
   double 50, 81, 83, 88, 89, 141, 159–62
   media 1, 5, 11, 13–15, 21, 25, 48, 49, 79, 81–4, 105, 111, 143, 145, 146, 149, 158, 166, 180 n.8
   performance 5, 10, 12, 13, 15, 21, 93, 110, 147, 166, 176, 177, 181 n.7
   specificity 14, 15, 45, 51, 169, 175–6
   technology 1, 3, 4, 8–11, 13, 14, 17–18, 20–3, 30, 36, 37, 39–41, 45, 46, 51, 56, 71, 75, 84–6, 92–4, 96, 99, 108, 111, 112, 114, 115, 118, 122–4, 142, 151, 165, 167, 171, 175, 178, 179, 180 n.3, 182 n.18
display technologies 141, 187 n.12
Dixon, Steve 12
dramaturgy 2, 32, 35, 43, 45, 49, 51, 81, 84–6, 93–6, 98, 102, 108, 114, 115, 125, 150, 155–6, 167, 178, 179
dualism 50, 81, 88, 158

Electronic Cafe International (ECI) 29, 30, 35, 38, 42, 45, 46, 51
electronic circuitry 73
Emshwiller, Ed. 27
entropic process 163, 177
entropy 163, 164, 188 n.9
Environmental Theatre (Schechner) 150
epigenetic layer 69
epiphylogenesis 69–71
Event 2, 51, 60, 85, 119, 175, 180 n.1
exosomatic environment 59, 66, 68–70, 73, 102, 157, 178, 183 n.3
expanded scenography 16, 85
experimentalism 4, 5, 10, 12, 13, 35, 42, 43, 114, 170, 173, 174
exteriorization 62, 69, 70, 136, 137, 160

Extra Ear (Stelarc) 53–77
Eyecon 106

Fancher, Hampton 139
feedback 37, 48, 68, 144
   loop 68, 94–5, 114, 120, 158, 162
Feral, Josette 15
Fernandez, Aleix 128–9
Fisher, Mark 100
five-factor model 156, 188 n.4
Forum Theatre 150
Foucault, Michel 132, 133, 158
Frankfurt School 131, 132, 136
Freud, Sigmund 136–8, 187 n.7, 187 n.9

Galloway, Kit 29, 30, 31–2, 34, 35, 37, 181 n.7
geminoids 185 n.4
genotype 69, 102, 184 n.12
Georges Coates Performance Works 9, 35
Gesture and Speech (Leroi-Gourhan) 61–2
Gibson, William 57
global connectivity 12, 17
Gough, Richard 10
grammatization 108–10, 124, 165–6
Green, Michael 139
Grusin, Richard 123
Guattari, Felix 47, 137

Haraway, Donna 4, 15, 55–6, 73, 81
Haring, Chris 80–6
Hayles, N. Katherine 4, 15, 55
Heidegger, Martin 118
Her (Jonze) 153
hominization 70, 177
homogenization 6, 131, 134
Horkheimer, Max 130–2
human
   and automaton 173
   consciousness 40
   and feedback 68, 120
   genotype 69, 102
   human–computer 16, 42, 79, 94, 114, 120, 153, 175, 179
   individuation 48, 65, 66
   and non-human 67, 94, 101, 115, 120

INDEX

performativity 174
phenotype 67
and software 45, 111
and technology 61, 62, 67, 101, 102, 179
and world 63–4
human–machine interaction 12, 16, 42, 43, 79, 94, 114, 153, 179
Hungers (Emshwiller) 27
Husserl, Edmund 186 n.6, 188 n.6
hybrid knowledge 115
hylomorphism 64–5
hypercapitalism 162, 163, 172, 173, 176
hyperindustrial 101
　capitalism 159, 163, 171
　economy 163–6
　epoch 75, 101, 110
hypermodernity 75, 165, 166
hyperprofiling 188 n.7
hyper-rationalization 110, 131–2, 170, 175
hyper-synchronization 134

IDAT '99 (International Dance and Technology 1999) 49, 183 n.20
indeterminism 43, 44, 95, 113–15, 121, 173–5
individuation 47–9, 63–6, 74, 102, 105, 106, 119–21, 125, 134–8, 147, 159–61, 163, 165, 171, 172, 176–8
industrial temporal objects 133, 136, 139, 142, 160, 170, 186 n.6
In Plane (Troika Ranch) 26, 45–7, 49–51
intelligent personal agents (IPAs) 156
Intel Research 143
Interactor (Coniglio) 28–9, 181 n.4
intermedial 11, 13, 14, 170
internet 2–4, 12, 15, 17, 25, 30, 52, 53, 71, 105, 154, 174, 180 n.7
intersubjectivity 3, 15–18, 39, 40, 42, 45, 54, 55, 61, 72, 75, 84, 94, 99, 101, 133, 136, 160, 166, 178
invention 1–5, 8, 10, 17–19, 24, 26, 30, 41–4, 53, 63, 77, 107, 113, 126, 164

Invisible Theatre 151
Irigaray, Luce 55, 73
Ishiguro, Hiroshi 112–13
Itseez 143

Jameson, Frederic 100
Jonze, Spike 153

Kalypso software 106–7
Kant, Immanuel 70, 116–19, 130, 158, 170, 185 n.6
Karatani, Kōjin 144–5
Karen (Blast Theory) 147, 151–62, 166, 167
Kelman, Scott 35
kinaesthetic technique 11, 27, 30, 32–4, 38, 42, 44–5, 95, 106, 122
Klich, Rosemary 11, 12, 79
Kongerød, Desirée 93
Krapp's Last Tape (O'Dwyer) 111

Lavender, Andy 83
Lehmann, Hans-Thies 2
Leroi-Gourhan, André 61–3, 65, 67–70, 73, 183 n.8
liberalism 126, 147, 158
L'individuation Psychique et Collective (Simondon) 64
Living Theatre 35, 181 n.10
logos 46
Lotker, Sodja 10
Lyotard, Jean-Francois 118

McKinney, Joslin 11, 16
Mac Plus 28
Mann, Paul 5–7
Manovich, Lev 37
Marx, Karl 8, 130, 131, 135, 186 n.5
Masura, Nadja 186 n.2
mathematical sublime 118–19
'MEDPOR | Stryker' 59–60
Mee, Erin B. 157, 158
metastasis 9, 68, 162
microchip 1–3, 52, 142
microelectronics 40, 113
microprocessor 41, 44
MidiDancer technology 25, 28–30, 32–5, 38, 42, 43, 45, 49–50
Midiphone 182 n.18

INDEX

mise-en-scène 2, 11, 16, 31–3, 49, 50, 80, 84–5, 87, 93, 95, 113, 119, 120, 153–5, 174
mitosis 121, 186 n.7
Mortal Engine (Obarzanek) 105–8, 115–19, 124–5, 185 n.1, 185 n.2
motion-tracking 93, 95, 97, 109, 123–5, 143, 174
multimedia 11, 86, 124, 185 n.3, 186 n.1
Musical Instrument Digital Interface (MIDI) 27, 28, 34, 178, 182 n.18

nanosecond 40, 182 n.14
Need, The (Troika Ranch) 25, 27–9
Neganthropocene 164
negative entropy 163, 189 n.10
Nelson, Robin 13–14
neoliberalism 168
Netflix 188 n.7
neuro/cognitive-capitalism 100, 185 n.6
Neuromancer (Gibson) 57
'New Media performance' (Causey) 15
Nietzsche, Friedrich 47, 69, 171, 184 n.15, 189–90 n.1
Nikolais, Alwin 80, 86, 87, 106, 115, 185 n.3
noetic reactivation 176–7
noise-based scenography 114–15
Note Complémentaire (Simondon) 66
numerical output 44

Obarzanek, Gideon 106–8, 112, 114–16, 119, 120, 123, 124
Obermaier, Klaus 4, 9, 16, 21, 22, 51, 77, 79–80, 87–91, 105–8, 111, 112, 114, 120, 123, 126, 128, 140–2, 152, 161, 169, 173, 175, 185 n.6
    Apparition (see Apparition (Obermaier))
    D.A.V.E. (see *D.A.V.E.* (Obermaier))
    projection-mapping 97–9
    responsive scenography 94–7
    symbiosis/organology 101–3
    Vivisector 79, 85–93, 98, 123
OnionLab 4, 16, 21, 22, 127–30, 169, 173, 175

and Adorno 130–2
Blade Runner 139–41
computer vision 143–5
cultural and program industry 132–4, 138–9, 146–7
desire 136–9
projection-mapping 146–7
software 141–3, 145–6
symbolic misery 134–6
ontogenesis 72, 172, 184 n.14
Open Computer-Vision (OpenCV) 143–6
Open Theatre 181 n.9
organology 102
    Chunky Move 119–21
    Extra Ear (Stelarc) 66–8
Orlan 9, 59, 184 n.17
over-rationalization 142, 177

Paik, Nam June 35
Palmer, Scott 11
Parker-Starbuck, J. 15–16
performativity 20, 60–1, 71, 75, 101, 124, 161, 169, 174, 177–9
Phaedrus (Plato) 181 n.12
pharmacology
    of automation 141
    digital technology 122–5
    of software 141–3, 145–6
    telecommunications 39–41
Pharmakon 39, 41, 124–6, 137
Phelan, Peggy 182 n.16
phylogenesis 68–70, 72, 172, 184 n.13
plastic surgery 19, 67, 72, 174
Plato 181 n.12
Poggioli, Renato 5
Poincaré, Henri 189 n.11
political
    agency 170–2
    efficacy 189 n.12
postdigital 14, 55, 72
postdramatic theatre 2
posthumanism 55, 99
postmodernism 43, 52, 73, 102, 103, 182 n.17
post-production 3, 20, 141
practice-as-research (PaR) 2, 10, 12, 23, 25, 26–9, 43, 46, 51, 60, 73–4, 79, 85, 93, 124

pre-individual milieu 65, 68–71, 134, 138
Processing 187 n.13
program industry 132–4, 138–9, 146–7
projection-mapping 77, 80, 84, 89, 92–3, 97–9, 125–30, 159, 174, 175
   Adorno's theory 130–2
   Blade Runner 2049 139–41
   computer vision 143–5
   cultural industry 132–4
   desire 136–9
   program industry 132–4, 138–9, 146–7
   software development 141–3, 145–6
   symbolic misery 134–6
proletarianization 8, 40, 141, 144, 159–62, 164, 165, 186 n.5
protentions 160, 162–3, 165, 172, 184 n.9, 188 n.6
Pure Data (PD) 187 n.13

quasi-organic scenography 113, 116, 119, 121, 122, 179

Rabinowitz, Sherrie 29, 30, 31, 35, 37, 181 n.7
radio transmitter 25, 28, 42, 181 n.2
real-time data analysis 12, 19, 20, 29, 30, 36, 37, 39, 97, 106, 107, 110, 141, 151, 154, 162
realtime video analysis technique 93
repurposing 17, 18, 43, 72, 74, 76, 79, 103, 124, 142, 146, 147, 166–9, 174–5
responsive scenography 94–7
retention 65–6, 160, 162, 165, 167, 184 n.9, 188 n.6
rupture 17–18, 21, 25, 29, 39–41, 45, 51–2, 56, 71–2, 76, 79, 85, 119, 122, 146, 163–6, 171, 172, 179
Russell, Charles 5

Salter, Chris 11–12, 15, 180 n.4
Saltz, David Z. 5–7
scanning process 88–9
scenography 1–3, 9–17, 53–4, 169, 170, 172–4
   ambivalences of 91–3
   body 81–2
   cyborg 56, 57, 74
   embodied
   expanded 16, 85
   noise-based 114–15
   quasi-organic 113, 116, 119, 121, 122, 179
   responsive 94–7
   specificities of 111–15
Schechner, Richard 150
Scheer, Edward 11, 12, 79
Schrödinger, Erwin 189 n.10
scientific knowledge 71, 76, 173
Scott, Ridley 139
second-order cybernetics 66, 184 n.11
Simondon, Gilbert 47, 48, 62–7, 69, 73, 136–8, 182 n.19
singularity 18, 37, 42, 53, 68, 69, 72, 73, 88, 103, 110, 134, 138, 160–5, 171–3, 175, 177
slow-scan videophone 29–34, 38, 42, 43, 159
Smith, Barry 12–13
Smith, Matthew 93
society machine model 66
socioculture 5, 8, 17, 18, 42, 56, 70, 72–7, 100, 103, 124, 125, 158, 162, 167, 171
socio-economics 3, 8, 9, 39, 42, 45, 68, 83, 100, 101, 109, 110, 118, 132, 142, 144, 156, 163–5, 170–3
socio-ethnic groupings 62, 157
socio-political subject 5, 6, 8, 17, 22, 23, 38, 40, 41, 51, 64, 73, 74, 76, 103, 131, 132, 134, 146, 147, 162, 167, 168, 170–2, 176, 177
soft prosthesis experiments 57, 72
software development 141–3, 145–6
special effects 20, 141
Speculum of the Other Woman (Irigaray) 55
Stelarc 4, 9, 16, 21, 51–4, 81, 102–3, 169, 172, 173, 175, 178. *See also Extra Ear* (Stelarc)
Stiegler, Bernard 1, 7–8, 39, 40, 47, 48, 61–7, 69–71, 73, 99, 100–1, 105, 108, 118, 120, 132–7, 139, 140, 142, 143, 146, 147, 157–9,

INDEX

161–5, 171–2, 176, 177, 182 n.13, 183 n.8, 184 n.9, 186 n.5, 187 n.7, 188 n.6, 189 n.1, 190 n.1
Stoermer, Eugene F. 188 n.8
Stoppiello, Dawn 25–35, 38, 42, 43, 45–6, 48–51, 181 n.7
Subotnick, Morton 27, 46, 48–9
subversion 12, 71–2, 174
surveillance model 88, 99, 100, 106, 108–10, 139, 147, 152, 158, 159, 167, 178
Svoboda, Josef 86, 107, 108
symbiosis 3, 24, 80, 94, 95, 101–3, 120
symbolic misery 134–6, 142, 163
systems art 43–4, 95
systems theory 44, 163, 164, 172, 189 n.11

Tactile Diaries (Troika Ranch) 26, 28–31, 35, 36, 38, 42–5
Tannion, Robert 93
technical
    evolution 44, 63, 68–9, 118, 125, 147
    tendency 62–3, 65
technicity 20, 63–6, 106, 115, 124
techno-cultural paradigm 141
technology
    agency 51, 77, 94, 158, 178
    cutting-edge 2, 21, 23, 29, 110, 122–3, 130, 131, 142, 143, 174, 175, 179
    cybernetic 3, 4, 11, 15, 16, 41, 43, 52, 55, 66, 74, 83, 111–13, 122, 133, 174, 178, 180 n.2, 184 n.11
    determinism 62
    digital 1, 3, 4, 8–11, 13, 14, 17–18, 20–3, 30, 36, 37, 39–41, 45, 46, 51, 56, 71, 75, 84–6, 92–4, 96, 99, 108, 111, 112, 114, 115, 118, 122–4, 142, 151, 165, 167, 171, 175, 178, 179, 180 n.3, 182 n.18
    display 141, 187 n.12
    efficacy 8, 19, 20, 63, 70, 94, 96, 101, 122, 133, 160, 161, 167, 168, 178, 179, 189 n.12
    human and 61, 62, 67, 101, 102, 179

MidiDancer 25, 28–30, 32–5, 38, 42, 43, 45, 49–50
performativity 15, 161, 169, 177–9
shock 17, 19, 41, 52, 71, 122, 164
Troika Ranch and 33–5
techno-scientific knowledge 3, 103, 114, 173
teleacting 36–9, 42
telecommunication 16, 19, 20, 30, 39–41, 70, 73, 75
teleconferencing 30, 31, 36
telematics 20, 30, 59, 183 n.4
telepresence 30, 36–8, 72
temporal objects 135, 157, 186 n.6
tertiary retentions 160, 162, 184 n.9, 188 n.6
Theatre of the Oppressed (Boal) 150
Third Hand (Stelarc) 56–7
Third Industrial Revolution (Rifkin) 17, 21
This Sex Which Is Not One (Irigaray) 55
transindividuation 105–6, 135, 176–7
transitional object 137, 138, 158
Troika Ranch 4, 9, 12, 16, 21–3, 25–6, 51–3, 95, 106, 111, 114, 126, 152, 161, 169, 172, 173, 175, 177, 181 n.6
    and avant-garde 35–6
    CalArts 26–7
    choreography 45
    experimentalism 42–3
    individuation and influences 47–9
    invention 42–3
    mise-en-scène 31–3
    Need, The 27–9
    In Plane 45–7, 49–51
    process 43
    systems art 43–4
    Tactile Diaries 29–31
    and technology 33–5
    telecommunications 39–41
    videoconferencing 36–9
24/7 capitalism 141, 157, 159–63, 177

unboxing 137, 187 n.8

video broadcasting 31, 35–9
videoconferencing 30, 36–8, 42, 151
videograms 33, 34, 44, 154

videophone. *See* slow-scan videophone
Villeneuve, Denis 127, 139, 141, 147
Virilio, Paul 37–9
virtual 9, 11, 15, 38, 50, 53, 54, 96, 140, 141, 149, 175
Vivisector (Obermaier) 79, 85–93, 98, 123
Von Forester, Heinz 184 n.11
Vostell, Wolf 35

Wagner, Richard 5–6
Weiss, Frieder 103, 105–9, 112–16, 119–25
Wiener, Norbert 41, 66, 174, 180 n.2
Wikileaks 186 n.4
Willow Garage 143
Wilson, Robert 14, 87
Winnicott, Donald Woods 137
Wooster Group 9, 12, 14, 35
World Wide Web 3, 18

www.ingramcontent.com/pod-product-compliance
Lightning Source LLC
Chambersburg PA
CBHW051810230426
43672CB00012B/2678